CU00821284

Disarmament, Demobilization, and Reintegration

Disarmament,
Demobilization,
and Reintegration

Theory and Practice

Desmond Molloy

To Gordon, his.
This ought offer some
insight as to why DDR
won't be happening in Myanmar
over tend soon.
D.M.
Desmond Molloy

Kumarian Press

A Division of Lynne Rienner Publishers, Inc. • Boulder & London

Published in the United States of America in 2017 by
Kumarian Press
A division of Lynne Rienner Publishers, Inc.
1800 30th Street, Boulder, Colorado 80301
www.rienner.com

and in the United Kingdom by
Kumarian Press
A division of Lynne Rienner Publishers, Inc.
3 Henrietta Street, Covent Garden, London WC2E 8LU

© 2017 by Lynne Rienner Publishers, Inc. All rights reserved

Library of Congress Cataloging-in-Publication Data
A Cataloging-in-Publication record for this book
is available from the Library of Congress.
ISBN: 978-1-62637-568-0 (pb)
ISBN: 978-1-62637-567-3 (hc)

British Cataloguing in Publication Data
A Cataloguing in Publication record for this book
is available from the British Library.

Printed and bound in the United States of America

The paper used in this publication meets the requirements
of the American National Standard for Permanence of
Paper for Printed Library Materials Z39.48-1992.

5 4 3 2 1

Contents

Acknowledgments

My friend, brother, jazz partner, and mentor, Kenji Isezaki, of Tokyo University of Foreign Studies has encouraged me from our first meeting in East Timor in 2000. He brought me to Sierra Leone in 2001 and later offered refuge and a new direction in Japan. In Sierra Leone, Bengt Ljunggren stimulated a curiosity about and intellectual approach to disarmament, demobilization, and reintegration (DDR).

My DDR families in Sierra Leone, Haiti, and Nepal and my friends in DDR through the years—Kelvin Ong, Ayaka Suzaka, Simon Yazgi, Chris O'Donnell, Sophie da Camara, Luc Lafreniere, Daniel Ladouceur, Dean Piedmont, and Kees Steenken—all offered professional support, guidance, advice, and, more important, friendship. DDR masters Kees Kingma, Nat Colletta, Walt Kilroy, Rich Bowd, Rob Muggah, Jim Kovar, Stavros (Aki) Stavrou, Macartan Humphreys, and Jeremy Weinstein gave encouragement over the years. Richard Millett and Eric Shibuya gave me confidence to follow the qualitative track.

At the Centre for Peace Studies at Tromsø University, Tone Bleie, Stina Torjesen, Vidar Vambhein, and the International Research Group on Reintegration have pushed me to reach further. At the Hiroshima Peacebuilders Center, Hideaki Shinoda and Yuji Uesugi have encouraged and facilitated me since I arrived in Japan in 2007. In Tokyo, my faithful friends Maja Vodopivec, Gunnar Rekvig, Muzafary Sayed Ahmad, and Mohamed Omar Abdin have been there for me. David Baxter and Mike Martin gave early editing advice. My colleagues at the Nippon Foundation in Tokyo and Myanmar have offered encouragement and patience in seeing me complete this work.

My copyeditor, Tara Joffe, has made my book readable. I am in awe. Any remaining faults are my own. I am grateful also to my publisher, Lynne Rienner, for her personal attention, kind guidance, and encouragement and for having faith in me that I could deliver.

This book is dedicated to my two families, who have loved, supported, and encouraged me throughout, carrying the can when I was in distant places, keeping the home fires burning, coming when needed, understanding and removing stress: Anne, Elizabeth, and Desmond in Dublin, and Sopha, Kiri, and the extended clan in Phnom Penh and Kampong Speu. I am twice blessed.

Early in 2005, while struggling to design and lead the hybrid DDR process in Haiti in addressing the violence of criminal gangs, a local politician associated with the gangs asked my DDR team to talk to a group of child armed gang members from Port au Prince who were seeking alternatives. We met more than thirty children between the ages of ten and thirteen. Three weeks later, we received unsubstantiated reports that five of these children had been executed by their gang leader for having spoken to us without his permission. While never positively confirmed—bodies rarely turn up in this voodoo environment—we believe it to be true. This shock caused us to reassess all aspects of the design and implementation of our approach to DDR, to cease making contacts with gangs other than through gang leaders, and to generally reconsider our conflict sensitivity.

1

Disarmament, Demobilization, and Reintegration

For decades, scholars and practitioners of disarmament, demobilization, and reintegration (DDR) processes have been searching for an elusive success. In their search, they have consistently focused on striving for and counting the metrics of quantitative results—those results that can easily be enumerated. The most popular quantitative metrics—the "easy" options—have included the number of guns collected, the number of combatants demobilized, and the number of former combatants securing sustainable livelihoods as a result of reintegration support. Such quantitative results fit neatly into the logical framework of a program document as indicators of achievement that make sense to donor and program evaluators. The United Nations (UN), World Bank, and main bilateral donors continue to support DDR in a common belief that it forms a critical element of postconflict intervention. Practice demonstrates that DDR contributes to the initial cessation of fighting and to progressively stabilizing the postconflict environment in addressing the most volatile potential spoilers. Thus, DDR practice has predominantly focused on former combatants in addressing short-term imperatives. In measuring the quantitative indicators, however, a decade of scholarly investigation using refined empirical methodologies has failed to identify clear, generically applicable evidence that DDR, among a multitude of violence-reducing and peacebuilding processes, actually contributes to postconflict stabilization and the socioeconomic reintegration of former combatants.[1] DDR is therefore a highly disputed concept in terms of its effectiveness and its translation from theory to practice.

For me, as a practitioner fully immersed in the design, implementation, and consideration of DDR processes (including in Sierra Leone, Haiti, the Central African Republic, Somalia, the Niger delta, Sri Lanka, and Colombia) and who is convinced of its efficacy, this scholarly failure to confirm evidence-based metrics that indicate success in DDR has been a puzzle. If answers cannot be found, perhaps the wrong questions are being asked. Burned out from the attrition associated with implementing a type of

1

DDR in Haiti in 2007, I retreated to the comfort of scholarship at the Tokyo University of Foreign Studies to deeply contemplate this conundrum. What is successful DDR? When is DDR successful? What causes DDR failures? Is the "leap of faith" of DDR, which involves a series of risks, worth taking in addressing armed violence? Do the benefits outweigh those risks? In the course of my search for answers, additional questions arose: Is there a place for DDR in the evolving dynamic of global violence? Is evolving UN policy on DDR undermining its potential? *Disarmament, Demobilization, and Reintegration: Theory and Practice* takes you along my journey through these questions.

DDR has become an essential aspect of many postconflict peacebuilding efforts. After twenty years of UN and World Bank institutional engagement in the practice of DDR, a body of guiding theory has grown from scholarly analyses and practice-based evidence. In the practice of DDR, *success* is a subjective word, the definition of which depends greatly on the perspective of the relevant actors. Kenji Isezaki, in considering a combatant-focused perspective, contends that the use of the terms *success* or *failure* in relation to DDR is irrational and naive.[2] What is achieved, he says, in implementing DDR is neither success nor failure, though it may be some level of both. DDR is a vital series of processes offering breathing space in which political and security outcomes may be achieved. Socioeconomic outcomes, however, are incidental; the expectations of short- to medium-term socioeconomic achievement through DDR in a very disadvantaged postconflict socioeconomic environment are often unrealistic.

However, even in achieving short-term, combat-centric results, scholars have learned from practice-based evidence that the predominant determinants of success in DDR hinge not on quantitative aspects but rather on the qualitative aspects of program planning, implementation, and achievement. The impact of DDR is contingent upon the belief, perception, and mutual trust among direct stakeholders that both security and related human security have improved as a result of DDR implementation. Success in DDR is about the vertical and horizontal relations between and among the stakeholders involved in the process—state and nonstate, local elites, former combatants, communities, and, indeed, the implementing agencies. Addressing perceptions, attitudes, and aspects of trust in order to achieve sustainable results is about addressing human relations; it requires systems thinking that applies an integrated consideration of these qualitative elements across the range of stakeholders. The perceptions of those stakeholders depend on the management of multiple inherent dilemmas—security, moral, cultural, ideological, legitimacy, and interpretational (hereafter, collectively referred to as security dilemmas).

This book traces the evolution of the theory and practice of DDR by considering selected case studies, related literature, and professional documentation. It also draws on personal experience and peer consultation. It finds that the critical factors in achieving optimal outcomes in DDR are indeed the perceptions, attitudes, and trust of the stakeholders, including the often-neglected host communities in which the former combatants are being reintegrated. The crux in applying the theory in practice exists in how to manage a range of associated security dilemmas, which result from the conundrum of deciding the appropriate action for addressing the pros and cons of the trade-offs associated with operational phenomena. Neglecting the trade-offs results in a failure to "win the people," including their perceptions, attitudes, and trust. This book demonstrates that prioritizing the phenomenon of security dilemmas in DDR offers an opportunity to address the right questions and to contribute to improved results.

Over the past decade, the evolution of DDR theory has moved toward recognizing the criticality of the qualitative elements of stakeholder perceptions, attitudes, and trust. This recognition is reflected in a growing consensus regarding the benefits of and the moves toward bottom-up approaches and conflict sensitivity in addressing the multiple security dilemmas. Such bottom-up approaches include the establishment of second-generation DDR and community security approaches. In 2005–2009, the attempts at DDR and the reduction of community violence in Haiti (a countercriminality environment) as considered in Chapter 5, which were then tentatively adapted to Somalia and Côte d'Ivoire, reflect the complexity and risks associated with addressing such security dilemmas. In practice, however, in light of the expediency of addressing competing political imperatives and resource and time constraints, the security dilemmas are often neglected.

Attempts to implement DDR in conflicts such as the counterinsurgency environments in Afghanistan and Colombia provided stern lessons regarding how ongoing conflicts enhance security dilemmas and pointed toward the apparent incompatibility of security approaches with human security approaches. The introduction of the robust, innovatively mandated UN combat unit, the Force Intervention Brigade, in the Democratic Republic of Congo (DRC) emphasized uncertainty regarding the legality—at least in the context of international humanitarian law—of UN offensive operations. It also raised further questions regarding the potential for implementing DDR in conflict.

Addressing the security dilemmas associated with DDR through innovative bottom-up approaches is time consuming and labor intensive. Doing so requires a high level of expertise, capacity, and deep consideration of the crosscutting issues. It demands a conflict-sensitive approach, local agency, and long-term commitment. It is also expensive. For all of these reasons, it is often placed on the back burner, which constitutes a deficit in addressing perceptions, attitudes, and trust. This failing is often deemed justified in an effort to gain quick fixes in politically charged, volatile environments. Yet, this deficit can actually accentuate the security dilemmas that undermine the DDR process. The relegation of efforts required to manage the security dilemmas contributes to stakeholders' negative perceptions, attitudes, and distrust. Favoring an apparent quick fix or seeking immediate political wins by focusing directly on former combatants in DDR processes constitutes a decisive deficit that reduces the quality, impact, and sustainability of outcomes.

Greater recognition of the role of the perceptions, attitudes, and trust of stakeholders—in particular, of host communities—in achieving desired outcomes, and thus moving toward next-generation DDR—an evolution beyond second-generation—is offering the opportunity to strengthen the conceptual foundations of DDR. This recognition points out the direction for applying resources, time, and training appropriately in planning for next-generation DDR. It also permits the development of the most effective metrics—quantitative and qualitative—for designing new approaches to implementing and evaluating DDR. These new metrics will contribute to improved outcomes, including lives saved, the establishment of functional normative systems for people living in postconflict environments, and the enhancement of both security and human security.[3]

Within the UN system, the human security agenda is a highly contested concept originally adapted from Franklin Roosevelt's Four Freedoms—in particular, the freedom from fear and the freedom from want. This agenda was relaunched into the world via the *Human Development Report* of 1994.[4] In considering humanitarian action, the report places responsibility to the individual above responsibility to the state. The fact that this agenda implies a move away from the international recognition of the primacy of the state is a major element in the argument against it, as this change poses a threat to states that do not ascribe, generally or occasionally, to Western-imposed liberal standards—that is, universal values in the area of human rights.

The new context of the network mobilization of the ideologically and theologically driven Islamic State (IS) caliphate in Syria, Iraq, and now Libya (and moving toward West Africa) has led to the prickly conundrum of how to address the issue of terrorist infiltration, returning foreign fighters or indigenous radicalized youth associated with violent extremism, beyond the geographic caliphate. In light of the high-profile terrorist outrages and the sowing of panic being committed by or attributed to IS, some consider this as the emerging greatest threat to a global societal sense of security. There is broad consensus that the geographic caliphate—the Islamic State's area of operations, currently primarily in Syria and Iraq—must be attacked militarily and its foundations destroyed. Addressing the network-mobilized global caliphate—its outreach through infiltration, through returning fighters, or through the activities of locally radicalized youth—is far more complex than addressing the geographic caliphate. Can any evolution of next-generation DDR cope with this complexity?

For many scholars of postconflict recovery, DDR is often seen as being closely linked to the security sector reform (SSR) process. SSR, largely necessitated by the changing nature of global polarity following the collapse of the Soviet Union, initially focused on the resizing and retasking of military forces in addressing a changed security environment. SSR was operationalized by reducing host country recurring security/defense budgets to allow a greater contribution to social spending and development in a rapidly democratizing world. SSR has evolved to include the reform of the broader security system, as reflected in the seminal *Handbook on Security System Reform* of 2008, published by the Organisation for Economic Co-operation and Development's Development Assistance Committee (OECD/DAC).[5] This broader security system, together with military forces and armed national security resources, includes law enforcement services, correctional services, and the judiciary; it also enables and directs the reform of legal frameworks. A close proximity between SSR and DDR, however, is rarely the case in practice, as the two tend to be planned and implemented in parallel rather than convergently. Both are highly charged elements of the security and political landscape contributing to postconflict recovery. Nat Colletta and Robert Muggah discussed the evolving ideas regarding the relationship between DDR and related postconflict activities and SSR in their article, "Rethinking Post-war Security Promotion."[6] They consider a shift from classic state-centric thinking about the security sector to include interim stabilization measures and second generation security promotion. This idea mirrors a similar evolution in DDR toward implementing bottom-up, area-based interventions—also known as the maximalist approach.

DDR is seen as essential in preventing the return to hostilities by dealing with surplus arms and fighters through a human security–guided approach. SSR, in contrast, shapes the sustainability and functionality of the state security apparatus for the state's future stability and development. Although SSR envisages human security outcomes, those outcomes are usually implemented in the context of a national security strategy. Attempting to address SSR and DDR as intractably linked processes has occasionally created a critical mass necessitating urgent reconsideration. Even when the UN has launched peacekeeping operations with the intention of combining the planning and implementation of DDR and SSR under the management of a unified director of SSR/DDR, it has been necessary to subsequently separate the functions. The reasons are primarily the incompatibility of the principles guiding implementation, security, and human security; conflicts of interest among responsible state institutions, supporting agencies, and lead countries; diverse and differing priorities and time frames; and differing mindsets of the professional individuals involved in the implementation.[7] Although DDR may be implemented in the context of SSR, the two do not necessarily occur together. Although this book does not dwell on SSR, the concept is introduced incrementally as a crosscutting issue.

The theory and the practice of DDR are not evolving in a linear progression. Lessons learned from and contributing to practice are drawn incrementally in evolving and eclectic contexts. Neglected ideas from former experiences often come to the fore to be reestablished in new contexts. As such, the structure of this book is eclectic; although it is broadly chronological, it occasionally backtracks to demonstrate incremental learning and the evolution of the application of relevant existing or emerging concepts.

Scholars have been skirting the pertinent questions for decades. They have admonished the practitioner to improve the metrics with more relevant, evidence-based indicators of success. However, they have not suggested what successful DDR looks like. They have counted the weapons collected, considered the numbers of combatants entering the process, and counted the percentage of participants achieving sustainable livelihoods as a result of DDR. They have looked at the numbers and talked to the fighters and applied refined regression analysis in seeking the answer. But they have not found an answer. What is successful DDR? There is no one answer. Has DDR achieved success once its impact as a confidence-building measure has drawn the fighting parties into a cessation of violence in which they work toward a comprehensive peace accord? Does success occur once fighters are disarmed and demobilized? Is it when former fighters are in sustainable, decent alternative livelihoods? Is it when the progress of the postconflict environment becomes irreversible?

The practitioner seems to have a different perspective than the scholar on what constitutes success in DDR. The practitioner sees a series of targeted milestones and achievement, with each one marking a level of success. However, the nature and level of those targeted indicators change progressively in dynamic postconflict environments, in each case-specific context, and in accordance with what is deemed normative in that flux. The qualitative elements of trust and perception have major and heretofore underestimated affects on the achievement of those milestones. Thus, it is not easy for the scholar to investigate, remotely or retrospectively, a DDR process using the quantitative indicators of achievement from the logistical framework of a program document. It is also difficult to measure the qualitative indicators, including levels of trust and people's perceptions from an earlier period, in a dynamically evolving context.

The daily decisions made by the practitioner in struggling for positive results—that is, for success—are often choices between less-than-optimal options based not only on the changing conditions but also on the levels of risk and opportunity at a specific moment. The prioritization of achieving one result often necessitates shifting resources and partly sacrificing some other desirable result. It is a process of addressing a continuous series of dilemmas, and it implies a leap of faith, based on a subjective assessment of the moment, to grasp a fleeting opportunity. This opportunity is often dependent on the qualitative and transient elements of human relations.

Although practitioners feel the pressures of making such choices on a daily basis and experience the sense of risk, the self-doubt, and the sense of moment, they have poorly articulated these frustrations to the scholars. For practitioners, success occurs when one of their many decisions leads to a positive result contributing somehow to the desirable outcome, which can be any of the milestones. Knowing that DDR is only one of multiple processes and influencers contributing to a stabilized postconflict normative environment, these lesser, more attributable milestones are essential in assessing manageable achievement.

DDR was spawned in a series of peace processes in South and Central America, the end of apartheid in South Africa, and the changing environment of bipolarity with the collapse of the Soviet Union at the end of the 1980s. Here the early evolution of theory and practice of DDR was applied in implementing confidence-building measures as an aspect of SSR. These confidence-building measures were perceived to contribute to the stabilization of immediate postconflict environments. Coalescing into DDR, it became a darling of the UN, particularly in the General Assembly, where it was seen as a silver bullet for addressing issues of arms, ammunition, and surplus former combatants in the context of a peace process.

From the practitioner's perspective, however, DDR was not a smooth ride. Over the subsequent two decades, lessons were drawn from trial and error; technical toolboxes and guidance documents were compiled; and the foundations of the theory were laid down. Some of the programs implemented were deemed critical in guiding the transformation of conflict into peace and in rebuilding the social fabric of communities through enhanced trust and reconciliation. In the optimistic post–Cold War era, DDR practice evolved in a somewhat template format, with the human security agenda emerging as an overarching philosophical guide.

With the proliferation in demand for DDR, planners, trainers, and practitioners struggled for coherence in designing efficient, effective approaches to implementation that would contribute to successful outcomes without having to reinvent the wheel each time. Such cases included South Africa, Angola, Mozambique, Sierra Leone, Liberia, the Great Lakes region of Africa, and current-day South Sudan—all considered by the practitioner as cases of classic DDR.

Attempts at implementing DDR along classic postconflict lines using template assumptions in a less-than-classic environment came to a head in Haiti in 2004–2005, an environment of criminal chaos. This situation required a sea change toward an innovative, context-specific community security approach to achieve community violence reduction. While the chaos prevailed in Haiti, the struggle for coherence and results led to the evolution of a new approach to DDR, called second-generation DDR, which took DDR toward a systems approach to conflict sensitivity in addressing armed violence. Such a direction enhanced the opportunity for community and civil society engagement in DDR.

From 2010 to 2013, my DDR team in Nepal used the opportunity of a small-scale DDR program as a laboratory to test many of the lessons learned to date in addressing an array of the topical crosscutting issues in DDR, such as effective information management, implementing dynamic monitoring, evaluation and adjustment, dynamic management, addressing the gender perspective and psychosocial issues, and improved job placement support. Practitioners took risks and elements of DDR theory were prioritized or abandoned in light of context in order to ensure acceptable outcomes. In a major failure, however, the larger group of qualified Maoist combatants that had remained as pawns of the political process in cantonment were ultimately treated to a quick fix by being bought off with a cash lump sum. The concept of using cash incentives for engagement in DDR will merit some scrutiny.

Neither classic DDR nor second-generation DDR can prepare practitioners to implement DDR in ongoing offensive operations. In such situations, the security perspective remains dominant, as the transition to a post-conflict environment has not yet been achieved, and the human security agenda is suppressed. This throws up a major dilemma to DDR implementers in what appears to be a premature environment for DDR. Attempts at DDR in Afghanistan and Colombia offer contrasting examples of DDR in war that exude the complexity and frustration of such efforts. The aggressive mandating of the UN Force Intervention Brigade in DRC in 2013 contributed to further complications in implementing DDR.

How has the DDR theory dynamically evolved in response to diverse, dynamic contexts and perspectives? How has this evolution influenced policy development, particularly in the latter half of its twenty-year evolutionary period? In compounding the complexity of evolving DDR, no two contexts are the same. In this flux, can the UN's Integrated DDR Standards of 2006 (IDDRS) keep pace with the theory? Are those standards still relevant? Such concepts as interim stabilization mechanisms, the value of former combatant cohesiveness, the reality of UN commitment to the gender perspective in DDR, and the role of reintegration in transforming social capital and contributing to reconciliation in the community further influence that policy development. Key organizing concepts to facilitate the study of reintegration—political economy, context, separation trajectories, and the multicentric notion of community—have arisen. Both scholars and practitioners continue to struggle with the conundrum of devising criteria and agreed-upon metrics to permit evidenced-based analysis of the achievements of practice for planning and evaluation purposes. However, a new school of DDR is suggesting that both scholars and practitioners have been asking the wrong questions. The functional metrics are not the quantitative ones that have heretofore been the subject of focus, but the qualitative ones—that is, the perceptions, attitudes, and trust of the stakeholders, particularly within the communities, that DDR is contributing to their interests in creating normative systems.

DDR is not an end in itself. Its successful implementation means that it acts as a contribution to the delivery of a peace process or to the reduction of armed violence, while also mutually supporting and affecting other practice areas associated with the same objectives. How should DDR be included in pre-ceasefire peace mediation? Why do the complementarities and tensions experienced as a result of the association between DDR and justice, transitional justice, and the impact of amnesties raise much current debate? How does the folly of convoluting SSR and DDR and addressing them en masse from a security perspective threaten practice? How does the privatization of elements of SSR and DDR to profit motivated private military security companies threaten to erode human security motivation? Can support for regionally, culturally, and religiously sensitive designed approaches to something beyond a perceived Western orientation of DDR be garnered and be applied to Islamic DDR? Can a heightened sensitivity to local solutions lay the foundations for next-generation DDR? It is time to reboot both the theory and practice of DDR to address a dynamically evolving global environment. DDR implementation must involve genuine attention to the qualitative metrics of the perceptions, attitudes, and trust of the people and stakeholders in order to address risk and security dilemmas.

Next-generation DDR may have to contend with demands for implementing DDR to address the contexts of violent extremism and organized crime. However, evidence indicates the incompatibility of concurrently embedding DDR's human security approaches into security operations. Trust does not exist in these cases, and DDR is about trust. Western states are awaking to, and perhaps overhyping, the imminent threat presented by the return of foreign fighters or indigenous youth inculcated by the ideals of the caliphate. What have we learned in recent second-generation community security approaches to DDR that may help us create an effective next-generation DDR? How can this contribute to global policy in addressing violent extremism? Ultimately, the ability to apply a new generation of DDR methodologies to armed violence reduction and in supporting disengagement of fighters, criminals, or radicalized youth in evolving complex contexts will depend greatly on levels of trust between stakeholders and on the willingness and capacity of actors to take multiple leaps of faith.

Notes

1. Stabilization here implies an intervention that is designed to solidify the capacity and legitimacy of a host government in a conflict or postconflict environment.

2. Kenji Isezaki, formerly chief of DDR in Sierra Leone, led the Afghanis New

Beginning Program's DDR process on behalf of Japan in Afghanistan and has written extensively on peacebuilding. He is currently head of the Peace and Conflict Studies faculty at Tokyo University of Foreign Studies. He has been my friend and inspiration for many years. He introduced me to DDR and ultimately drew me into scholarship in Japan in 2007. He also plays a mean jazz trumpet.

3. See David Kilcullen's theory of normative systems: "The population wants predictability, order and safety and that safety comes from knowing where you stand and knowing that if you do this or don't do this, following the rules, you will be safe." "Interview with Dr. David Kilcullen," Octavian Manea, Small Wars Foundation, November 7, 2010, accessed July 4, 2012, http://www.smallwarsjournal.com/blog /journal/docs-temp/597-manea.pdf.

4. UN *Human Development Report* is published annually by UNDP and provides one of the world's top sources of international development data.

5. OECD/DAC, *Handbook on Security System Reform: Supporting Security and Justice* (Paris: Organisation for Economic Co-operation and Development, 2008).

6. Nat Colletta and Robert Muggah, "Rethinking Post-war Security Promotion," *Journal of Security Sector Management* 7, no. 1 (2009).

7. In the 2013 UN mission in Côte d'Ivoire, under operational pressure, the combined tasking as director of SSR/DDR was eventually split into two posts addressing parallel rather than converged processes.

2

The Foundations of
the Theory

DDR is often considered to be an essential aspect of stabilizing
immediate postconflict environments and preparing the way for transition
through peacebuilding to development. For the past twenty years, the practice has been applied in both nationally driven and international interventions to end the scourge of armed violence and to achieve a broad range of
security, political, and socioeconomic objectives. In a dynamically evolving
world, the complexity of the practice has grown exponentially. Through
trial and error, and with occasional success, lessons learned and scholarly
analysis have been cobbled together into a body of theory in an attempt to
ensure that the vast resources and energy being expended on implementing
DDR provide an acceptable return on investment, not just to direct stakeholders but also to humanity.

This chapter offers an introduction to the foundations of DDR theory,
locating the beginnings of the specific practice of DDR to the mid-1980s
and a series of peace processes in South and Central America that heralded
a changing post–Cold War conflict dynamic. These peace processes saw the
initiation of mutual confidence-building measures and the rationalization of
creating the appropriate size (often termed "rightsizing") and re-tasking of
armed force from both the economic and security perspectives through
processes of security sector reform (SSR) supported by DDR. The brief case
study of El Salvador, described later in this chapter, offers insight into the
complexity and limitations of applying the nascent practice of DDR, a practice that gave rise to the theory.

From a Discrete Postconflict Stabilization Practice
to a Body of Theory

Tracing the evolution of a body of theory that has soared a considerable dis-
tance from practice is a complex undertaking for a practitioner. Practice of

DDR, an inherently political activity, has always struggled in a volatile political world far from the ideals and ethics of the human security agenda–driven theory. The imperatives of security, power, and economics have complicated many efforts at implementation. Conventionally, DDR has occurred as one aspect of a comprehensive peacebuilding intervention in a postconflict environment, though it now occurs during conflict. A postconflict environment is often highly charged with political, economic, and social dysfunction, with predatory neighbors, absence of rule of law, devastated vital infrastructure, and the pervasive presence of illicit arms, ammunition, and explosives. The situation is further complicated by a volatile and uncertain combatant/former combatant community and a civil population hoping for some level of predictability and safety to permit ascension to an acceptable level of existence in a normative system.

Studying the practice and theory of DDR represents one of those clear scholar/practitioner gaps common in technical practices, with scholars and practitioners living in very different worlds. In the mid-1980s, scholars and practitioners of DDR were leading the World Bank's entry into demilitarization and conversion in global postconflict environments. These founding members and collators of lessons learned crossed the scholar/practitioner gap at a time when the early-engaged institutions were reacting to an exploding post–Cold War DDR practice area. They were seeking lessons and the creation of an effective toolbox to develop a theory that would deliver DDR efficiently, effectively, and, just as important, economically.[1] This period was followed by the ascendance of scholarly young bucks testing empirical methodology, while drawing on the practice and support of the amenable practitioners in the proliferating DDR programs. These young scholars focused on developing academic rigor and seeking evidence-based analysis. They challenged the often intuitive, gut-originated claims of the practitioners and exasperatedly called on practitioners to plan more carefully, monitor more systematically, and account for their decisions. They pushed the practitioners toward a more results-based implementation.[2]

Many academic and technical institutions and research networks have been following the scholar's and practitioner's lead and are invigorating the development of the overarching theory.[3] However, the theory reaches the practitioner only in a nebulous way. Theoretically, the practice follows the theory; in reality, however, it does not. The scholar/practitioner gap in DDR is real, though thankfully tangibly diminishing. DDR practitioners operate at several different levels. One is in the headquarters of the international organizations: the UN and World Bank in Washington, New York, or Geneva. These practitioners swim in a politically charged cauldron of high international bureaucracy and interests. They seek international political imprimatur and funds to pursue the desired intervention to contribute to the required outcomes—that is, the stabilization of a peace process and the establishment of a political process. Often these required outcomes are associated with a lead nation's interests.

A second level is in the respective country office, dealing with the country team, UN, international organizations, and diplomatic missions, in addition to the national political elites, in encouraging national ownership of, or at least support for, the DDR program.[4] At the third level, the coal face, they eyeball the former combatant and the community. They seek rapid solutions for the implementation of a complex human experiment. They address daily crises by managing a team under constant threat and by dealing with maneuvering local military, militias, and political leaders. They strive for results within the constraints of program budgets, limited resources, tight time frames, disputed approaches, and conflicting local interests. And they do all this while keeping a tentative group of risk-averse organizational heads, UN resident coordinators, heads of engaged UN agencies and nongovernmental organizations (NGOs), and interested ambassadors on board. These stakeholders need constant reassurance that their investment in funds, time, and political and professional capital will not come to grief.

Practitioners at the coal face have not read the scholar's papers. These papers are written in the language of the political or social scientist for peer consumption, are published in inaccessible specialist journals, and exist just beyond the reach of the field practitioner, who does not have the time or inclination to search for the studies. But things are changing.

The following chapters consider the work of the scholars and the rare breed of scholar/practitioner as they have developed the evolving, ragged-edged theory of DDR. One cannot talk about doctrine in the case of DDR. Doctrine implies a universal practice and acceptance, disseminated from an authoritative source for compliance by majority practitioners. No such body of doctrine exists for DDR. Despite the development of the evolving but currently stalled UN Integrated DDR Standards, published in 2006, there is no cookie-cutter approach to DDR. The Integrated DDR Standards are ostensibly a dynamic toolbox of basic principles and ideas of areas to be addressed in developing case-specific responses to very different contexts. Input to its development is derived from multiple sources with various motivations. International institutions and organizations, programs and funds, departments within those organizations, governments, academic and training institutions, and practitioners all make their play to contribute to the evolving theory of DDR, mainly through a process of postimplementation review in drawing lessons. These contributions are often biased toward consideration of "turf" issues or areas of practice deemed, by themselves, as their exclusive territory. In its current state of evolution, DDR, as a body of theory reflecting practice, is bursting beyond the limits of the Integrated DDR Standards to the point at which, in its next generation, it must contribute to addressing the evolving contexts of global strategic and security concern.

The Beginnings

When did DDR start, and who wrote the early theory? One hears from mature and early practitioners that DDR first reared its head in the UN Observer Group in Central America (ONUCA). This was in the context of post–Cold War security readjustments, which gave rise to what Dean Piedmont called "proxy DDR," or a type of DDR that occurred by default.[5] The book *Confidence-Building Measures in Latin America* offers a window onto that maternity.[6] From the turn of the twentieth century, Central and South America ("Latin America") was a cauldron of decolonization, dictatorship, revolution, democratization, and the emergence of new independent democratic states. The United States, which marked its sphere of influence in the two American continents with the Monroe Doctrine in the early nineteenth century, still took seriously its interests in the development of the states of South and Central America in the mid-twentieth century. Perhaps it considered the Central American states, given their proximity and political fungibility, most seriously. As the Cold War ebbed and the Soviets dealt with their own "Vietnam" in Afghanistan, confidence for a more self-determined independence arose among the states of Central America. They learned from the techniques of their neighbors, the Southern Cone states, a capacity to deal with the multiple interstate and intrastate conflicts that unsettled the region. These conflicts were accentuated by the existence of extremes of wealth and poverty, which prevented the establishment of a relatively normative environment that would offer an acceptable level of human security.

As Central America moved into the era of democratization in the early 1980s, the myth that democracies do not face off against each other militarily proved just that. Central American countries therefore sought "soft" mechanisms to allay their own concerns and move toward the desired "relations of cooperation."[7] With the growing levels of independence and the professionalization of militaries, the increasing scope for related interstate tensions necessitated an increase in the coordination of government policies, including with the United States, and the development of "non-confrontational mechanisms for military interaction in the region."[8] The end of the Cold War and the demise of military bipolarity did not end the conflicts in Central America in the mid-1980s; if anything, as traditional geostrategic interests gave rise to increasing tensions, the need for those nonconfrontational mechanisms became even more important.

Augusto Varas, James Schear, and Lisa Owens defined confidence-building measures as "agreed military and non-military measures to enhance mutual understanding, convey non-hostile intentions, define acceptable norms of behavior, and allay excessive fears and suspicions."[9] This much-used tool of diplomatic dialogue dates from the eighteenth century to the current day and includes the Strategic Arms Limitation

Treaty (SALT) and the Strategic Arms Reduction Treaty (START).[10] Confidence-building measures have been exceptionally well used among and within the states of Central America to address the post–Cold War environment. They are particularly in evidence in the delivery of the Central American peace process of 1983 in Nicaragua that spread into El Salvador and Guatemala. Indeed, the use of this tool in facilitating hemispherical cooperation and tension reduction is visible in the resolutions of the Organization of American States of June 1991 in relation to security matters. This practice was subsequently taken up by many Latin American states in their interstate security management.[11]

As Jack Child notes:

> Confidence-building measures exist in an international environment in which tensions and mistrust, often in the context of security dilemmas, exist between potential adversaries who lack adequate information on their enemy's intentions and even their military capabilities.[12]

Left to its natural progress, such an environment could, "in a mutually reinforcing spiral of mistrust," escalate rapidly into an unstoppable military conflict. Confidence-building measures reduce the risk of such an eventuality. Therefore, such mechanisms were recommended for contributing to peace between states in the June 1992 Report of the UN Secretary-General, *Agenda for Peace*.[13]

Child listed the following essential characteristics for confidence-building measures: transparency, openness, reciprocity, balance, and adequate communications. He noted that confidence-building measures are just one aspect of a series of other conflict-resolution approaches, both soft and hard, which include peace enforcement, peacekeeping, peace observation, peacebuilding, and peacemaking.[14] The confidence-building measures associated with the Central American peace process that combined the Contadora process and the Arias and Esquipulas processes merit particular mention. They used such devices as peace verification, in which a neutral third party verifies that the conditions of a particular treaty are being complied with, and "zones of peace," an extensive geographic area in which confidence-building measures have been successful to the extent that the threat level in that area has been considerably lowered. Concepts associated with this somewhat utopian idea of zones of peace include disarmament, interdependence, and integration.[15] Child mentioned the notion of confidence-building measures within peace zones metaphorically as "peace dominoes," as opposed to "conflict dominoes."[16] Zones of peace are also associated with the Tlatelolco Treaty, which proscribes nuclear weapons in Latin America, and the Antarctic Treaty, which keeps Antarctica demilitarized.[17] In considering the limitations of confidence-building measures, Child pointed out that they will only function if there is genuine political will to make them work, if the tendency for mistrust in the context of the "prisoner's dilemma" is allayed, and if civil primacy is functioning in terms of the authority of military hierarchy within the state.[18]

Following the breakthrough in addressing the several Central American conflicts at the conference attended by the foreign ministers of Colombia, Mexico, Panama, and Venezuela on the Panamanian island of Contadora in January 1983, further progress was made at the meeting of foreign ministers in Cancún, Mexico, in July 1983. The ministers incorporated confidence-building measures to conflict resolution by agreeing to the provision of third-party peacekeeping and verification, the creation of joint boundary commissions, mutual notice regarding certain sized troop movements near frontiers, and direct communications between governments. They also addressed the following specific concerns:

> controlling the regional arms race; ending arms trafficking; eliminating foreign military advisors; creating demilitarized zones; prohibiting the use of one state's territory to destabilize another's and prohibiting other forms of interference in the internal affairs of countries in the region.[19]

Over the following years, while aspects of the adversarial position between Nicaragua and the more US-friendly Central American states persisted, the efficiency and effectiveness of confidence-building measures were strengthened with UN support and expanded into further agreements, contributing to increased regional cooperation and a reduction in the chances of conflict outbreaks. To a large degree, these confidence-building measures were included in the Esquipulas (Arias) Peace Plan of 1987, which led to cooperation among Costa Rica, El Salvador, Guatemala, Honduras, and Nicaragua in "security, verification, control and limitation of weapons" and which continued on to discuss "arms reduction, force levels and the international military presence in the region."[20] This process facilitated the demobilization of the Contras in Nicaragua from the early to mid-1990s, when confidence-building measures were extensively used to encourage their disarmament.

According to Child, confidence-building measures were often "heavy on symbolism," such as using scrapped Contra weapons to make prostheses.[21] He also described a ceremony in Managua, Nicaragua, in November 1990. In the presence of ONUCA, all stakeholders, and the media, 10,000 rifles surrendered by the Contras were cemented into a monument, as the creation of a representative National Disarmament Commission was announced.[22] Thus, the links between confidence-building measures in addressing security dilemmas, disarmament, and the reduction of intrastate and interstate armed violence in Central America were established.

Confidence-Building Measures in DDR

DDR grew out of the use of confidence-building measures in Central America in the mid-1980s and early 1990s. Since then, confidence-building measures for addressing security dilemmas have continued to be an aspect of DDR. A primary objective has been to establish a level of trust between parties to the conflict that will encourage the belief that the decision to cease the conflict is real and not just a ploy to permit consolidation. The potential for the absence of trust has been the inherent security dilemma in DDR from its outset. Confidence-building measures have been making their contribution to security across the globe and have spread beyond being an element of international treaty mechanisms and peace accord negotiations. They have now entered the arena of peacebuilding in intrastate postconflict environments and in addressing the proliferation of small arms in the context of DDR and small arms collections programs.

Ineffective disarmament as an aspect of a cessation of violence in a postconflict environment indicates an absence of confidence by the warring parties; in such cases, the potential for the reversion to armed violence is high. Confidence-building measures can contribute to restoring that confidence or ensuring that it is not lost in the first place. Transparency in the provision of information and the confirmation of reciprocity between parties is a critical aspect of confidence-building measures. Meek mentioned the device being used during the disarmament of the Revolutionary United Front and the Civil Defence Forces in Sierra Leone in 2001.[23] In that situation, units of the opposing forces were disarmed simultaneously in a process of rolling disarmament, moving slowly across the country, thus avoiding the distrust common in a mutual disarmament process with the onset of the prisoner's dilemma. The detailed arrangements were worked out between the parties at the Tripartite Committee on Conventions in the presence of the UN. The UN then supervised the implementation of the disarmament, which led to a relatively smooth disarmament operation in phase three of the Sierra Leone DDR process.[24]

Further, in light of the several conflicts raging in West Africa in the late-1990s and the porous borders and uncontrolled trafficking of illicit arms, the Economic Community of West African States unilaterally declared a moratorium on the import, export, and manufacture of light weapons in 1998; a commitment to share information on small arms among states; and a clear declaration of intent to address the problem. Although this was probably an impossible measure to enforce, its declaration did constitute a higher-level attempt to build confidence.

Between states, the existence of transparency in terms of security expenditure is a significant confidence-building measure. The establishment of the

UN Register of Conventional Arms established in 1991 through the UN General Assembly, goes some way to offering such transparency. For the 2010 consolidated report of this Register of Conventional Arms, the General Assembly, received reports from sixty-four states (not including the nil reports), which offered a legitimate overview of each state's import, export, and manufacture of small arms.[25] This mechanism, together with complementary global and regional measures to control the trafficking of illicit small arms and light weapons, is considered a major contributor to global transparency and confidence building regarding the manufacture and movement of small arms.

Small arms disarmament has moved from being a specific technical area of practice to being recognized as having a crosscutting impact, particularly associated with development, crime prevention, and postconflict stabilization. Thus, confidence-building measures are being used imaginatively in many areas. Meek mentioned such examples as the UN Development Program's various weapons for development programs, which have been particularly successful in Nicaragua, Albania, and Sierra Leone, and the NGO-implemented tools for arms programs in Mozambique. Meek also mentioned the implementation of confidence-building measures between the governments of South Africa and Mozambique and between South Africa and Lesotho in agreeing to mutually verified weapons cache destruction operations.[26]

The value of applying the confidence-building measure concept to DDR planning was increasingly being realized with the example of Sierra Leone's innovative community-focused, context-specific disarmament for development programs, which are complementary to DDR. Success breeds success, and resulting mechanisms of armed violence reduction were repeated in other DDR processes, including Democratic Republic of Congo and Burundi, where it was used as an element of the Multi-Donor Demobilization and Reintegration Program. Implementation of the confidence-building measure concept as an aspect of DDR can contribute to breaking the cycles of insecurity and related poverty, with transparency and communications being the critical elements.

However, disarmament can also contribute to increasing insecurity if the security dilemma elements of the process are not well considered, anticipated, and addressed. An example is the disarmament of the Northern Alliance in Afghanistan in 2004–2005, which did not contribute to broader community confidence-building but which did create a vacuum that facilitated the return of the Taliban.

El Salvador

Of the multiple implementations of treaties in Central America, the example of conflict resolution in El Salvador in the early 1990s illustrates a cross-section of the dynamics of DDR's early evolution. Stiles, in a chapter for Richard Millett's (ed.) forthcoming book, reviewed the DDR process in El

Salvador, noting that it is considered to have been successful, with no reversion to politically motivated guerrilla activities.[27] This success was achieved, despite the major escalation of drug-related gang crime shifting the center of gravity from civil war–related violence to gang violence and bestowing on El Salvador the reputation as one of the most dangerous places on Earth. This crime-related violence reflects the continuing reversion to the lesson learned in the previous eighty years in El Salvador that "killing can resolve social and political issues."[28]

The Cuban-inspired revolution of the early 1980s led to a fluctuating level of US intervention and support for the right-wing government in El Salvador, depending on the political imperatives associated with the US electoral cycle. Cuban support for the rebels waned parallel to the demise in its bolstering by the USSR. This change in the global political environment opened space for the development, with support of the George H. W. Bush regime, of a negotiated settlement in El Salvador. By the early 1990s, sensing a stalemate, exhausted, and losing popular support, all parties to the conflict were ready to seek a resolution, supported by both Washington and Moscow and a diminishing Cuban capacity. This was after the atrocities committed by both the government of El Salvador and the guerrilla Frente Farabundo Marti para la Liberation Nationale (FMLN) led to domestic pressure—notably, from the Catholic Church—to end the conflict. Multiple efforts were launched to establish a peace agreement, with the groundwork being laid to secure a ceasefire in July 1990 that recognized the FMLN as a legitimate negotiating partner. Major elements of constitutional reform were agreed upon, including bringing the national police under civil primacy, some demobilization of existing defense forces, reform of the judiciary, and the establishment of a Truth and Reconciliation Commission. The UN Observer Mission in El Salvador was also established. Efforts were made to demilitarize the state, reform the judiciary and electoral processes, and address human rights issues. Talks ensued regarding the details for the demobilization of the FMLN, the selected units of the government armed forces, and the creation of the new civil police force. All of this resulted in the Chapultepec Agreement of 1992, which offered a comprehensive approach to addressing concerns and which launched the DDR program. The UN and regional organizations, such as the Organization of American States, with the backing of the United States, supported these efforts.

From the Chapultepec Agreement, the provisions of the subsequent DDR in the context of an SSR process were to include a 50 percent reduction of the armed forces; the creation of civil primacy, with the removal of law enforcement–related tasking; increased human rights education for the armed forces; an investigation into previous human rights breaches; and an end to national conscription. Decisions were also made regarding the proportion of former forces to be recruited into the new police force—an issue that, together with the vetting process, was to prove temporarily contentious. Reform of the judiciary, that conservative element of society that thrives irrespective of the system, proved a crux that remained unresolved.

The demobilization process established several phased milestones, such as confidence-building measures between government forces and the guerrilla movement, with reciprocal demobilizations occurring simultaneously. Government forces reduced from 63,000 to 31,000 troops, while the FMLN reduced by 10,000 cadres. With some obstructions arising in 1992, the demobilization continued haltingly, with ongoing demobilization continuing along with steady disarmament, despite clear evidence of reserve arms caches being maintained. By 1993, the UN had collected almost 10,000 weapons, including artillery pieces; four million rounds of ammunition; 9,000 grenades; and more than 5,000 assorted explosive devices.[29]

The Chapultepec Agreement had not considered the inclusion of a reintegration process. Instead, it called for collaboration between the government and the FMLN in a national reconstruction plan that offered official personal documentation and limited subsistence support to demobilized former combatants and supporters. Skills training workshops were established, and access to microcredit was supported. Midlevel commanders were offered business training opportunities and access to credit. Business start-up opportunities and access to jobs market were supported. Access to land and land reform was another major issue in a country with a very high density of 300 people per square kilometer. This difficult and controversial provision was partially resolved by a scheme of access to credit to purchase land, rather than providing direct access to land. Agricultural technical assistance was also offered, as were vocational and higher education opportunities and scholarships.

Organizations were established to support and represent the interests of the demobilized and disabled former combatants. The issue of dealing with child soldiers proved particularly difficult, as 9 percent of the government forces and 20 percent of the FMLN had been recruited under the age of fifteen years.[30] More than 62 percent of the child soldiers were released from service without inclusion in any rehabilitation program other than limited access to education, some support by bilateral agencies (such as GTZ, a German government development implementation agency), and some food subsidies.

According to Stiles, although the levels of crime in El Salvador in 2012 were extraordinary, it was difficult to attribute any of this crime to the results of the DDR program; many other subregional geopolitical and crime-related influences were at play, including the endemic narcotics trade. Despite clear weaknesses in the DDR program, there was no return to guerrilla activity. The common challenge, as with all DDR processes, has been the provision of employment for the demobilized and the impact of the influx of demobilized former combatants into the labor market on the opportunities for the broader youth. The mass repatriation of criminals from the United States has also negatively affected both the labor market and the domestic crime rate. Although Stiles did not see simple answers to the problems of crime and violence in El Salvador, he contended that the DDR effort offers an example of sound application with acceptable levels of success.

The practice of DDR grew from the successful application of confidence-building measures in a series of peace processes in South and Central America, necessitated largely by the changing global bipolarity at the end of the Cold War. Confidence-building measures were found to strengthen the perceptions of actors that the peacebuilding efforts were genuine. SSR was critical in resizing and retasking respective security sectors. This combination of confidence-building measures with SSR was also applied in various peace processes in southern Africa. DDR in El Salvador demonstrates the numerous challenges arising in such applications. Outcomes illustrate the limitations of DDR in consideration of the broader postconflict socioeconomic and security environment. DDR, an innovative practice area, and its related body of theory evolved from these origins.

Notes

1. These scholar/practitioners included Nat Colletta, Kees Kingma, Mats Berdal, Nicole Ball, Guy Lamb, and Bengt Junggren, among others.

2. The young scholars included Robert Muggah, Macartan Humphreys, Jeremy Weinstein, Sarah Meek, Walt Kilroy, and James Pougel, among others, together with practitioners such as Kees Steenken, Sofie da Camara, Luc Lafrenier, and Daniel Ladeuceur, who have worked to integrate the lessons learned into practice.

3. For example, Bonn International Center for Conversion, Clingendael Institute, Escola de Cultura de Pau, Center for Peace Studies, Tromsø University, Folke Bernadotte Academy, Pearson Centre, Norwegian Defence International Centre, and many others.

4. *National ownership* implies that the processes are compatible with the national postconflict recovery plan and are supported by a broad cross-section of local actors.

5. Dean M. Piedmont, formerly senior DDR desk officer at UN Development Programme, in comments on an early draft of this work, May 9, 2013.

6. Augusto Varas, James A. Schear, and Lisa Owens, eds., *Confidence-Building Measures in Latin America and the Southern Cone*, Report No. 16, Henry L. Stimson Center/FLACSO-Chile (Washington, DC: The Henry L. Stimson Center, February 1995).

7. Ibid., 2.

8. Ibid.

9. Ibid., v.

10. Jack Child, "Confidence-Building Measures and Their Application in Central America," in Varas, Schear, and Owens, *Confidence-Building Measures*, 6.

11. Ibid.

12. Ibid., 7, and also referring to the Report of the UN Secretary-General, "Agenda for Peace: Preventive Diplomacy, Peacemaking and Peacekeeping," by Boutros Boutros-Ghali, 17 June 1992.

13. UN Secretary-General, "Agenda for Peace."

14. Child, "Confidence-Building Measures," II.

15. Ibid.

16. Ibid., 12; "peace dominoes," originally coined in Fernando Cepeda, *Democracia y Desarrollo en America Latina* (Buenos Aires: GEL, 1985).

17. Ibid.

18. Child, "Confidence-Building Measures," 13.

19. Ibid., 17.

20. Quotes from Child, "Confidence-Building Measures."

21. Ibid., 19.

22. Ibid.

23. Sarah Meek, "Confidence-building Measures as Tools for Disarmament and Development," *African Security Review*, no. 1 (2005), 14.

24. Personal experience, Sierra Leone, 2001–2004.

25. UN Office for Disarmament Affairs, "UN Register of Conventional Arms," accessed July 25, 2012. Document A/65/133/Add.1, September 15, 2010. http://www.un.org/disarmament/convarms/Register/.

26. Meek, "Confidence-building Measures," 19, 20.

27. Thomas Shannon Stiles, "DDR in El Salvador," in *Demobilization, Disarmament, and Reintegration (DDR): Case Studies of Partial Success and Enduring Dilemmas*, ed. Richard Millett (Fort Leavenworth, KS: Combat Studies Institute Press, forthcoming 2017).

28. Ibid.

29. Ibid.

30. Ibid.

3

The Evolution of
the Practice

Since ancient times, victorious armies have imposed the practice of disarmament and demobilization on the vanquished, often with terminal results for the vanquished. Rather than reintegration, the Romans occasionally preferred to offer mass crucifixion. More recent examples of large-scale disarmament and demobilization operations include Prussia in 1807, Germany in both 1919 and 1945, and Japan in 1945. In the recent era, the biggest logistical operation associated with disarmament, demobilization, and repatriation was the return of Japanese troops from the Asian war theater to Japan in the aftermath of the 1945 Potsdam Proclamation. Potsdam saw the unconditional surrender of Japan and the division of spoils of war—the Asian territories—for administrative purposes, among the Allies. The proclamation was issued by the United States, the United Kingdom, and the nationalist government of China and was subsequently adopted by the USSR based on that nation's secret agreement with the Allies, formulated at the Yalta meeting of February 1945. The Potsdam Declaration, which laid out the terms for a Japanese surrender at the end of World War II, was initially met with silence from Japan and was only accepted days after the devastation of Hiroshima and Nagasaki by atomic bombs in August 1945.

At that time, in addition to approximately two million troops in Japan, there were about three million Japanese troops throughout Asia—in China, Manchuria, Korea, Formosa, Southeast Asia, and the East Indies.[1] Nearly two million who fell to the Russians in or around Manchuria (the Japanese puppet state of Manchukuo) were transported to Siberian concentration camps, often as slave labor. By the end of 1947, only 625,000 of these prisoners of war had been repatriated; more than 200,000 were retained in the Asian theater by Allied forces and the Chinese as slave labor, with some held for as long as two years after the war's end. By 1948, approximately two million Japanese troops were disarmed, demobilized, and repatriated to Japan.[2] They arrived, frequently into the remains of Hiroshima port, vanquished and ashamed, to find their homeland devastated and under occupation. Their repatriation benefits consisted of a cursory medical examination, delousing, and a train ticket to their home city. Their longer-term reintegration to sustainable livelihoods depended on the economic recovery of Japan, which, thankfully, was phenomenal. The operation of their repatriation was implemented efficiently, largely by the acquiescent, postsurrender Japanese administration, as the Allied supreme command under General Douglas MacArthur exercised indirect rule.

DDR as we know it today is a more recent evolution of such reintegration. Having seen how DDR per se originated in the confidence-building measures of the Central and South American peace processes (see Chapter 2), this chapter now launches a literary review that considers the writings of early DDR practitioner/scholars, who recorded the policies devised at the highest levels of government and by planners in international institutions, as well as the implementation methods tested by practitioners. These scholars listed the lessons learned at the field level that contributed to the evolution of the theory of DDR. This theory draws primarily on the evaluation reports of early DDR processes in southern and sub-Saharan Africa, mainly written for the World Bank and the Bonn International Center for Conversion (BICC). Such reports offered lists of constraints to implementation and rec-ommendations for good practice, and their contributions strengthened the foundations of the theory. A seminal contemporaneous literary review, by Guy Lamb, offered a view of the state of that theory in 1997.[3] In this way, a new practice area of DDR evolved, built on the foundations of a practice-tested theory. DDR, established in the minds of the implementers of post-conflict peacebuilding interventions during the 1990s, set the stage for what have since been termed as classic DDR processes.

The Early Days

Surplus arms and combatants in the context of a post–Cold War cessation of primarily intrastate violence in the developing world resulted in associ-ated excessive, recurring security budgets. Disarmament was identified as a critical need for both regional security and governments in seeking post-conflict stabilization. However, the process of demobilization—that is, the separation of the soldier from the military, both physically and mentally—was identified as an intrinsic aspect of reducing the potential for remobi-lization and the resumption of armed conflict, as it would take the peace process past the tipping point of irreversibility. The question of what to do with the demobilized former combatants gave rise to the development of a process of reintegration support that would assist former combatants in finding a sustainable livelihood in civil society.

The ending of the Cold War proxy wars in the early 1990s led to the requirement for demobilization of armies and armed groups, particularly in several African countries. This necessity arose especially in the strategic geopolitical area of the Horn of Africa. Driven by security, economic, and financial pressures, Eritrea, Ethiopia, Mozambique, Namibia, Uganda, Angola, Chad, and Somaliland had already completed or were engaged in demobilization processes. The future needs of Sierra Leone, Liberia, Somalia, Zaire (Democratic Republic of Congo), South Africa, and Sudan were beckoning. The World Bank was heavily engaged with governments in the region in stabilizing the economies and moving toward poverty reduction and development in the context of structural adjustment. German bilateral aid in particular focused on the region and the practice area of demobilization through the technical division of its international aid effort, the German Technical Cooperation Agency (GTZ). BICC was also engaged in much research in developing a systematic response to the demobilization needs of the Horn of Africa and undertook several studies.

A 1994 workshop report by Kees Kingma and Vanessa Sayers, titled "Demobilisation on the Horn of Africa," reflects the developing theory that was to be brought forward as the basis for DDR practice for subsequent decades.[4] The workshop's objective was to learn from global successes and failures in demobilization and the reintegration of former combatants, considering the Horn of Africa's minimal historical experience of the practice in contributing to increased human security and development. The purpose of the workshop was to avoid reinventing the wheel in designing demobilization and reintegration programs globally. Where long-running conflicts were ending and democratic practice was spreading, the call for demobilization of armies and armed organizations was increasing throughout Africa. This need demanded greater participation of a broad range of actors, including governments, bilateral supporters, international organizations, and NGOs. These positive developments required support for postconflict countries in developing the capacity for the design and implementation of effective programs.

Subsequently, such scholars as Nat Colletta and Mats Berdal have generally accepted the following basic tenets as identified in the workshop report: DDR, or the process of transforming a soldier to a civilian, is a continuum rather than a set of separate processes. It requires sound planning; reintegration, in particular, needs a culturally sensitive reorientation toward civilian life, in addition to material and technical support. Related decisionmakers must remain cognizant of the broader political and security concerns, including factors such as the ethnic makeup of the new security forces after demobilization, which is an SSR issue. It requires strong management of the relevant security dilemmas when addressing the sensitivities of the demobilizing forces engaged in the cessation of violence. Further, the potential security and economic impact of releasing a large number of former combatants into the community must be considered. Political will and cooperation between states are vital in addressing cross-border issues, managing surplus weapons, and preventing arms transfers. If the results are to be sustainable, national institutional capacity building for government and civil society sectors in supporting these efforts is vital to ensure national ownership of the DDR processes. Such efforts at national governance capacity building have often been referred to as "state building." However, this term, which was promoted by David Petraeus in his *Counterinsurgency Field Manual* of 2006, is now more associated with the US counterinsurgency efforts in Iraq and Afghanistan and has since been denigrated as representing a myth of the agency of expeditionary interventions in addressing their own interests.[5] The failures of those efforts were to have considerable bearing on reinforcing such cynicism.

The principal lessons learned in the Kingma and Sayers report, which generally approaches DDR as a perspective of SSR, are listed here briefly. For demobilization to succeed, unambiguous cessation of violence is necessary. Regional security and stability contribute to the success of demobilization. Demobilization, including the institutional framework required for implementation and any relevant SSR concerns, should specifically be mentioned in the comprehensive peace accord. Credible central authority is also necessary. DDR forms a continuum and requires a voluntary disarmament. Effective demobilization depends on effective rehabilitation and reintegration. Any type of lag between the processes constitutes a threat to the entire endeavor. In the Horn of Africa, a cultural affinity to arms is a complicating factor, and legislative arrangements are necessary to address this matter sensitively. Such arrangements may include, for example, an acceptable and nonthreatening registration and licensing procedure, as was somewhat successfully implemented in Somaliland. Initial creation of a unified national armed force—that is, the integration of forces—before implementing demobilization also avoids subsequent stigmatization and offers improved control mechanisms on combatant eligibility for the processes. Funds required to implement demobilization and reintegration processes should be confirmed up front to avoid insecurity driven by a cash-flow crisis. International commitment to the completion of the processes must be confirmed. The implementation of the processes should be nationally led and should take into consideration the appropriate political, social, and cultural context. Although central assembly points, such as cantonment sites, are useful to facilitate documentation, orientation, and counseling, they offer specific security, logistical, and social challenges; thus, the concept of concentrating even disarmed combatants in one location must be approached with great caution. Security and transparency in relation to arms collection and storage are critical. Disarmament should not focus simply on individual former combatants but should be considered comprehensively in a national and regional context; it should address the broader phenomenon of surplus weapons and porous borders, preferably in the context of regional security arrangements.

The reintegration program must fit into the national development plan. Initial socioeconomic profiling of the caseload is essential in supporting sound planning for socioeconomic reintegration. Demobilization and resettlement packages should be uniform across the range of direct beneficiaries. Career and sustainable livelihood counseling and access to microcredit are important. Governments should facilitate access to land, housing, or business space. In designing and implementing reintegration programs, local social and cultural values of both the individual former combatants and the communities of resettlement must be considered. The problem of AIDS/HIV must be considered, especially in the Horn of Africa. Vocational and managerial training is vital; sometimes such training can be offered even before demobilization. Management of reintegration support must be decentralized. The needs of female and child combatants and dependents must be considered, and psychosocial support will be crucial to successful reintegration. Although it may seem desirable to implement reintegration quickly, the determinant of the time needed is the achievement of the objectives of successful, sustainable socioeconomic reintegration. The report advises that sustainable reintegration requires a "general process of democratization,"[6] though this issue will be open to debate as contexts evolve.

According to Colletta, work really started on the development of DDR theory in Uganda in 1992.[7] This work was initially driven by what would now be considered SSR considerations in trying to divert public expenditures from nonproductive areas, such as defense, through a process of rightsizing the military. But this work was not done in pursuit of peace per se. The word *peace,* along with *conflict* and *security*, did not exist in the World Bank's lexicon in those days. Instead, the recurring budgetary implication of oversized militaries was a common theme for the Bretton Woods Institutions. Early scholar/practitioners of DDR got busy, with their output really starting to flow in 1994–1996 with a series of case studies on Uganda, Namibia, and Ethiopia, published by the World Bank's Africa Technical Unit. These case studies later emerged in Nat Colletta, Markus Kostner, and Ingo Wiederhofer's *The Transition from War to Peace in Sub-Saharan Africa,* which remains a seminal publication on the theory of DDR in Africa.[8]

In the foreword to the book, Kevin Cleaver outlined the environment of a changing and fragile Africa.[9] He referred to twenty-five million refugees and child soldiers, twenty million land mines, a huge percentage of arable farmland remaining fallow, and severe limitations on freedom of movement in many areas. Long-running wars, some as long as thirty years, were drawing to a close in the context of the end of the Cold War. An environment of weakened civil and national institutions and a breakdown in rule of law gave rise to warlord rule. The structure of human and social capital in communities was disrupted, with limited coping mechanisms to deal with disaster, whether natural or manmade. Countries in Africa were seeking ways to reduce the capital expenditure and recurring budgets, which until recently had been expended on a now-unsustainable security apparatus. In this climate, demobilization and reintegration programs, the downsizing of militaries, and a focus on economic revitalization were crucial for the continental transition to development. Under the leverage of structural adjustment, African countries were seeking World Bank leadership in the design and implementation of demobilization and reintegration programs, with specific requests for direct support coming from Uganda, Rwanda, and Mozambique. This launched the development of a model program in Uganda and the start of reintegration in Mozambique. Support for Rwanda was delayed by the political crisis and genocide of 1994.

Baseline lessons were drawn from an earlier World Bank study, titled "Demobilization and Reintegration of Military Personnel in Africa: The Evidence from Seven Country Case Studies."[10] As the study continued, additional candidate countries arose—Angola, Liberia, Sierra Leone, Djibouti, South Africa, and Togo. Namibia and Eritrea also sought further support. Beyond Africa were Cambodia, Bosnia, and Sri Lanka.

The World Bank Africa region established a postconflict rapid response team, facilitated by the Post-conflict Fund, to address the gap between relief and reconstruction. The guidelines for this team were developed through a three-country study (Uganda, Ethiopia, and Namibia) that analyzed three different demobilization and reintegration environments. In Uganda, these processes addressed a peacetime restructuring of military forces driven by macroeconomic constraints and political consensus—clearly, SSR processes. Ethiopia was responding to emergency conditions, with the sudden victory of the government of the day creating the need to demobilize approximately 450,000 combatants of the defeated Dergue army. In Namibia, the settlement negotiated by the UN and South Africa was followed by a UN occupation and UN-managed repatriation and demobilization process; the complex reintegration process, however, was left to the new government.

The primary findings of this study were that demobilization and reintegration programs contribute constructively to supporting the transition from war to peace. In the context of a comprehensive peace accord or in the peacetime restructuring of public finances in favor of poverty reduction and peacebuilding, demobilization and reintegration programs facilitate a movement toward development. Reinsertion (the absorption of former combatants into the civilian community) and reintegration (the actual "civilianization" of former combatants) are both part of the continuum in the transition from military to civilian life. Although these two were not initially identified as distinct processes from demobilization, Colletta et al. identified from the outset that the demobilization and reintegration processes are more broadly concerned with rebuilding the communities' social fabric—that is, rebuilding trust and contributing to national reconciliation. The process requires several integrated actions: the classification of former combatants, the provision of a preliminary transition safety package to each former combatant, support from a simple delivery system, sensitization of communities, and building on existing social capital. Thus, demobilization and reintegration programs must be coordinated centrally, while also offering decentralized implementation and decision-making authority. Demobilization and reintegration programs must be fully integrated with ongoing national development efforts.

The comparative study opens with an overview of the postconflict political status of each country and the status of combatants. Ethiopian economy and society had been ravaged by a twenty-nine-year guerrilla war, until the Ethiopian People's Revolutionary Democratic Front seized power and established the transitional government of Ethiopia in 1991. Faced with almost half a million former combatants of the defeated Dergue army, the transitional government of Ethiopia established a commission to design and implement a demobilization and reintegration program. The immediate objective was to restore security and stability by restricting the movement of former combatants to transit centers, with the longer-term goal of facilitating their social and economic reintegration into society.

In Namibia, after the UN brokered independence in 1990, the repatriation and reintegration of combatants coincided with the creation of the new nation after seventy years of South African rule. Reinsertion and reintegration were not well planned, however, and many former combatants failed to reintegrate economically. Pressure from disaffected veterans forced the government to act, unfortunately in a patchwork of ad hoc activities. In 1996, the government commenced to redesign what was hoped to be a more effective reintegration program.

In Uganda, after fifteen years of guerrilla war, the National Resistance Movement came to power in 1989. However, sporadic rebellion continued across the country until 1991, causing a spiraling increase in capital needs for recurring defense budget. When the military opposition was defeated in 1991, the government refocused national expenditure on social and economic development. Between 1992 and 1995, this focus required a resizing by demobilization of 36,500 of the 90,000-strong National Resistance Army. The Uganda Veterans Assistance Program was launched to implement this demobilization, with the objectives of (1) effecting the demobilization and resettlement of the former combatants and their families, (2) facilitating sustainable social and economic reintegration, and (3) restructuring public expenditure, redirecting funds to priority programs such as economic and social infrastructure and services.[11]

Colletta et al. asserted that the most important factors in determining the success, or otherwise, of a demobilization and reintegration program are the political commitment, realism, and pragmatism of the national government and international community toward implementation. A government must not promise more than it can deliver. A program that is ineffectively coordinated will lead to duplication of payment and effort and a waste of resources. Thus, sound strategic planning is critical. Swift cost-benefit analysis must be undertaken during the design phase of the demobilization and reintegration program, and trade-offs have to be made in such areas as coverage versus sustainability, expedience versus relevancy, and control versus initiative. Successful strategy is related to providing the minimum assistance package, simplicity in delivery, and decentralized decisionmaking, while also building on existing social capital and the reorientation of local institutions. Program implementation should be prioritized by simplicity first—completing simpler tasks first—while optimizing use of resources and timely delivery of assistance. Long-term reintegration of former combatants should not be neglected in favor of short-term pacification and repatriation. DDR programs should stick to program guidelines and should not create a dependency syndrome.

The transition from soldier to civilian can be differentiated into three phases—demobilization, reinsertion, and reintegration—with distinct safety requirements and individual needs for each phase. Transitory safety allowance must be provided to bridge the gap between demobilization and reintegration. Baseline data for program design, socioeconomic profiling, job opportunity, and market information, both rural and urban, are essential. Reliable, durable, nontransferable identification documents with a photo (indisputable identification) are essential. Veteran associations, such as comrade committees, can facilitate identification at the point of entry to the demobilization and reintegration program.

Specific needs of females and children associated with the fighting groups should be addressed as a priority issue. This step takes the approach to DDR beyond the minimal focus, purely on the former combatants, to what Robert Muggah termed the "maximalist" approach.[12] This approach has huge implications not only on the potential impact but also on the scope, complexity, and cost of the processes. Any cantonment of former combatants should be for as short a period as possible, as this stage has security, logistical, and cost implications. Urban reintegration—particularly if the former combatants are from rural backgrounds and opt not to relocate to their communities of origin—is more complex than rural reintegration and needs due consideration (planning, counseling, placement support and referral, vocational training and employment subsidy schemes, community preparation, and so forth). Demand-driven skills training—that is, training that addresses skills gaps in the market—and job placement schemes should be linked.

An effective, technologically advanced information and dissemination system, especially one that targets beneficiaries, is essential to offer accurate information on opportunities, constraints, procedures, and time frames, such as schedules for benefits payment. Such a system can reduce frustrations and enhance client-program collaboration, thereby supporting the social and economic reintegration. The interplay of community physical and social capital, together with the influx of former combatants' financial and human capital, will determine the success (or otherwise) of reintegration.

Support for nonpolitical social networks among former combatants can contribute to social and economic reintegration. Governments and donors need to avoid placing labels on former combatants that can stigmatize and alienate. Coordination within and between governments and all relevant actors is important for maximizing the effectiveness of interventions. A single civil agency tasked with the design and implementation of the demobilization and reintegration program can serve this purpose best. Central coordination, balanced by decentralized decisionmaking and implementation authority to districts, contributes to an effective institutional structure. Decentralized field offices are necessary to reach the client load and to understand the local contexts.

Demonstrating that participative approaches are not new to DDR theory, Colletta et al. advised that local communities should be directly involved in decisionmaking related to the community. Communities should be mobilized as intermediaries for problem solving through such vehicles as community advisory committees, which can positively influence and guide former combatants. Community support should be fully utilized, and former combatant groups should ideally have elected representatives who liaise with the program and represent their interests in the community.

The peace dividend needs to be understood by all actors and appreciated not only in social and economic terms but also in financial terms. Unless social expenditures are allocated effectively, a high ratio of social-to-defense spending does not necessarily translate to benefits for the poor.

In another seminal study of the pre-DDR era, Mats Berdal built on the lessons listed by Kingma and Sayers (1995).[13] Berdal provided analysis of the efforts to disarm, demobilize, and reintegrate both government and guerrilla forces after prolonged internal conflicts in Angola, Mozambique, Somalia, and Central America. He considered the impact of the continuing influence of the belligerents where a cessation of violence is achieved but without a decisive victory by either side. In doing so, he emphasized the dependence of successful demobilization and reintegration on its linkages with parallel efforts of political, social, and economic reconstruction aimed at addressing root causes of the conflict. He advised that disarmament must be voluntary, because coercive disarmament will offer only short-term results. Instead, the focus should be on devaluing the necessity of arms in society, contributing to consent-based disarmament, rather than seeking to eliminate them altogether. Demobilization and reintegration processes must be better managed than heretofore, and international support efforts must focus more on SSR, including advocacy for civil primacy and respect for human rights, local capacity, and infrastructure building, rather than on implementation of the processes. The processes of demobilization and reintegration have been difficult, and internationally supported initiatives experienced considerable setbacks during the 1990s. These concepts will need to be addressed moving forward.

In 1997, Guy Lamb surveyed the literature on the interrelated concepts of demilitarization and peacebuilding in southern Africa in order to determine the state of scholarly affairs in these matters at the end of the Cold War and "to possibly contribute to the general dynamic of demilitarization and peacebuilding."[14] His findings reflected on how, in scholarly literature at a global level, southern Africa is contributing to the evolution of DDR theory in the practice of demobilization and peacebuilding.

The end of bipolar rivalry has offered unprecedented opportunity for peace, both locally and globally, while at the same time opening the gates for fresh interstate and intrastate conflicts. Through the production of a substantial volume of interdisciplinary literature, scholars have focused on how to encourage the opportunities, while restricting fresh outbreaks of violence. This research has resulted in a fundamental shift in the direction of the theory of security, peace, and conflict, including raising the concept of peacebuilding. The new global environment has also given rise to demilitarization, particularly in those states that were affected by proxy conflicts, as occurred in much of southern Africa. Lamb classified the literature into several categories: mechanisms for peace and security, case studies, and policy recommendations. He noted the empirical wealth alongside the dearth of theory in the literature.

Lamb noted an absence of consensus regarding definitions, which, in turn, has led to analytical ambiguity. He drew on the UN discussion on peacebuilding from the Secretary-General's report of 1992, "Agenda for Peace: Preventive Diplomacy, Peacemaking, and Peacekeeping," which outlines a comprehensive list of activities and a range of mechanisms contributing to peacebuilding, including DDR, election monitoring, protection of human rights, government institutional capacity building, social and economic reform, and reconciliation. The term *peacebuilding* had become "a 'catchall' concept for a range of vague theories about security, development and conflict prevention."[15]

After World War II, the concept of demilitarized zones was realized as a confidence-building measure and as a buffer between belligerents. During the Cold War, the concept of demilitarization became the almost exclusive domain of peace studies scholars. After the Cold War, the concept of demilitarization was being analyzed from the social and cultural perspective, along with ideas such as civil primacy, demobilization of combatants, disarmament, cuts in military spending, and the conversion of security industries, as well as a growing debate on the ideology that views violence as a legitimate projection of politics. Lamb argued that the linkage of demilitarization and peacebuilding was symbiotic because a focus on demilitarization narrows the vagueness of the catchall nature of peacebuilding, whereas linking the contested concept of demilitarization to peace reduces the conceptual confusion.

The bulk of the relevant literature in southern Africa, predominantly on peacebuilding, arrived in the 1990s, with the dominant themes being regional security, confidence-building measures, demobilization and reintegration of combatants, military review and reconstruction, peacekeeping, disarmament and arms control, and civil-military relations.[16]

Mechanisms for Peace and Security

Dramatic change was occurring in southern Africa by the end of the 1980s and early 1990s. The thawing of the hostile environments and ideologically based distrust common to the Cold War period and the dismantling of apartheid required a redefinition of *security*. A new security paradigm was devised that

> perceived security from being synonymous with defence, to a more inclusive understanding that took into account the political, economic societal and environmental dimensions as well. Such a framework envisages human security as ultimately more important than state security.[17]

Peacekeeping

This area includes many reviews of regional UN peacekeeping missions, in addition to the ideas of building capacity of regional peacekeeping partnerships, such as the Southern African Development Community.

Disarmament

With small arms seen as a major destabilizing factor in southern Africa, the reduction of illicit weapons and the strengthening of arms control were major issues. Weak frontiers and the unaccountable trafficking of the newly surplus arms were leading to a proliferation of arms and localized destabilization. With the growing perception that arms control was essential to the maintenance of peace, means of containing and controlling small arms—seen as an intrinsically political and long-term process—was a focus of research.

Conversion

Closely related to disarmament and a broader aspect of SSR, conversion focuses on how resources heretofore applied to security might be converted to economic benefit. A small amount of this literature—in particular, from BICC—considers the macroeconomic contribution of conversion to social benefits, such as poverty reduction and development.

Peace Dividend and Economic Development

Although a range of literature has pursued the peace dividend associated with demilitarization and peacebuilding, Lamb claimed that, in reality, the peace dividend has been negligible for southern Africa.

Demobilization and Reintegration

These two are the most popular subjects of literature associated with demilitarization and peacebuilding. Lamb mentioned that these processes are context specific and that often the "distinction between where the demobilization ends and social reintegration begins differs . . . and leads to a degree of confusion." The processes are volatile, but if well managed, they can create opportunities for sustainable peace and development.

Civil-Military Relations

This tends to be a scholarly (sociology and political science) approach that centers on the analysis of the relationships between the military and civil society. Its modern focus is on the concept of civil primacy, the depoliticization of the military, and the creation of smaller professional military forces.

Most of the available literature on DDR is in the form of case studies—either single country or comparative cases—with Zimbabwe, Namibia, Mozambique, South Africa, and Angola featuring in southern Africa. Although a few of the studies are in-depth analyses through multi-country studies—particularly those initiated by the World Bank, BICC, and so on—most are merely descriptive of the problems, with little attempt to collate the analysis into a body of guidelines. With the collapse of the Bicesse Accords of 1992 and the return to violence between the National Union for the Total Independence of Angola and the Popular Movement for the Liberation of Angola, much study focused on the reasons for that failure, as opposed to the relative success of South West African People's Organization in Namibia, a productive UN peacekeeping intervention in Mozambique, the DDR program in Zimbabwe, and South Africa's demilitarization, military restructuring, and peacebuilding.[18]

Lamb considered the case studies of Berdal and Colletta, Kostner, and Wiederhofer. Despite conceptual confusion between the terms *demilitarization* and *peacebuilding* and their relationship, the case studies tended to be rigorous in data collection and descriptive presentation, offering insightful policy recommendations. However, Berdal tended to focus on South Africa, was vague, and did not reflect long-term vision. More pointedly, his review lacked a theoretical outlook, with only limited effort to formulate propositions, hypotheses, and general guidance, reflecting an ad hoc approach to addressing demilitarization and peacebuilding rather than "a coherent and theoretically driven approach that addresses the interrelated phenomena of peace-building and demilitarization in a systematic and co-ordinated fashion."[19] Lamb noted that this lack is due to it being a relatively new field of study and the fact that only a few individuals are focusing on it. He did predict that with an improvement in general quality, it would develop into a field of research in its own right.

Review

Those case studies of the early practice of DDR collated the lessons learned, laid the foundations of the theory, and added to a vibrant field of research. The programs, mainly in southern and sub-Saharan Africa, were deemed critical in guiding the transformation of conflict to peace and in rebuilding the social fabric of communities—that is, trust and reconcilia-tion. They occurred in the context of an end to hostilities in postcolonial readjustments of internal power structures in weak or conflict-affected states or the petering out of post–Cold War proxy civil wars. The studies led to a more structured approach—some would say a template or cookie-cutter approach—to the international community delivering DDR as an aspect of a comprehensive peace accord. These are the classic cases of DDR. The evolution of DDR saw a growing focus on human security–related outcomes and contribution to sustainable peace.

Human Security

Human security is a contested concept that is often considered as the repackaging and relaunching, by the UN Development Program in the 1994 *Human Development Report,* of two of the most universally acceptable of Franklin Roosevelt's Four Freedoms—Freedom from Fear and Freedom from Want. The human security agenda emerged in an optimistic and enlightening post–Cold War Western world. It strove to securitize a rights-based approach to development that addressed the plight of humans rather than focusing purely on macro aspects of state physical, political, and eco-nomic security. The desired outcomes were represented in the Millennium Development Goals (MDGs), which stated seven objectives: universal eco-nomic security, food security, health security, environmental security, per-sonal security, community security, and political security. The human secu-rity concept has been championed by specific states—in particular, Canada, Thailand, and Japan. And yet, although it was a foundational concept for planning and implementing DDR since the mid-1990s, it is currently a con-cept under threat. The MDGs were superseded in late 2015 by the new expanded list of Sustainable Development Goals, a complex list of 17 goals and 169 targets. These SDGs are sufficiently amorphous to offer less of a challenge to the security versus human security debate and its implication for the primacy of state sovereignty.

Paul James's definition of *human security* is appropriate:

> Human security can be defined as one of the foundational conditions of being human, including both (1) the sustainable protection and provision of the mate-rial conditions for meeting the embodied needs of people, and (2) the protection of the variable existential conditions for maintaining a dignified life.[20]

From the perspective of the humanitarian practitioner, human security and responsibility to protect are more than cold concepts;[21] they are a state of mind that offers an overarching people-centered philosophy and personal commitment in planning and implementing humanitarian interventions. This understanding of the impact of the human security agenda, together with the even more contested concept of responsibility to protect, are the overarching philosophical guidance to my consideration and insights on DDR that will permeate this book.

Notes

1. Statistics from Gunnar Rekvig, PhD candidate at Tokyo University of Foreign Studies, "Aspects of DDR in a Historical Context: Post–World War II Japan" (presentation to Peace Studies Masters Course, Hiroshima University, Japan, October 11, 2009).

2. Adapted from John W. Dower, *Embracing Defeat: Japan in the Wake of World War II* (London: Allen Lane, 1999), 50–54.

3. Guy Lamb, "Demilitarisation and Peacebuilding in Southern Africa: A Survey of Literature," CCR Staff Papers, Center for Conflict Resolution, University of Cape Town, South Africa 1997.

4. Kees Kingma (BICC) and Vanessa Sayers (InterAfrica Group), "Demobilisation on the Horn of Africa" (proceedings of the International Resource Group on Disarmament and Security in the Horn of Africa, Workshop Brief No. 4, December 4–7, 1994, Addis Ababa, Ethiopia, published June 1995).

5. General David H. Petraeus and James A. Amos, *FM3-24 MCWP 3-33.3 COIN: Manual of Offensive, Defensive, and Stability Operations* (Washington, DC: Headquarters, Department of the Army, December 2006).

6. Kingma and Sayers, "Demobilisation," 7.

7. Nat Colletta discussed these issues in an e-mail to the author, July 21, 2012.

8. Nat Colletta, Markus Kostner, and Ingo Wiederhofer, *The Transition from War to Peace in Sub-Saharan Africa* (Washington, DC: World Bank, 1996).

9. Ibid. Kevin Cleaver was the director of the World Bank, Technical Department, Africa Region.

10. World Bank, "Demobilization and Reintegration of Military Personnel in Africa: The Evidence from Seven Country Case Studies" (discussion paper, Africa Regional Series No. IDP-130, October 1993).

11. All statistics from World Bank, "Demobilization and Reintegration of Military Personnel in Africa."

12. Robert Muggah, ed., *Security and Post-Conflict Reconstruction: Dealing with Fighters in the Aftermath of War* (London: Routledge, 2009), 3.

13. Mats Berdal, "Disarmament and Demobilization After Civil Wars," Adelphi Paper 303 (London: Oxford University Press, 1996).

14. Lamb, "Demilitarisation."

15. Ibid.

16. Ibid.

17. Ibid.

18. UNITA, National Union for the Total Independence of Angola; MPLA, Popular Movement for Liberation of Angola; SWAPO, South West African People's Organization (Namibia).

19. Lamb, "Demilitarisation."

20. Paul James, "Human Security as a Military Security Leftover, or as Part of the Human Condition?" in *Human Security and Japan's Triple Disaster,* eds. Paul Bacon and Christopher Hobson (London: Routledge, 2014), 87.

21. Responsibility to protect (R2P or RtoP) is a contested concept initiated by the UN and launched at the World Summit in 2005, contributing to perceived emerging humanitarian norms based on an assertion that sovereignty cannot merely be an absolute right, but also a responsibility.

4

The Classic DDR Approach

A dramatic increase in the demand for DDR interventions arose in the early to mid-1990s in the context of UN peacekeeping missions—in particular, those missions that addressed the reduction in armed conflict in the bubbling cauldron of sub-Saharan Africa. In response, planners and practitioners struggled for coherence in designing approaches. They used existing skill sets and avoided reinventing the wheel to make the best use of limited resources to stabilize political environments and achieve degrees of sustainable peace. The lessons learned had evolved while addressing the cessations of violence predominantly through the implementation of SSR processes. The political environments, which were mainly associated with residual post-decolonization stabilization in places of inequity and deprivation, were ripe for social revolution that often spawned rural insurgencies opposing entrenched urban elites. All of this coincided with the evolving post–Cold War dynamics as proxy wars ran out of steam.

A common wisdom had arisen that, in order to facilitate successful DDR, certain prerequisites were necessary, including a cessation of violence in the context of a comprehensive peace agreement, the need for a secure environment, the need for national ownership demonstrating sufficient political will to see the processes through, and the voluntary commitment of participants. In seeking these prerequisites, the resulting DDR interventions assumed elements of a template approach. This chapter considers some of these template cases, referred to by practitioners—perhaps nostalgic for the associated technical coherence—as classic cases of DDR. These cases include events in Sierra Leone, Liberia, and the Multi-country Demobilization and Reintegration Program (MDRP) and the follow-on Transitional Demobilization and Reintegration Program (TDRP) in the Great Lakes Region of Africa, as well as the difficulties for DDR in current-day South Sudan. This chapter also lays the basis for the subsequent evolution of a DDR theory broadening toward an emphasis on community security and community-based approaches, as well as DDR in contexts other than postconflict environments.

"Classic" DDR

The continuing armed violence of the post–Cold War era was often related to decolonization and postindependence readjustments of power. In this context, rural masses often perceived themselves as marginalized by urban elites and strove for social, economic, and political inclusion through insurgency. This era was then followed by a changing post–Cold War dynamic, as proxy insurgencies closely associated with those social revolutions suddenly ran out of steam.

DDR planning had drawn largely on the experience of the related security- and conversion-driven SSR processes implemented early in the DDR era from the mid-1980s—that is, the rightsizing of national armed forces to address readjusted and reduced security needs and the conversion of resources toward social spending. But by the turn of the millennium the focus of international interest was shifting from those earlier SSR considerations in the new postconflict contexts. Struggling to address the proliferating demand for large-scale international DDR interventions associated with UN peacekeeping missions, planners and practitioners sought levels of technical coherence through the development of road maps for DDR in evolving postconflict contexts. This evolution saw a greater focus on stabilization and peace per se, which were now assumed to be critical elements, or prerequisites, for development. Also coming to the fore was a consideration of the impact of the imposition of large numbers of underemployed former combatants on that peace, as well as the socioeconomic impact on their communities.

Common wisdom drawn from experience assumed the necessity of prerequisites for DDR implementation. These prerequisites generally included that DDR must be implemented after the cessation of armed violence in the context of a comprehensive peace accord; broad political will must exist for DDR to be viable; and the processes of DDR must be nationally owned, with national stakeholders viewing them as essential to national recovery. It was also considered necessary to have unitary command of each participating armed group so that agreed-upon decisions could be enforced. Voluntary commitment by participants to the DDR process was vital. Further, DDR had to be implemented in a secure environment. Planners drafted a range of documents incorporating these prerequisites to offer field and classroom guidance to practice.[1] This cumulative guidance subsequently coalesced in contributing to the Integrated DDR Standards of 2006.

Such prerequisites have rarely all been in place or have existed to fluctuating extents, even in early DDR processes. However, practitioners came to consider the DDR processes implemented with a focus on these prerequisites as relatively simple to rationalize and address with technical template responses as examples of classic or traditional DDR. A brief review of a cross-section of those classic DDR processes will set the stage for the transition using second-generation DDR to address the emerging complexity of DDR in nonpermissive environments, particularly in situations other than postconflict.

Sierra Leone

The ten-year civil war in Sierra Leone launched in the late 1980s, not as an aspect of the diminishing post–Cold War proxy conflicts but largely as a genuine social revolution of a disenchanted rural youth excluded from the political, social, and economic life of the state, in their view, by a corrupt and avaricious urban elite.[2] As such, that civil war may reflect a paradigm shift away from the post–Cold War dynamic. The conflict was greatly encouraged by the goading and support of neighboring strongman, Charles Taylor of Liberia, who was seeking to fund his own internal conflict through control of the rich Sierra Leonean diamond fields in the northeast provinces of Kono and Kailahun, where hordes of hungry youth were scraping the now-infamous blood diamonds from muddy waterholes. The conflict in Sierra Leone was noted for its brutality, with the Revolutionary United Front terrorizing the civilian population through wanton destruction, abduction, enslavement, enforced child combatants, rape, amputation, and mass murder. With the minor players being a weak state defense force (the Sierra Leone Army) and a splinter group (the opportunist Armed Forces Revolutionary Council), the Civil Defence Force, a loosely organized force of mobilized population largely comprising traditional hunting groups, mounted a defense that often offered similar brutality in response.

In achieving the semblance of a negotiated settlement to a protracted conflict, particularly one in which there may not be genuine "good guys" and in which an outright victory by either side is unlikely, the sacrifice of justice over peace often becomes a recurring theme. The extraordinary scene after the signing of the Lomé Peace Accord, the negotiation of which was facilitated by Jesse Jackson of the United States, saw Foday Sankoh, the notorious leader of the Revolutionary United Front, enthroned as the minister for natural resources and virtual vice president of Sierra Leone. This gave him control over his prime resource and the basis of fraternity with Taylor—the blood diamonds. The elevation of Sankoh, the instigator of the most brutal crimes against humanity during the civil war, was a macabre projection of black humor that led to an arrogant sense of empowerment within the Revolutionary United Front. It encouraged their return to gross violence with the kidnapping of UN peacekeepers and the 1999 brutal attack on Freetown, which resulted in the murder of more than 6,000 citizens. In his account of his time as chief of UN DDR in Sierra Leone from

2001 to 2002, Kenji Isezaki was incredulous at the amnesty for Sankoh.[3] He equated it to the idea of the United States nominating Osama bin Laden as vice president in an attempt to end the War on Terror, a suggestion he had heard during a BBC radio show soon after 9/11. Isezaki mentioned that whereas approximately 3,000 people died in the Twin Towers attack, Sankoh was responsible for performing thousands of amputations on children and more than 50,000 deaths in Sierra Leone.

In light of its impact on regional security in neighboring Guinea, Liberia, and Côte d'Ivoire and the potential for broader associated humanitarian crises, the UN Security Council encouraged a series of negotiations and approved intervention in Sierra Leone. This series of negotiations, which was done with the support of the Economic Community of West African States (ECOWAS), resulted in the UN Development Programme (UNDP) launching a DDR program that targeted more than 75,000 combatants. The National Committee for DDR was established as an authoritative institutional structure, and the World Bank was tasked with marshaling resources through the management of a Multi-Donor Trust Fund.

The Lomé Peace Accord of 1999 had offered an effective comprehensive peace accord, with international support authorized by Security Council Resolution 1270 (October 1999). This accord was put into effect by a multiagency joint operational plan involving the government of Sierra Leone, the ECOWAS Monitoring Group, the UN Assistance Mission in Sierra Leone (UNAMSIL), and other partners.[4]

The DDR process progressed in three attempts with two false starts punctuated by the Revolutionary United Front's attacks on Freetown, the massacre of civilians, and incidents that included the mass kidnapping of UN troops. The resurgence ended when the Revolutionary United Front was finally defeated in robust action by Nigerian troops under the auspices of ECOWAS and British Special Air Service, leading to the start of effective DDR at its third attempt in 2001.

The launch of the Special Court for Sierra Leone in January 2002, a mechanism of transitional justice under the auspices of the International Criminal Court, greatly subdued the leaders of the Revolutionary United Front and contributed to their subsequent low profile and the organization's rapid demise. At this time the DDR Section of the United Nations was concerned that the speed with which the Special Court was mobilizing to indict senior leadership of both the Revolutionary United Front and the Civil Defence Forces for war crimes and crimes against humanity would discourage participation of former combatants in the DDR process. However, the influence of the Revolutionary United Front leadership over its cadres was much diminished, and the court did not appear to have noticeable adverse impact. In the initial postconflict general election of May 2002, the Revolutionary United Front, in the absence of any political platform or legitimacy, evaporated. Isezaki contended that the Revolutionary United Front leadership, after the removal of the charismatic and deemed-as-mystical leader, Sankoh, conceded to the earlier lunacy of the conflict and did not seriously contest the election.

The national DDR program recognized that demobilization would require not only the formal break in the command, control, and communications capacity between the armed group hierarchy and the former combatants, but also the adjustment of the mind-set of the former combatants to allow reorientation as a civilian. If the former had not been broken, it could have resulted in a rapid remobilization. As the Revolutionary United Front evaporated as a cohesive military and political entity, the former cadres found themselves cast adrift and dependent on the DDR process; therefore, aspects of their demobilization occurred by default. The demobilization of the Civil Defence Forces was a more nebulous affair, however, with rumors of their community-based militia activities lingering long after formal demobilization. The demobilization of mind-sets was to be a result of time and a successful reintegration process after seeing former combatants take their place in civil society.

Upon demobilization, former combatants were granted a transitional security allowance of $150, later termed in Phase III as reinsertion benefits. This amount was based on the estimated cost of living while awaiting take-up in a reintegration option package and the start of the associated monthly allowance. The United Kingdom's Department for International Development, a senior partner in reintegration, was concerned that such an allowance might be associated with the concept of weapons buyback and thus enhance the regional market for weapons, rather than discourage it. Thus, great effort was made to dissociate this allowance from the disarmament process, which gave rise to a broader consideration of the pros and cons of using cash incentives with former combatants in DDR processes. (For more information, see Chapter 7.) Isabela Leao found that the transitional security allowance/reinsertion benefit in Sierra Leone had a positive impact that was sometimes more significant than the formal reintegration education or skills training packages, in that the former provided the microcapital to permit former combatants to launch their desired small businesses.[5]

The stated objectives of reintegration in Sierra Leone was to support the return of former combatants to their home communities or communities of choice; to assist former combatants to become productive members of their communities; to use the potential of former combatants to enhance human and social capital in the community; to promote community-based reconciliation; and to spread the peace dividend. The choice of livelihood support options offered to each former combatant included education, agriculture, fisheries, vocational training, and microentrepreneurial support, together with the payment of subsistence allowances for a period of six months and the issue of tool kits related to the specific vocational training in most cases.

Between 1999 and 2001, when the disarmament phases were completed, the National Committee for DDR had registered 76,000 former combatants of all factions, including 6,000 children. (Note that this number may include some double-counting of combatants during the three phases of DDR.) By 2001, 67,000 former combatants were disarmed, and 57,000 opted for inclusion in the reintegration. Of the remaining 10,000 former combatants, 2,500 were absorbed into the newly tasked and restructured Sierra Leone army.[6] It is difficult to account for the remaining 7,500 former combatants. Some may have died or emigrated between 1999 and 2001. Some self-reintegrated, having their own coping mechanisms or wishing to avoid the stigma of former combatant status. Others may have seen greener pastures in joining the conflicts in Liberia and Côte d'Ivoire. Certainly, I met a few of the latter prior to the initial chaotic disarmament at Camp Schieffelin in Liberia in December 2003.

Thorsten Benner, Stephan Mergenthaler, and Philipp Rotmann presented a considerable potpourri of speculation about Sierra Leone's DDR program in relation to the missing numbers of former combatants and other elements of the DDR process in order to provide an example of lessons learned from incomplete reintegration.[7] An initial error in their piece, however, is in their reference to the *UN's* DDR program in Sierra Leone. This was a program owned and led by the government of Sierra Leone, with funding coordinated by the World Bank through the Multi-donor Trust Fund, with support from UNAMSIL and development partners; the UN mission in Sierra Leone was not responsible for the fundraising. The problematic hiatus of funding that occurred at the beginning of the Sierra Leone program was associated with World Bank systems rather than having anything to do with UNAMSIL. Benner et al. also referred to disgruntled former combatants who were awaiting support of the DDR process and who became easy prey for Charles Taylor's Liberian recruiters.[8] Indeed, some Sierra Leone former combatants joined several factions in Liberia, including the rebel group Liberians United for Reconciliation and Democracy, while others went farther afield to what may have appeared to be a more lucrative conflict in Côte d'Ivoire. However, the authors ignored the extraordinary achievement of the Sierra Leone DDR in processing 57,000 former combatants through a reintegration process that contributed to the sustainable cessation of armed violence. Instead, they focused on the few thousand who may have crossed the frontier into Liberia, some of whom may never have opted to enter the reintegration process in the first place. It is a long stretch to this situation reflecting "the disastrous consequence of the DDR program in Sierra Leone."[9]

The UN DDR role was to support the nationally led DDR effort by mobilizing partners to address funding and capacity gaps in delivery. The parameters for UN DDR were to contribute to the broader stabilization of peace by ensuring that the DDR process had a positive impact on the communities of Sierra Leone in the context of the human security agenda; thus, it was a people-centered approach.

However, there were serious constraints and planning difficulties associated with the program. Whereas the National Committee for DDR had estimated that 28,000 former combatants would present for Phase III of registration, 47,000 turned up and met the criteria. This misjudgment in the numbers contributed to initial funding difficulties. Furthermore, as the program launched, two-thirds of the country was still under Revolutionary United Front control with the government gaining access only in mid-2001. In response to these challenges, the National Committee for DDR, with partner support, accelerated the delivery of reintegration support.[10] The delays in cash flows, particularly the late delivery of subsistence allowances, led to intimidating, high-profile local outbreaks of vocal aggression by groups of volatile, angry former combatants. Decentralized staff of the National Committee for DDR and of the UN DDR Section that operated regional offices dealt with some tricky situations, such as the blockading of offices and the intimidation of both national and international staff members.

To help address the specific centers of concentration of the most volatile former combatants—that is, those whose spontaneous return to armed violence could derail the process—Isezaki and the UN DDR Section, in collaboration with UNDP and the UK's Department for International Development, launched the Stopgap Program. This series of targeted, community-based local infrastructure and mass employment projects covered about three months of employment, each project valued at a total of about $30,000 and engaging approximately 100 workers, both former combatants and community members. These were not like the quick-impact projects being implemented by the Civil Affairs office of UNAM-SIL and local NGOs that were geared toward the rehabilitation of vital infrastructure. Instead, they were more focused on the process of engagement, contributing to reconciliation, and demonstrating the benefits of the peace dividend. They were planned and implemented through a community participative process engaging local government, traditional leadership, and a representative committee, including sages, women, youth, vulnerable groups, and community-based organizations. The program had positive effects beyond the original objectives and won a prestigious UN21 Award for project implementation and impact; it also helped launch the stopgap concept in many subsequent DDR programs.[11]

One particular area in which the DDR process in Sierra Leone failed was in not ensuring the equitable, not to mention equal, treatment of female former combatants and women associated with the fighting groups. Women were generally omitted in the peace negotiations, with cursory paternalistic and patronizing mention in the Lomé Peace Accord. Whereas the DDR program emphasized from the outset the early release of children associated with the armed groups, addressing the issue of women associated with the armed groups was approached much more tentatively, perhaps in deference to local cultural sensitivities and to avoid creating unnecessary dividers that could obstruct the process. In addition to being neglected by the DDR process, many female former combatants and enforced bush wives, who are often among the most vulnerable of society, were stigmatized and rejected by their own communities or were hidden by armed group commanders throughout the reintegration process. Frequently, in preparing for the DDR process, female former combatants were either deprived of their entitled benefits or had their entitlement handed over to a male who had not earned it, as chosen by the commander. These women were frequently left without any support or were totally dependent on the amazing work of NGOs, such as Caritas Internationalis in the town of Makeni. The clear disparity and injustice associated with this issue in Sierra Leone drew considerable focus to the gender perspective.[12] Since then, much has been studied regarding this neglect, and much, as we shall see later, has progressed in the practice of DDR in reforming the failure to adequately consider the gender perspective.

A specific feature of the Sierra Leone DDR process that contributed to the trend within the UN of moving toward agency-integrated programming was the close relations that the DDR Section of UNAMSIL maintained with its development partner, UNDP. This informal institutional relationship was nurtured through good personal relations among the relevant technical officers in both organizations. This integrated approach was greatly encouraged by Alan Doss, the senior deputy special representative of the UN Secretary-General (DSRSG). Doss was also the first of the triple-hatted DSRSG, concurrently serving as resident humanitarian coordinator and resident representative of the UNDP, in the UN's experiment in encouraging the various divisions of the UN to "act as one." Through this relationship, the two UN entities combined resources to develop synergy in delivering the Stopgap Program. They then set a further example by working in collaboration to deliver follow-on small arms control programs. One such program was the Community Arms Collection and Destruction program, in which the UNDP contributed to the capacity building of the Sierra Leone police force in addressing small arms control issues. This coercive measure immediately followed the DDR process and involved police cordon and search of houses after a given amnesty period for the hand-in of small arms and respective sanctions for offenders. Following this program, by way of developing synergy, the Arms for Development program was a sweep-up process involving the strengthening of the community's will to ensure an arms-free community. Each chiefdom community that was declared arms free after a police investigation was then given the opportunity of a self-chosen infrastructure project, planned and implemented in a participative and representative way. This successful program has been replicated in many other DDR processes.

A process of defense sector reform, an aspect of SSR, was launched by the government of Sierra Leone to restructure the Sierra Leone army and was supported bilaterally by the UK's International Military Advisory Training Team, a team of mixed commonwealth training troops. Through this reform, approximately 2,500 of the demobilized former combatants were absorbed into the Sierra Leone army. However, neither the planning nor the implementation of this process included consultations or any significant level of collaboration with the DDR process. In fact, the relationship between defense sector reform and DDR was hardly considered. Looking back on the specific context in Sierra Leone and in light of the total demise of the Revolutionary United Front, any large-scale absorption into the downsizing Sierra Leone army would have been inappropriate. Considering the clear control of the government of Sierra Leone over the Sierra Leone army at this stage, it is doubtful that there existed any scope for significant collaboration between the defense sector reform process and DDR; therefore, DDR was not implemented as an aspect of SSR. This gives some indication of how far the classic model of DDR had evolved from its forbearers in South and Central America and in Southern Africa, which had revolved around SSR in the context of post–Cold War readjustment.

Did DDR work in Sierra Leone? Scholars debate the impact of the DDR process in Sierra Leone, especially focusing on its objectives. Macartan Humphreys and Jeremy Weinstein applied rigorous scholarly methodology based on a refined regression analysis of the results of a large-N survey of more than 1,000 former combatants of "what the fighters said."[13] The authors could find little evidence that reintegration support had any impact on contributing to sustainable livelihoods for former combatants in Sierra Leone; these findings were subsequently reinterpreted to suggest that there was little evidence of DDR contributing to the peace process. Although it is indeed difficult to apportion the impact of a DDR process on the stabilization of a peace process because it is just one of the relevant interventions, the DDR in Sierra Leone did create a broad confidence in the commitment of the fighting groups to peace.

Sufficient levels of trust were developed through the institutional structures supporting the planning and implementation of the DDR process. The president's office had executive responsibility; the Tripartite Committee made up by representatives of government, the Revolutionary United Front and the UN defined policy; and the National Committee for DDR handled implementation. In the Tripartite Committee's discussions of the methods of operationalizing each DDR element, the main security dilemmas could be addressed right from the disarmament and cantonment phase. Furthermore, the DDR process removed many surplus weapons from the theater and contributed to positive perceptions in civil society of better potential for the constructive engagement of former combatants in civil society. It can therefore be considered that this DDR process did contribute to reducing the odds of a return to armed violence. Indeed, Sierra Leone has never returned to organized armed violence and has seen a relatively peaceful transfer of power in successful elections; thus, the DDR process implemented in Sierra Leone in the context of the Lomé Peace Accord (1999–2004) can justifiably claim success. The country continues to face extraordinary challenges, as demonstrated by the Ebola outbreak. However, remembering the futility of one of the most brutal civil wars in recent history, it is clear that things have changed for the better in terms of armed violence in Sierra Leone.

As the DDR process in Sierra Leone drew to a close in mid-2003, the UN, driven by energetic individuals in the UN Department of Peacekeeping Operations and the UNDP, such as Kelvin Ong and Spyros Demetriou, was planning the development of a body of policy guidance to offer some conceptual coherence and institutional direction for the ever-expanding practice of DDR. Much was drawn from the lessons being learned in Sierra Leone and apparently being concurrently unlearned in Liberia. This work was to later emerge as the Integrated DDR Standards (IDDRS), a body of guidance agreed to by a majority of UN agencies and international collaborating organizations. The standards, once published in December 2006, drew together the most critical lessons learned and the division of labor for DDR implementation, while reviewing the standards in a systematic, dynamic way to support timely evolution of that guidance to match evolving contexts in other nations. The debacle in the launch of the DDR process in Liberia in late 2003 drew UN headquarters management support to the drafting process and added impetus to the urgency of developing the IDDRS.

Liberia

Observing the launch of DDR in Liberia in late 2003 was like having the overview of a preplanned train crash.[14] Although the dynamics of the tribal conflict in Liberia were different from the social revolution in Sierra Leone, the unbridled ambitions of Charles Taylor were a common denominator. As mentioned earlier, Taylor was able to retain his dominance thanks to the wealth of the Sierra Leonean diamond fields. With the demise of the Revolutionary United Front, however, Taylor's fortunes were also doomed. In opposing Taylor in early 2003, the covert hand of regional support from Republic of Guinea to the north together with some apparent US logistical engagement was discernable. Taylor was overcome and, after a sojourn in Nigeria, is now and for the foreseeable future a guest of the International Criminal Court. Taylor's removal opened the doors for a peace process.

With Liberians United for Reconciliation and Democracy bearing down on Monrovia from the north and others pressuring from the east, a peace accord between belligerents was negotiated and signed in the Accra Comprehensive Peace Accord of August 2003. A Security Council resolution immediately established the UN Mission in Liberia (UNMIL), the deployment of which was slower than anticipated, as is frequently the case. Early during this deployment, retired US Air Force Reserve Major General Jacques Klein, the mission's special representative of the Secretary-General, was seen to be under exceptional pressure by US ambassador John Blaney to collect weapons quickly and at all costs.[15] It was clear to me, visiting occasionally from Sierra Leone as external DDR adviser, that disarmament was being viewed as a solution to the potential for the reemergence of violence in the absence of an adequately negotiated political solution. With no experienced DDR expert in the mission, the top management of UNMIL, under bilateral pressure, pushed to disarm groups in what amounted to a cash buyback program. Although I advised against this course of action, UNMIL went ahead and advertised a cash reward for the surrender of weapons and struck a minimum criterion for entry into the process of the hand-up of 150 rounds of ammunition.

In early December 2003, UNMIL launched the DDR process at Camp Schieffelin, a military camp about 60 kilometers north of Monrovia. The operation planned to receive 1,200 participants; over three days, 13,150 armed elements came forward, many clearly not belligerents but meeting the generous criteria set forth by the mission. They all claimed the immediate cash benefit. This action reflected the success of the reinsertion allowance device used in Sierra Leone to address immediate subsistence needs and to act as encouragement to go forward with the reintegration phase; however, it did so without robust entry criteria. In Sierra Leone, $150 was paid up-front to clearly identified combatants, with $150 more being paid on the first visit to the relevant regional reintegration office to launch the process of entering into the selected reintegration package. UNMIL management saw this payment more as a transitional security allowance—that is, a device to defuse an immediate security threat posed by the large numbers of unpredictable marauding armed groups. In other words, they used it in an attempt to defuse the threat of armed violence and to get arms rapidly turned in, rather than as the application of negotiated political solutions. The huge numbers of people turning in arms were unmanageable, and UN staff in the field were under threat. A few volatile days ensued that included nightly riots in Monrovia in which at least eight people were killed. The angry mob fired weapons in the air around UNMIL headquarters in Monrovia.

With UNMIL in panic and with a cash shortage, they agreed that all claimants meeting the minimum criteria would be paid half the initial promised cash incentive immediately ($75) and the balance later. Because such cash was not readily available to UNMIL, however, a helicopter was dispatched to Freetown to borrow from UNAMSIL's bank account. Over a very dangerous few days, with UN staff continuously under threat of violence, the payments were made. The cash benefits were even paid out to children, against the basic principles of DDR pertaining to children, as then articulated and broadly accepted in the Cape Town Principles.[16] During this phase of the DDR process, more than 8,600 mixed-quality weapons, some of which were unserviceable, and more than 2.7 million rounds of ammunition were collected. There are tales of former faction leaders and acting ministers, who had held significant stocks of weapons, getting relatively rich at this time by employing gangs of youth to come forward, on a commission basis, with a weapon for this virtual "buyback" process.

At the early stages of the process, the coordination between UNDP, the agency tasked with delivering subsequent reintegration packages, and UNMIL, which had responsibility for the disarmament and demobilization aspects of the process, was, to say the least, poor. This fact did not improve with time, as the relationship between the UNDP DDR coordinator and the individual selected to lead UNMIL's DDR effort was openly hostile.[17] The same can be said of UNMIL's initial relationship with the agencies and NGOs that were to provide specialist support to the demobilization phase, including camp management, catering, medical support, handling of children, and so forth. The mission's initial coordinating efforts with these agencies were dictatorial and, in some cases, threatening. This attitude had a lasting adverse effect on levels of collaboration among the mission, UNDP, and NGOs in delivering reintegration.

The integrated vision for the DDR process, which was guided by people-centered conceptual parameters, that was used during the UN's DDR support in Sierra Leone was replaced with a blind focus on immediate disarmament, collection of weapons, and immediate security. This focus led to available resources being used to fund the virtual buyback, with little left for the subsequent—and, at the time, poorly planned—reintegration process. By the end of disarmament in 2005, 102,200 eligible claimants had entered the process, and 27,000 assorted weapons had been collected. These weapons included more than 3,100 (or 63 percent of a shipment) high-quality Serbian Zastava M70 AB2 assault rifles for which import records exist and 6.15 million rounds of assorted ammunition.[18]

If the success of Liberia's DDR process was to be measured solely by the numbers of beneficiaries absorbed, as the special representative of the Secretary-General saw it, then UNMIL could claim success. However, other criteria are more telling. The low ratio of just better than one weapon for every four "former combatants" (the Sierra Leone ratio was approximately 1:2) points to the inappropriateness of the entry criteria. It is clear that the policy of accepting 150 rounds of ammunition as the entry criteria, without any mechanism for confirmation of entitlement, to a program with an initial cash payout of $300, in addition to subsequent inclusion in a reintegration option valued at about $1,000, was attractive and was well exploited by a very UN-savvy people. Some sources claim that up to 60 percent of the total caseload consisted of people who had never been affiliated with any fighting force in what has been referred to as a commercialization of the DDR process.[19] The regional market for ammunition was well stimulated, and sources in Sierra Leone were aware of the movement of ammunition out of Sierra Leone to Liberia to take advantage of the benefits of Liberia's DDR program. It is also clear that many of the heavy weapons used early in Liberia's conflict—120-mm mortars and field artillery pieces—had been transported to Guinea and Côte d'Ivoire early in the intervention process, before the effective deployment of UNMIL force and military observers to the remote and rebel-held areas of Liberia.

The misdirection of this DDR process seems to have originated with the traditional pitfall of attempting to develop a solution to a political and security problem using a disarmament mechanism. This is a critical and classical error in any volatile postconflict scenario, driven in part by the illusion that the collection of weapons will resolve the security problem. In this case, the need for the United States to remove weapons that might be traced back to them was another alleged issue.[20] DDR must be the result of political agreement and must follow the political and stabilization process. The absence of any accredited DDR expert in UNMIL, from its inception, was an extraordinary failing for an organization with the UN's resources.

The UN interagency evaluation on the progress of DDR in Liberia was convened after the Camp Schieffelin debacle of December 2003. It confirmed that many causes of the problem were predominately due to external pressure and abysmal planning. The damage was done, criteria had been established, and the following years of implementation consisted largely of damage limitation and knock-on impact. However, one spin-off benefit of the huge numbers of beneficiaries included in this DDR process, even if it broke the bank and extended the period of the DDR process to 2009, is that subsequent analysis—in particular, by James Pugel—identified clear, positive impact from the provision of reintegration support to a large proportion of the population.[21]

Multicountry Demobilization and Reintegration in Africa's Great Lakes Region

After two decades of multiple violent conflicts affecting half the countries in Africa and a third of its population, the World Bank's Multi-country Demobilization and Reintegration Program (MDRP) was the most ambitious DDR response ever undertaken in partnership with national governments, donors, and international institutions. In fact, MDRP was the largest DDR program undertaken in the world, with a total budget of $450 million.[22] It brought together unprecedented partnership with forty-three partners, seven national governments, thirteen donors, eleven UN agencies, regional organizations, and NGOs.[23] It took a regional approach that covered seven countries—Democratic Republic of Congo, Republic of Congo, Burundi, Central African Republic, Uganda, Angola, and Rwanda; however, it was implemented based on the principle of national ownership of the processes affecting each specific country. Each country, with assistance, established its own demobilization, reinsertion, and reintegration program. Significant cross-border learning was realized and networks established to address security, political, and development issues in the most volatile areas of the world. Multiple issues were addressed, many in innovative ways. These included dealing with foreign combatants; addressing elements of the gender perspective and child soldiers; operationalizing transitional justice mechanisms; coordinating cross-border issues requiring negotiation and diplomacy; and addressing country-specific objectives through regional action. After seven years in operation in the Great Lakes Region of Central Africa, from April 2002 to June 2009, MDRP closed after demobilizing close to 300,000 former combatants.

With the imprimatur of the World Bank offering strong political signals to actors and donors at the outset, funds were pledged in advance and donor resources pooled. Overarching management institutions were established in Washington, DC, an Advisory Committee and a Technical Coordinating Group. These institutions functioned efficiently but could have had greater direct impact if more policy discussions had been held in the field. The post-program evaluators suggested that despite its huge scale, MDRP had low visibility within the World Bank structure. Furthermore, diverse reporting lines complicated the program's management structure, as these were often interdepartmental within the World Bank rather than internal to the MDRP hierarchy. In addition, external experts did not often know of World Bank procedures, which led to bureaucratic tensions. Better decentralization, away from Washington, would have made more sense, with a visible and high-level field presence put in place.

MDRP offered daunting challenges with extreme logistical and operational complexity. Delays were often caused in specific country programs by political logjams and poor management at national levels. Yet, it was able to meet most of the demobilization and reinsertion targets. Clearly, the greatest challenge lay in delivering sustainable reintegration of former combatants. The Scanteam report advised that livelihood support must be realistic and market friendly, suggesting that this may not have been the case. However, livelihood viability cannot be delivered by a DDR program focused on former combatants; rather, it is dependent on dynamics in the larger economy. Further, technology must be practical, given local conditions and capacities. Resources must be earmarked for special groups, as was the case of child soldiers—though this did not work so well for female former combatants. As with the program in Sierra Leone, much of the support that female former combatants did receive came later from outside the program. It is also critical to develop a more professional approach to monitoring and evaluation; this stage must be programmed into implementation and not considered as an ad hoc afterthought. Perhaps the monitoring and evaluation function within MDRP could have been contracted to specialist agencies. Considering the program's extraordinary security, political, and development challenges, the design was inadequate.

Bilateral donor commitment, in particular, tended to fluctuate with political interests, electoral cycles, and changing attitudes toward the targeting of overseas development aid.[24] This fluctuation occasionally led to uncertainty regarding cash flows and planning for subsequent phases of programming. Dedicated donor staff seemed to rotate frequently, leading to occasional poor interpartner communications, as well as poor communications with headquarters. Host governments, while welcoming DDR support, were sensitive to policy decisions and perceived incursions into their sovereignty. Strong stable governments were better able to participate constructively than were weak ones. Thus, it was necessary to take account of specific country capacities and ambitions for the program to be scaled appropriately. In such a complex environment, roles and tasking needed to be spelled out in a broad operational plan early in the program.

The MDRP's regional approach to DDR, while contributing to the complexity of implementation, was critical in light of the volatility, the porous borders, the transferability of combatants, and the range and interconnectedness of local conflicts in the Great Lakes region. Due to the varying levels of national cohesion, interests, and chronologies regarding implementation, continuous negotiation was needed to achieve the regional outputs. Thus, country-specific outputs were more easily realized than regional ones.

According to the evaluation report by Scanteam, MDRP was an efficient vehicle offering financial transparency and accountability, consistent management, and harmonized reporting. In its cross-border functions, it offered opportunities for peer learning and intercountry trust- and confidence-building measures.[25] All mechanisms had to be adapted to country-specific contexts and requirements, and national ownership was deemed an essential quality. However, the dilemma of government ownership versus broader national ownership was ever present and was initially poorly defined, often leading to tensions. Taking into consideration the broader community, including civil society, could have brought in the potential spoilers and built trust.[26]

The devastated postconflict countries of MDRP faced significant capacity constraints—political, management, technical, and physical capacity needs. Because capacity development is a long-term commitment, judicial consideration was needed regarding the amount of capacity development the program should invest. However, knowing that DDR tends to extend beyond the initial planned time frame and that reintegration is not a time-bound process, Scanteam advised that capacity development could well prove a sound investment.

Further consideration was needed in the establishment and maintenance of knowledge management mechanisms. Although the World Bank was proactive in knowledge management, the UN and donor countries could have contributed more in this area. Although the regional approach was the big success of MDRP, upstream considerations (policy and SSR) and downstream links to DDR (sustainable reintegration) needed to be systematically identified and addressed. The impact and sustainability of steps taken under DDR could increase with inclusion into these broader agendas.[27] The institutional memory of MDRP must be retained. The report noted that this DDR effort was the most high-risk endeavor ever undertaken by the World Bank.

Quality Enhancement and Innovation in Regional and Community Approaches

When MDRP closed operations in June 2009, it had coordinated and provided assistance to more than 300,000 former combatants in seven countries in the Great Lakes Region. It had also generated much literature offering lessons, good practice, and recommendations.[28] And yet, the job was incomplete. A four-year follow-on program called the Transitional Demobilization and Reintegration Program (TDRP) was launched with a multidonor fund of US$33.2 million provided by the African Development Bank, Belgium, Finland, France, Italy, Norway, and Sweden. This program was managed by the World Bank with the aim of building on the lessons learned and the regional peacebuilding networking of MDRP. The TDRP represents a financing mechanism of last resort, intervening only when country-level and regional resources could not address critical needs in DDR.[29] The primary objectives were to continue to provide technical assistance and support to ongoing demobilization and reintegration programs in the Great Lakes Region; to expand demobilization and reintegration coverage by providing emergency financing to demobilization and reintegration programs with funding gaps; and to facilitate dialogue, information exchange, and learning on demobilization and reintegration through a process of "quality enhancement and innovation."[30] This process of quality enhancement and innovation included supporting and building the capacity of local and collective initiatives for reintegration and peacebuilding, working together with academic institutions and community organizations, and thus deriving synergies.

TDRP focused its efforts on Central African Republic, Rwanda, Burundi, Uganda, and Democratic Republic of Congo in supporting specifically designed efforts toward capacity building for the reintegration of former combatants.[31] In Central African Republic, which returned to conflict after the overthrow of François Bozizé in March 2013, a community reintegration program was being implemented by international NGOs with an established foothold primarily in the communities. Such an approach made great sense in light of the recent abortive efforts at DDR by UNDP in Central African Republic. The initial process of DDR of combatants in 2004–2007, known by the French acronym PRAC, demonstrated the complexity of attempting to deliver DDR in an environment of instability and extraordinary obfuscation in the absence of political will and a penchant for prebendalism, where the elite feel that they have a right to share in the state's revenues. The second effort, in 2008–2009, funded by the UN Peacebuilding Fund, was based on the comprehensive peace accord signed at Libreville, Gabon, in June 2008; its implementation was to be supervised by the oversight committee. But, again, this attempt offered DDR in an environment of continuing instability and extraordinary obstruction.[32] Initially, rapid progress was made in establishing the appropriate national institutional structure (specifically, the National DDR Steering Committee); developing the necessary documentation, including a joint operational plan; setting the parameters for DDR with the belligerent factions; establishing weapons criteria; securing lists of eligible combatants; and planning a validation process to confirm eligibility.[33] However, the process was halted in an environment of elite capture of resources and rent taking, both by the government and rebel commanders, with a perceived level of regional collusion. In such conditions, the community-based approach being pursued by TDRP was probably the most appropriate solution that could see benefits reach the most vulnerable war-affected communities and offer reintegration opportunities for former combatants, especially in the informal economy that existed in the absence of a functioning formal economy.

In Rwanda, after having demobilized and reinserted relevant former combatants, the focus was on continuing reintegration support for former combatants, including children, women, and disabled people, through programs led by the government of Rwanda. The program successfully mainstreamed the former combatants into the state social services system. Likewise, the UN Organization Stabilization Mission in the Democratic Republic of Congo saw the World Bank's TDRP respond to requests for assistance in DDR. In driving toward regional ownership of the efforts, TDRP has been collaborating with the UN Department of Peacekeeping Operations to develop capacity within the African Union through DDR training. In addition to the five focus countries, such capacity building was also undertaken in Côte d'Ivoire, Niger, and South Sudan.

With innovative approaches bearing fruit and demonstrating the development of regional capacity, TDRP extended operations beyond its planned completion date of 2012. The complexity and challenges of the multicountry DDR environment and the continuing volatility in the Great Lakes Region remain daunting and offer a clear indication of how difficult it is to quantify an adequate return on investment. However, this innovative approach for providing international organization technical assistance (advice) and support (training, material, and on-the-ground management support) to regional DDR, as well as developing regional capacity using community approaches through quality enhancement and innovation, represents the application of lessons, potential good practice, and a positive development within the evolution of the DDR theory.

During TDRP's delivery of reintegration support in multiple countries from 2010 to 2012, the World Bank coordinated the creation of an extraordinary data set based on the responses of almost 10,000 former combatants and community members to more than 100 questions concerning the socioeconomic aspects of the reintegration process and the transition from military to civilian. This is the largest such data set ever compiled. The first classification and presentation of this data set, including some preliminary comparative analysis, was completed by Randolph Rhea and Qinyu Cao of Tromsø

University's Centre for Peace Studies and was published by the World Bank in July 2014.[34] The initial analysis of this huge data set offers useful evidence-based findings regarding the impact of reintegration support in the TDRP. Further, it provides the material for scholarly mining and analysis for years to come and offers a new resource—"the cutting-edge of empirically driven quantitative research on the reintegration process of former combatants"—to support research and planning for DDR processes into the next generation.[35]

DDR Stalemate in South Sudan, 2015

In Sudan, prior to the separation into two states, the UN initiated a DDR process along "classic" lines targeting 90,000 combatants.[36] This program, launched in 2004, reached only 25 percent of that caseload in a contrary environment that included an absence of political will and local ownership, intractable disagreement between the government of Sudan and the UN regarding the approach to be taken, funding delays, and low national capacity. Dysfunction in the institutional relationship, manifest in personality clashes between the DDR chiefs of the UN Department of Peacekeeping Operations and the UNDP, initially undermined the effort to enforce institutional integration. This was concurrent with the equally challenging piloting of such an integrated approach in Haiti. All of this was compounded by the imminent split of Sudan into two countries needing separate institutions and restructured approaches. Attempts to implement DDR in the nascent South Sudan were not going to be any easier.

DDR in South Sudan/Sudan Phase I (2005–2012) was approached from the perspective of the classic DDR process implemented following cessation of violence in a major civil war, postreferendum interstate war. Dean Piedmont suggested that this approach was wrong. The mistake was in pressing the classic approach against this conflict, as this approach did not address any of the following issues:

- a nonbinding comprehensive peace accord
- a referendum for a two-state solution
- the resulting two stronger armies
- the level of specific-needs groups (SNGs) and the need for strategic interim stabilization measures
- the necessity for four separate DDR processes in both countries (Sudan and South Sudan)
- the complexity of ongoing DDR in peacekeeping operations and non-peacekeeping operation missions in both countries
- international conflict and civil conflict occurring simultaneously
- the additional complexity of SNGs also prominent in the SSR caseload[37]

Despite an early virtual cessation of hostilities, there was little progress. The absence of elements of trust between belligerents and the birthing pangs of the newly established Republic of South Sudan resulted, despite the necessary national implementation and oversight institutions being established, in South Sudan's DDR process being all dressed up with nowhere to go. That process was constrained and delayed, largely impeded by the continuing security dilemma of whether to disarm or strengthen the Sudanese and the South Sudanese armies. Regional tensions and local conflict contributed to an absence of political will within both the Sudan People's Liberation Army (SPLA) and the government of South Sudan to implement either SSR or the associated DDR.

With the focus on the SPLA forces, which is now the national army of South Sudan, both the government of South Sudan and international donors considered DDR a vital process to contribute to the stabilization of the peace process and the transition to development, all to be implemented in the context of a comprehensive SSR process. The plan (Phase II DDR) targeted the disarmament, demobilization, and reintegration of 150,000 SPLA combatants and police. This aspect of SSR involved resizing and retasking in order to address the "four A's" of delivering an adequate, appropriate, affordable, and accountable armed force. This DDR process was to be implemented as a joint exercise by the government of South Sudan and the UN Mission in the Republic of South Sudan. It was envisaged to start in 2013 and to run for eight years with a budget of US$1.2 billion, of which 64 percent was to be covered by the government of South Sudan.[38]

In early 2013, continuing constraints and security considerations, including the continuing skirmishes in the Sudan/South Sudan conflict and tribal uprisings, resulted in continuous recruitment by SPLA, which created a negative environment for DDR. This was compounded by austerity resulting from the closure of the oil pipeline to the port in Sudan, due to a dispute between the governments, thus shutting off South Sudan's major source of revenue. In the absence of political will, capacity, or requisite resources, the UN and the government of South Sudan planned to launch a pilot phase targeting just 500 SPLA combatants, down from an initial target group of 4,500 combatants. Due to the inability to proceed with the main SSR/DDR of downsizing the SPLA by 150,000, the UN recommended refocusing on SNGs for 2013–2014, while continuing to engage with the government of South Sudan in planning the broader SSR/DDR process. These recommendations appeared to be based on the following factors:

- There were few resources (due to the oil shutdown of April 2013), nor was there evidence of political will to proceed with the main SSR/DDR. Therefore, it was unlikely to move forward in 2013.
- Interim DDR programs were already focused on SNGs, including aged, disabled combatants; women associated with armed forces; and

children associated with armed forces. National and UN capacities were already developed to address this reduced target.

- Focus on SNGs would allow for progress while emphasizing a human security approach, as there is an estimated caseload of 12,525 SNGs in South Sudan.
- The SSR/DDR process of downsizing by 150,000 would remain nationally owned, which is a critical factor considering the absence of UN leverage in driving it.

However, as civil violence re-erupted in early 2014, progress even on this limited scale was difficult. UN staffs were evacuated, and all effort refocused on the cessation of violence and the prevention of a looming massive humanitarian disaster.

With a DDR program in stalemate in early 2016, the UN was drawing lessons learned from many dimensions of the attempted launch of DDR in Sudan in 2004 to the current efforts in both Sudan and South Sudan. Such lessons include the need to analyze and strengthen aspects of UN-integrated programming, predeployment assessments, integrated mission planning processes, political analyses, national ownership, DDR timing, and realistic targeting. In light of the reversion to widespread civil violence in 2014 and 2015, it remains to be seen whether the proposed DDR in South Sudan can proceed. Although it no longer appears to meet the classic criteria, it may gradually shift into a new hybrid of next-generation DDR.

The dynamic evolution of the theory of DDR has shifted from the immediate post–Cold War focus on security, to a contribution to defense rightsizing and conversion as an aspect of SSR, to a peacebuilding focus in the context of human security. Sierra Leone, seen from the practitioner's perspective, demonstrated the effectiveness of the tested solutions to the many challenges and opportunities experienced. Such opportunities included the value of informal integrated relationships among UN agencies, the synergy of collaborative programs, and the beginnings of the development of the Integrated DDR Standards, which offer conceptual coherence within the UN system. Liberia offered an overview, from my own perspective, of the dangers of DDR driven by third-party interests, where the host government has little leverage. The World Bank–led MDRP in the Great Lakes Region of Africa offered the most complex DDR process ever yet attempted. Drawing on in-program and independent assessments, the follow-on TDRP saw theory evolving toward a greater commitment to nationally owned, case-specific, community-based implementation of DDR. In current-day South Sudan, I reviewed the challenges of attempting to implement DDR in an unstable conflict environment with limited international community leverage and ongoing civil war. The scene is now set for a consideration of the attempts to implement community-based approaches to DDR and the shift into second-generation DDR, which operationalizes conflict sensitivity in optimizing DDR's potential contribution to conflict transformation.[39]

Notes

1. Desmond Molloy, *The DDR Process in Sierra Leone: An Interim Report: Lessons Learned,* an internal document of UN Assistance Mission in Sierra Leone, UNAMSIL, Freetown, August 28, 2003; Ian Douglas, Colin Gleichmann, Michael Odenwald, Kees Steenken, and Adrian Wilkinson, *Disarmament, Demobilization, and Reintegration: A Practical Field and Classroom Guide* (Frankfurt: German Technical Cooperation Agency, Norwegian Defence International Centre, Pearson Peacekeeping Center, and Swedish National Defence College, 2004); among others.

2. Drawn largely from Desmond Molloy, *Sierra Leone and Discovering DDR: Conflict Resolution and Peace Building in Africa: Lessons Learned,* trans. Yujiro Tokumitsu (Kyoto: Ryukyu University Kyoto, March 2011); Desmond Molloy, "DDR in Sierra Leone 1999–2005 and an Overview of the Pitfalls of DDR in Liberia 2003–2009," (unpublished, Tokyo University of Foreign Studies, 2009); Desmond Molloy, *The Qualitative Quantitative Dilemma: Analysis of Indicators of Achievement as Used in DDR Programmes* (Tokyo: Tokyo University of Foreign Studies, 2009); and my contemporaneous notes as chief of DDR Section with UNAMSIL, Sierra Leone, 2002–2004.

3. Kenji Isezaki, *Disarmament: The World Through the Eyes of a Conflict Buster,* published in Japanese by Kodansha Gendhi Shinho in January 2004, translated into English in 2011, 54.

4. Including UN Development Programme (UNDP), UN Children's Emergency Fund (UNICEF), World Food Programme (WFP), Department for International Development (DfID), and German Technical Cooperation Agency (GTZ).

5. Isabela Leao, *Swimming Against the Stream: DDR in Sierra Leone* (PhD dissertation, State University of Milan, January 2011).

6. These statistics are drawn from National Committee for DDR, *DDR in Sierra Leone Final Report,* 2004, as published by the Office of the President.

7. Thorsten Benner, Stephan Mergenthaler, and Philipp Rotmann, "Reintegration: From Quick Fixes to Sustainable Social Reintegration," in *The New World of UN Peace Operations: Learning to Build Peace?* (Oxford: Oxford University Press, 2011), ch. 6.

8. Ibid.

9. Ibid.

10. Support to the DDR program came primarily from UNAMSIL, UNDP, UNICEF, DfID, US Agency for International Development (USAID), and GTZ.

11. The UN Secretary-General established the UN21 Award in 1996 to provide recognition to staff members for innovation, efficiency, and excellence in delivery of the organization's programs and services (accessed July 7, 2014, http://www.un .org/webcast/un21awards/).

12. Including Desmond Molloy, "The Gender Perspective in DDR: Lessons from Sierra Leone," *Conflict Trends,* Fall 2004, Accord, South Africa.

13. Macartan Humphreys and Jeremy Weinstein, "What the Fighters Say: A Survey of Ex-combatants in Sierra Leone" (CGSD Working Paper 20, Columbia University, Center on Globalization and Sustainable Development, with the Sierra Leonean NGO PRIDE-Salone, 2004).

14. As chief of DDR in Sierra Leone, I traveled as DDR adviser to Liberia. Advice rebuffed, I was subsequently a member of the UN interagency team sent to carry out the post mortem following the abortive launch of DDR in December 2003.

15. I met Ambassador Blaney two times while visiting Monrovia as UN DDR adviser to UNMIL in mid- and late 2003. However, on both occasions, it was Blaney who did the talking.

16. Cape Town Principles was an agreement among international NGOs of the criteria for defining *child soldiers* and the manner in which the international com-

munity should address the phenomenon. These criteria were later ratified as the Paris Commitments.

17. I kept close communication with the officer tasked with implementing UNDP's end of the DDR, a personal friend, and was approached by UN headquarters to mediate in the issue.

18. Wolf-Christian Paes, "Eyewitness: The Challenges of DDR in Liberia," *International Peacekeeping* 12 no. 2 (2005).

19. Ibid.

20. Richard Millett, ed., in his *Demobilization, Disarmament and Reintegration (DDR): Case Studies of Partial Success and Enduring Dilemmas* (Fort Leavenworth, KS: Combat Studies Institute Press, forthcoming 2017), chapter 11, Conclusions, 3, mentions that US ambassador Blaney says that he personally carried home some "Redeye" human-portable, surface-to-air missiles (ManPads, Man Portable Air Defense Systems), collected from Liberia.

21. James Pugel replicated the methodology that Humphreys and Weinstein ("What the Fighters Say") had used in studying reintegration in Sierra Leone (2005–2006), after having adapted the operationalization of the variables for Liberia in his *What the Fighters Say: A Survey of Ex-combatants in Liberia, February–March 2006* (New York: UNDP and ANPPCAN, April 2007).

22. Drawn from Scanteam Analysts and Advisers, *Final Report on the Multi-country Demobilization and Reintegration Program: End of Program Evaluation* (Oslo: Scanteam, June 2010).

23. These statistics are taken from a Skype discussion with DDR desk officer at UNDP's Bureau for Crisis Prevention and Recovery, New York, August 12, 2012.

24. Regarding fluctuating political interests, immediate postconflict environments can see the priorities of donors and lead countries change rapidly, as influenced by the Metropolitan Effect, the changing attitudes of its home electorate.

25. Drawn from Scanteam, *Final Report on the Multi-country Demobilization and Reintegration Program.*

26. The term *spoilers* can be very subjective, depending on perspective.

27. Scanteam, *Final Report on the Multi-country Demobilization and Reintegration Program.*

28. Guy Lamb, *Assessing the Reintegration of Ex-combatants in the Context of Instability and Informal Economies: The Cases of the Central African Republic, the Democratic Republic of Congo, and South Sudan* (Washington, DC: International Bank for Reconstruction and Development and World Bank, December 2011), 9.

29. Transitional Disarmament and Reintegration Program (TDRP), *Quarterly Report*, (Washington, DC: World Bank, July-September 2012), Annex II, 19.

30. TDRP, *Overview* (Washington, DC: World Bank, November 2011).

31. Technical details of the TDRP are drawn from TDRP, *Quarterly Report* (Washington, DC: World Bank, October–December 2011).

32. I was UN Senior DDR adviser in Central African Republic for the beginning of the latter effort.

33. Most technical data on the DDR process for 2008–2009 are drawn from "Update on DDR Process, CAR: 29 Apr 2009," my contemporaneous report to UNDP headquarters and the UN Peacebuilding Support Office.

34. Randolph Wallace Rhea and Qinyu Cao, *A Comparative Study of Ex-combatant Reintegration in the African Great Lakes Region: Trajectories, Processes, and Paradoxes*, TDRP/GLR Report (Washington, DC: World Bank Group, July 2014).

35. Ibid., 6.

36. Much on DDR in South Sudan is drawn from Jairo Munive, "DDR in South Sudan: Feasible Under Current Conditions?" African Arguments, Royal African

Society, February 6, 2013, accessed March 18, 2013, http://www.africanarguements .org/2013/02/06/disarmament-demobilisation-and-reintegration-in-south-sudan -feasible-under-current-conditions, and from personal interviews with relevant practitioners.

37. Drawn from Dean Piedmont in comments relating to an early draft of this chapter, May 5, 2013.

38. Statistics from Munive, "DDR in South Sudan."

39. Conflict transformation: See Christine Bigdon and Benedikt Korf, *The Role of Development Aid in Conflict Transformation: Facilitating Empowerment Processes and Community Building* (Berlin: Berghof Research Center for Constructive Conflict Management, 2004).

5

Operationalizing Community Security Approaches

The major challenges in attempting to implement a DDR program along classic lines using template assumptions in a less-than-classic environment came to a head in Haiti in 2004–2005. The violence was related to the activities of politically connected criminal armed gangs rather than military warring factions. The need for an innovative approach to deal with even a part of this constituency led to the development in 2006 of a purpose-designed community violence reduction program that was based on addressing community security. This chapter reviews the birth of that community-based approach to DDR in Haiti.

The environment in Haiti at the time thrived under a weak government attempting to survive in shark-infested waters, a predatory elite that coopted gangs into projecting its will, and a culture of criminality that was fueled by the transiting of cocaine from Colombia and marijuana from Jamaica to the United States in part exchange for weapons. In the absence of rule of law, the criminal gangs operated with impunity by controlling the communities of the urban poor quarters. The gangs maintained no-go areas for the state, controlling the communities through fear, murder, and rape somewhat tempered by creating dependence through the dispensation of often coopted humanitarian largess. The desired outcomes of the UN intervention in Haiti—a normative system operating within the rule of law—were not achieved. The limited progress made was severely knocked back by the chaos of the post-earthquake environment in 2010. However, the concept of operationalizing community security methods to address armed violence is reflected in the second-generation trend in DDR, led by the UN Department of Peacekeeping Operations.[1]

Haiti, 2004–2009

Attempting to assess the impact of the UN Stabilization Mission in Haiti (MINUSTAH) since 2004 throws up some perplexing and intriguing ques-

61

tions. What has the UN peacekeeping operation, a stabilization mission, achieved through its twelve-year, extraordinarily expensive presence in Haiti? Has it done more harm than good? In particular, why did it launch a DDR process in 2004 that failed to address the reality of the specific environment of violence? Although the UN military force eventually partly and temporarily "defeated" the armed criminal gangs that controlled the *bidonvilles* (shantytowns) of Port au Prince, its robust actions failed to address the underlying close relations between the controlling business elites and the armed gangs. The failure to break those relations allowed the gangs to reemerge after the earthquake in the absence of structural reinforcement of rule of law, reflecting the general thesis of James Cockayne's "The Futility of Force?" and coinciding with my own observations.[2] According to Dean Piedmont, despite the clear failings, one positive aspect of what started as a DDR process in Haiti may be that, after initially misidentifying the environment as requiring a classic DDR model, practitioners, who were under enormous pressure, demonstrated flexibility and ingenuity in turning the process from a classic approach to DDR to a more context-specific approach. They managed to bring the establishment, which included MINUSTAH management, the UN Security Council, lead countries, and the government of Haiti, toward an innovative, bottom-up approach to DDR that they called the Community Violence Reduction Program.[3]

In early 2004, the United States took a clear lead in removing from the presidency of Haiti Jean-Bertrand Aristide, its protagonist and that of its client elite in Haiti. Aristide, a liberation theologist priest, had lately been portrayed in US media as a political despot. The US intervention was initially covert, with empowerment allegedly through the support of the International Republican Institute and US Marine training of an armed group in the Dominican Republic. It involved a small team led by notorious thug and instrument of the Haitian bourgeoisie, Guy Philippe. In March 2004, within weeks of Aristide's exit, a multinational intervention force led by the United States, France, and Canada entered Haiti, legitimized by Security Council Resolution 1529. Pushing constitutional capacity to the limit, a motley crew of expatriate and bourgeois Haitians who were vehemently opposed to Aristide and his popular movement, *Fanmi Lavalas* (the flood), were drawn together to form the transitional government of Haiti. This transitional government was tasked with stabilizing the country and preparing for democratic elections. The international community mobilized donor countries to form the Interim Cooperation Framework, which, in June 2004, pledged more than US$1.3 billion to the reconstruction and democratization of Haiti.

Also in June, UN Security Council Resolution 1542 established MINUSTAH to replace the multinational intervention force. This stabilization mission, a new genre of peacekeeping operation, was to comprise more than 7,500 troops, 1,500 police officers, and 1,000 civilian substantive and support staff. In addition to stabilizing the country and supporting the transitional government in delivering the elections, the mission's mandate was to implement a comprehensive disarmament, demobilization, and reintegration of all illegally armed groups and to provide support for the women and children associated with the armed gangs. This DDR process was to be done in close collaboration with the national police of Haiti. However, planning for the DDR drew deeply from a flawed pre-mission assessment. Allegedly, the predeployment report of the UN Technical Assessment Mission for Haiti relied heavily on DDR planning formulated for the UN Mission in Sierra Leone, which had been a totally different context.[4]

The predeployment assessment, in line with the common wisdom of the international community and to the amusement of many of the Haitian bourgeoisie, identified the rearmed groups of the former military, les Forces Armées de Haiti, as the greatest threat to state security and to the delivery of elections. Aristide, with the assistance of the US Marines, had summarily demobilized this force in 1994–1995. Having been quiet for ten years, in 2004 this partially reconstituted force, ostensibly orchestrated by some notorious members of the elite, occupied government buildings—mainly police stations having expelled the police—in various towns throughout the country. In early 2005, with assistance of Muggah's Small Arms Survey publication, *Securing Haiti's Transition*, it was estimated between 1,500 and 2,000 soldiers were engaged in this rearmament.[5] These forces were more likely seeking possible reinstatement and recompense for the indignity of their unceremonious disbandment rather than any other political ambitions.

The basic prerequisites for classic DDR as outlined in lessons learned did not exist in Haiti. The Haitian environment in 2004 could not have been classified as postconflict; the intervention was not to address the culmination of a civil war but rather to address a period of national anarchy involving multiple political and criminal actors. There was no comprehensive peace accord, which is the usual starting point for DDR. There was not yet buy-in from the numerous armed gangs, whether those associated with the former military or those formed to engage in political or criminal activities. These gangs were holed up in the large slum areas of the major cities that they controlled, feeding on the communities with impunity. There was no way and no sense in gathering gang leaders collectively around a table to negotiate. Thus, each approach had to be on an individual basis.

In addition, the Haitian constitution guarantees the right to own arms for personal defense in one's home. It was estimated that whereas former military groups and armed gangs in 2004 may have held between 13,000 and 18,000 weapons, domestically and among private security firms, there could have been between 180,000 and 200,000 weapons.[6] Due to the ineffectiveness of the Haitian National Police's small arms registration system, fewer than 24,000 weapons were legally registered. It is possible that the primary sources of small arms in Haiti were retail outlets in Fort Lauderdale, Pompano Beach, and Miami, Florida, with others coming from South and Central America (in association with narco-trafficking), Israel, and South Africa.[7] Add to this cocktail the fact that in early 2005, approximately 15 percent of Colombian cocaine consumed in the United States was believed to transit Haiti, bringing with it all the associated criminal organization and high stakes. In the tenure of previous Haitian governments, it was alleged that government representatives—in particular, senior officers of the National Army of Haiti—were handling major aspects of this drug trafficking.

The transitional government never seriously tried to develop the appropriate political space for disarmament and reintegration. It was clearly biased against DDR and contributed to the polarization of the political environment, rather than developing any move toward national unity. Up to this point, the Haitian National Police, who were to be supported in delivering DDR, had been, to a significant extent, a criminal armed group contributing to the problem and not to the solution. In December 2005, during the lead-up to the presidential elections that were eventually held on February 7, 2006, there was a massive increase in crimes against the community by criminal gangs marking their territory and making their presence felt. Mario Andresol, the director general of the National Police, stated on national radio in January 2006 that he believed that in excess of 30 percent of the destabilizing crime, particularly kidnapping, was being committed by serving police officers. Although it may have been expected that, with the intense international focus, the implementation of a broad SSR program would have contributed to the professionalization of the police, this was actually progressing very slowly. Through the various regime changes of the previous thirty years, the Haitian National Police had been politicized, purged, and repoliticized. These changes left an unstable and undependable organization that had inherited much of the culture of brutality and impunity of the Tonton Macoutes, though without the underlying loyalty to the regime in power.[8] The Haitian judicial and penal systems were also in total disarray, reducing the odds of establishing legitimate rule of law and further complicating the chances of implementing a voluntary disarmament. In March 2007, more than 80 percent of all detainees in Haitian prisons, some locked up in excess of two years, had been on remand without any judicial process and often without any criminal file or record.

The DDR Section of MINUSTAH was established in late 2004 in an agreement between the UN Department of Peacekeeping Operations and the UNDP as an experimental pilot of *integrated* implementation. This agreement followed the direction of the Brahimi Report of 2000 to move toward the "UN working as one"—combining members of the peacekeeping operation and UNDP in a unified team—to derive synergies through their combined institutional strengths in delivering DDR. Concurrently, a similar experimental pilot of the integrated approach between the two organizations was being attempted in the DDR process tentatively launching in Sudan (see Chapter 4).

From the outset of the DDR programs, a lack of accurate or baseline data on the security environment, the situation of illicit small arms, the poor socioeconomic conditions, and the aspirations and expectations of former combatants and gang members were the scourge of DDR planning processes. Such data help to inform the conflict analysis, set the scope of the program, and set the parameters for establishing indicators of achievement for the DDR processes. Haiti in 2004 was no exception to this lack of data. The single relevant baseline data on the security environment concerning armed gangs in Haiti was Rob Muggah's 2004 study on the structure, armament, motivations, and prevalence of those armed gangs. This study was completed concurrent with the establishment of the DDR Section in Haiti and offered a starting point for the development of some level of appropriate response to the armed gang problems facing Haiti.[9]

Muggah's study took a broad view of the situation, using analyses of survey results with the application of tested academic multipliers. This information was combined with available statistics on weapons import and trafficking, drawn from regional law enforcement, concerned NGOs, and diplomatic agencies. These data were used to estimate the number of small arms and light weapons in Haiti, including their sources and impact. In his review of the levels of violence occurring in Haiti, Muggah studied the morbidity statistics in relation to armed incidents, available from functioning hospitals, the International Committee of the Red Cross, and Médicins Sans Frontières (Doctors Without Borders); he also sought figures from the Haitian National Police. The study included a review of the national legal framework in relation to the control and movement of small arms and light weapons. The study attempted to list the various armed groups in Haiti, including the former army; the former presidential guard; and the *chimères*, the informal armed groups encouraged by Aristide to support his personal powerbase and provide him with security and coercive capacity. It also identified other criminal armed groups and informal bodyguards used by various quasi-political and bourgeois personalities. It listed groups of redundant police officers purged from the force by Aristide and now engaged in criminal activities; in that list, Muggah also could have included, but did not, a good number of the serving police officers.

In the study, Muggah considered the dynamic structure of armed gangs in Haiti, which often had one famous and powerful main leader with three or four lieutenants to carry out his bidding. Those lieutenants, in turn, would have a few regular henchmen and a flexible number of women and children called in as required for various operations. The gangs were small and tight, following an efficient cell structure that some of the most effective terrorist groups in the world have found to be effective in reducing leakage of information or disloyalty of members. Most gangs were associated with particular communes of their quarter and tended to draw loyalty from that commune. They would, for instance, tend not to rape or murder to any great extent inside their own commune and would often distribute a percentage of the spoils of their criminal activity within that commune. An incident that is indicative of the relationship occurred in the Martissant neighborhood of Port au Prince in early 2006, when community members returned an escaped kidnap victim to the gang. Each gang normally would not have more than twenty close members but could have a considerable number of associates who would benefit from the gang's activities and could be depended upon to support its operations. This support could include providing early warning of danger, blocking and delaying police or UN infiltration to the slum quarters, holding and guarding kidnap victims, providing human shields against UN "seek and snatch" operations and impeding the return of fire, or transporting and hiding weapons and ammunition. Muggah estimated that the total number of gang members and all those associated with the armed gangs—and, therefore, those who would be directly addressed in a broad DDR program—to be as many as 31,000.

A surprising aspect of the gang dynamics identified in the study was the fluidity of apparent motivation. Although linkages with narco-trafficking were common, political allegiances tended to depend on who was paying. There was even evidence of collaboration between various gangs that were nominally from opposite ends of the political spectrum. There seemed to be little ideological motivation in Haitian society other than the *politique du ventre*, or the politics of the belly, a drive for self-aggrandizement in which the end justifies any means.[10] This motivation is prevalent not just among the armed criminal class in Haiti. An unfortunate fact in Haiti's environment of limited opportunity and abject poverty is that the most brutal gang leaders served as the role models of success for the youth of the *bidonvilles*.

From October 2004 through January 2005, the DDR Section, working with the ad hoc committee for DDR comprising transitional government representatives, struggled to devise a coherent, appropriate strategy to address the unique, complex environment of violence in Haiti. On May 11, 2005, the transitional government, MINUSTAH, UNDP, and the president of the newly established National Commission for Disarmament signed the program document that had been developed to establish Haiti's national program for DDR. This signing created a financial mechanism, to be operated by UNDP under a direct execution modality, that would channel voluntary contributions from donors to the DDR program.[11] Elements of MINUSTAH's contribution to the DDR process from the UN-assessed budget would be operated through the mission's financial mechanisms. In this untested integrated structure, the existence of parallel funding mechanisms created levels of confusion regarding the segregated funding of activities between the collaborating partners—UN Department of Peacekeeping Operations and UNDP.

As 2005 progressed, it became clear that a multidimensional, innovative approach to DDR and violence reduction was necessary for Haiti. Despite continued encouragement from the DDR unit based at UN headquarters in New York, the integrated DDR Section was unclear to what extent it had the support of the executive staff of the Department of Peacekeeping Operations; instead, it bobbed and weaved in trying to find a coherent way forward. This situation came to a head in the summer of 2005 during a visit by Jean-Marie Guéhenno, the assistant secretary-general for the Department of Peacekeeping Operations. In my formal presentation to Guéhenno, his staff, and the UN mission management, overcome by a wave of exhaustion and frustration, I shockingly blurted out the obvious and heretofore unspoken truth that nobody was going to do DDR in Haiti. This startling declaration was received philosophically by both UN headquarters and the Chilean head of the mission, Special Representative of the Secretary-General Juan Gabriel Valdés, who said, "Okay, now tell us what you are going to do." In subsequent reconsideration, the new approach to DDR that had been gestating within the DDR Section for previous months was coined *community violence reduction*, an idea that was supported by the Department of Peacekeeping Operations and was reflected in Security Council Resolutions 1702 and 1743.

A consensus developed among the main actors on the need to revise the approach; the focus would shift from a conventional logistical disarmament to addressing armed violence in all its aspects. It became understood that the threat of reemergence of a rearmed former army of Haiti was something of a paper tiger, devised by some of the clearly identifiable lead bourgeoisie to assist in reestablishing their primary coercive institution, the army. Instead, armed youth in criminal gangs were recognized as a significant threat to national security. In particular, young men were widely available, pliable, and cheap to recruit in order to undertake criminal activity or political coercion.

The DDR Section and partners sought every opportunity for progress in Haiti. They developed a partnership with the famous Brazilian NGO Viva Rio, which had achieved much success in working with volatile youth in the exceptionally violent *favelas* (shantytowns) of Rio de Janeiro. The most vibrant and influential area of Haitian life is the cultural sector—its music, art, poetry, and literature. Some of the people making the greatest impression on the youth of Haiti are the modern musicians, especially those of *rasin* (roots), *compas* (Haitian pop), and hip-hop music. In collaboration with Viva Rio and the Ministry of Culture of Haiti, the DDR Section contacted the most influential musicians and artists and included them in the DDR sensitization campaigns. These groups included Haitian roots music groups RAM, JahNesta, and Lolo from Boukman Eksperyans and popular Haitian writer Margaret Papillon. Discussions were also held with US-based hip-hop star Wyclef Jean, a Haitian expatriate who was committed to violence reduction in Haiti.

Also in collaboration with Viva Rio, the DDR Section considered the particular influence of the Afro-American cult tradition of voodoo on youth and gang leaders.[12] In discussions with senior *houngans* (voodoo priests), the partners in DDR learned that although the portals of violence had been opened to voodoo during the famous ceremony of *Bois Caïman*, which launched the anticolonial revolution of 1791, no consideration had since been given to how voodoo might be mobilized to diminish violence. It was agreed that the DDR program would sponsor, through Viva Rio, a ceremony of the Afro-American tradition that would explore the idea of voodoo contributing to violence reduction. The colorful event was staged in mid-August at the famous Hotel Oloffson (reputedly the location for much of Graham Greene's *The Comedians*), with the participation of many *houngans* and *mambos* (female voodoo priests). Although traditional voodooists considered this a tourist event, it did spark a dialogue within the tradition as to how voodoo could contribute to peace in Haiti—a dialogue that continues.[13]

In a further bohemian effort to harness the indigenous youth exuberance toward reducing violence, the program contracted a British expert on community peace communications, the amazing Bill Brookman.[14] Bill, the personification of youthful exuberance, works through the medium of street theater and street circus. In Haiti, he hired local artists to create a local street theater troupe that included clowns, fire breathers, and even street trapeze artists suspended from a crane. He adapted the popular Haitian Rara street music to contribute to community sensitization toward violence reduction and peace activities.[15] Bill's troupe, performing an exciting and colorful culturally adapted program full of positive symbolism, was the highlight of many *bidonville* community peace festivals; it also projected many unique personal injury– and public liability–related insurance threats for the legal department of the risk-averse UN mission.

In late 2005, it emerged that women were playing an active role in supporting the armed groups and their criminal activities. As anecdotal evidence of this, the UN Peacekeeping Force attacking the gangs in Cité Soleil reported that after "downing" a gang member that was shooting at them, a woman sprinted into the open, picked up the wounded member's firearm, and continued to shoot at MINUSTAH. Others reported that women and children were hired to feed and watch over kidnap victims and to offer human shields during MINUSTAH seek-and-arrest operations. However, women must also play important roles in restoring peace, as witnessed in Sierra Leone and Liberia, where women's associations and women in the home played a key role in promoting peaceful negotiations, and in Sudan, where women supported the Wunlit Accord.[16] The integrated DDR Section initiated an expert assessment by anthropologist Wiza Loutis to identify the impact of violence on women and their role in armed groups and to recommend appropriate interventions in the context of DDR.[17] Findings included that women themselves identified the worse form of violence against them not as being associated with the armed gangs and sexual abuse, but with their abandonment (and that of their children) by their men folk and the consequential social and economic difficulties. However, a common denominator in all of this hardship was the excessive use of arms. The major recommendation emanating from the study was the need to strengthen community-based capacity to address violence in general and not just violence against women.

The plight of children associated with armed gangs was a preoccupation of the UN family, not only in the context of the Convention on the Rights of the Child but also in adapting the provisions of the Cape Town Principles/Paris Agreement and best practices on the prevention of the recruitment, demobilization, and social reintegration of child soldiers.[18] Early in 2005, a local politician associated with the gangs asked my DDR team to talk to a group of child gang members from Port au Prince who were seeking alternatives. We met more than thirty children between the ages of ten and thirteen. Three weeks later, we received unsubstantiated reports that five of these children had been executed by their gang leader for having spoken to us without his permission. Although never positively confirmed, as bodies rarely turn up in this voodoo environment, we believed it to be true. This shock caused us to reassess all aspects of our design and implementation, to cease making contacts with gangs other than through gang leaders, and to generally reconsider our conflict sensitivity.

Building on the emerging concept that DDR is about putting weapons beyond use in the context of improving community security, from mid-2005 to mid-2006, the DDR Section developed its strategy while piloting DDR with several more accessible gangs in Port au Prince and with individuals throughout the country. The efforts bore limited results, as participants' security could not be guaranteed, and some were killed as a result of their efforts to leave the gangs.

The DDR team in Haiti drew on lessons learned from other community security programs around the world, such as initiatives undertaken by NGOs, and from its partner in the DDR process, Viva Rio. They also drew from UNDP projects in Somalia and Sierra Leone, such as Arms for Development and small arms control projects. The result was an enhanced strategy that combined the impact of classic DDR executed by the UN Mission with community disarmament and longer-term small arms control measures driven by UNDP. The UN, in partnership with the Haitian government, emphasized the need for a program that ensured that both grassroots communities and government institutions played an active, collaborative role. The DDR team adapted, in consultation with the transitional government, a multifaceted approach for the reduction of armed violence in Haiti through a strategy articulated in five complementary axes of intervention:

1. Reinforcement of the legislative and political framework to control the proliferation of small arms and to offer a legal basis for disarmament

2. Negotiation, disarmament, and reintegration of armed groups as opportunities arose to entice armed gang members into a reintegration process

3. Prevention of recruitment and the disarmament and reintegration of armed youth and those youth associated with armed groups

4. Reintegration of women associated with armed groups and reinforcement of their role as vectors of peace
5. Initiation of community disarmament and conflict-prevention activities

The objectives of this approach were to address concerns regarding the reduction and prevention of gang violence, particularly in the absence of the state, by empowering the community to address their fears. The approach encouraged engagement of a good portion of community women and the youth who formed the recruitment base and support for the gangs. Local representative committees were to be formed (called community committees for the reduction of violence and for development) in the most volatile quarters of Port au Prince. They would be provided with an operating base and would help identify and address those communities' vital needs. This goal would be achieved through microinfrastructural and social service projects, microentrepreneurial activities and local information, local confidence-building measures, and social and cultural peacebuilding activities. Concurrently, the state was to develop the appropriate institutional and legal framework to support the return of the state and the rule of law to the community, including legislation regarding local government, police, and small arms. All of this would discourage gang activities, while also creating an opening to attract gang members into a DDR process that would offer possibilities for alternative sustainable livelihoods.

Figure 5.1 illustrates the theory as designed by the deputy chief of the integrated DDR Section, Daniel Ladouceur. The central five parallel pillars are under their relevant headings, each listing its critical elements. Policy guidance percolates from government to local government to civil society organization to the community committee. The foundation of the effort is the community committee for the reduction of violence and for development, which operates in close consultation with community-based organizations, local government, and the central government represented by the National Committee for DDR. This model is informed by an open system of consultation, policy guidance from government, and goodwill stimulated through participation in community projects.

After the presidential elections on February 7, 2006, Haiti's president elect, René Préval, indicated that he intended to create the political space for increased national political reconciliation, including the implementation of a targeted disarmament of illegally armed groups and the reduction of violence in Haiti. Although levels of violent crime reduced immediately after the election, armed gangs apparently had taken a wait-and-see approach. After a hundred days of the Préval government, the gang leaders demonstrated their chagrin at the government's failure to offer them significant material incentives by staging some audacious mass kidnapping and other criminal attacks in Port au Prince. In early August, an infuriated Préval responded by announcing on the radio that gang members should

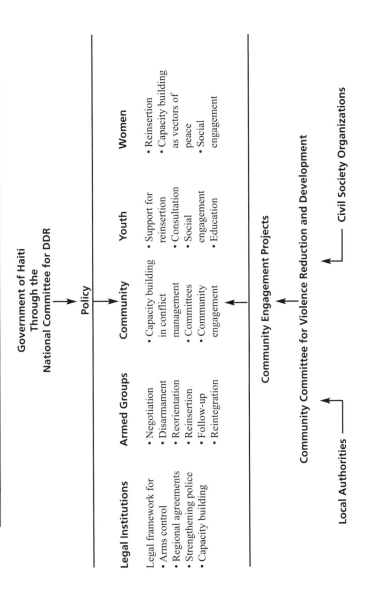

Figure 5.1 Community Security Through Management of Conflict and Small Arms Control

Government of Haiti
Through the
National Committee for DDR

Policy

Legal Institutions

Legal framework for
Arms control
• Regional agreements
• Strengthening police
• Capacity building

Armed Groups

• Negotiation
• Disarmament
• Reorientation
• Reinsertion
• Follow-up
• Reintegration

Community

• Capacity building
in conflict
management
• Committees
• Community
engagement

Youth

• Support for
reinsertion
• Consultation
• Social
engagement
• Education

Women

• Reinsertion
• Capacity building
as vectors of
peace
• Social
engagement

Community Engagement Projects

Community Committee for Violence Reduction and Development

Local Authorities

Civil Society Organizations

join the DDR process or the state would kill them. He then asked the UN, "What is DDR?"

Daniel Ladouceur and I presented to the Préval government the plan shown in Figure 5.1; this plan was presented to a new National Commission for DDR, having just been appointed by Préval, as a fully prepared concept. Préval agreed that this plan offered a broader approach to armed violence reduction than just focusing on the armed gangs and further, the plan could contribute to local government capacity and rule of law in inaccessible quarters of the cities of Haiti. The new Préval-led institutions had not been adequately consulted regarding the theory, as it had been devised during the transitional government period; thus, they felt little ownership of the proposed processes. The influential president of the National Commission for DDR, Alix Fils-Aime, gradually came to see the strengthening of a community's capacity to address violence—before the new government had had an opportunity to strengthen the capacity of under-resourced local government and social services sector—as undermining the state's institutions. This same tactic had been Aristide's strategy in building his personal support through gang mobilization in base communities. This fact, among a wide array of other constraints, greatly undermined the capacity of the DDR Section to implement the program. However, the concept did offer a new way to do DDR and represented a significant evolution of the theory that, with adaption to context and appropriate conflict sensitivity, has been applied in several more-recent DDR scenarios.

Meanwhile, Préval maintained discreet personal negotiations with gang leaders. In this context, from September to December 2006, 108 gang members from Cité Soleil were, by direction of gang leaders, passed to the newly established UN DDR processing center, a secure compound on the outskirts of Port au Prince. At the center, gang members who entered the DDR process could be assessed and orientated in a safe environment. Upon return to their communities or, where necessary, with their families to other, safer communities, they would be facilitated for sustainable alternative livelihoods through enrollment in skills training. Although this group behaved impeccably during orientation in the processing center and afterward showed great commitment to the livelihood training, in the upsurge of violence in late 2006, many were forced to return to the gangs by the gang leaders. By mid-2007, twelve were confirmed to be dead and fifteen more presumed dead as a result of intergang warfare or UN robust operations that applied the use of lethal force.

Clearly, as part of the stabilization and recovery jigsaw—in addition to strengthening rule of law through SSR, police, judiciary, and prison service and to reigning in the elites—violence reduction in Haiti must be addressed from a broad, community-based perspective. The dynamics of violence and gang activity in each quarter and each department, and their linkages with the controlling business elites, are all different, and no cookie-cutter approach will work across all the communities of Haiti. Capacity must be established in each community, together with the strengthening of local government to support local solutions through the mobilization of community-based initiatives supported by a strengthened rule of law—in other words, it must be a top-down/bottom-up approach.

Cockayne was critical that efforts through these community violence reduction approaches were not linked to the robust intelligence-based operations of the UN Peacekeeping Force or the policing tasks.[19] He stated that the "technocratic approach was reflected in the bureaucratic artefacts of managerial process . . . seen through the frame of technical assistance and capacity building—rather than as central to the strategic project of the mission."[20] Although this statement may have some legitimacy, Cockayne tends to view these processes through a securitized lens, reflecting elements of DDR in conflict. And yet, by 2007, DDR practitioners within the UN system still viewed DDR as a voluntary process and had not yet come to terms with the concept of delivering DDR in conflict, of prioritizing security over human security. Back then, even collaborating with the Joint Mission Assessment Cell, the intelligence-gathering function of the UN mission, proved a dilemma for DDR practitioners.

For the state to reclaim the volatile quarters of Haiti, it needs the support of the communities. The support and recruitment base for armed gangs must be gradually strangled by providing alternate and constructive engagement and role models in the context of a strengthening state presence and the establishment of the rule of law. The predatory elite must be brought to book. Impunity must perish, and credible deterrent against criminal activities—in particular, armed violence—must be established. The strategy as developed by the UN Integrated DDR Section, which was based primarily on practitioner experience, piloting, and broad consultation, acknowledged these necessities and laid out a road map for implementation. But the environment remained dynamic and the variables contributing to a complex environment of conflict were many, right to the devastating earthquake of January 2010. The earthquake certainly changed priorities and forced a step backward in addressing armed crime. In such an environment, a pragmatic, flexible approach to implementation is vital. Implementers and facilitators must weave their way through the dynamic environment in light of the variables, using their imagination and pragmatism. In this context, it is impossible to lay down a specific operational plan that can be implemented in a traditional way on a given time frame. Who has ever achieved sustainable results in Haiti with a traditional approach? Continuous adaptation to the changing reality is critical.

In early 2007, frustrated at the lack of progress, exhausted, and close to a breaking point, I resigned from my post as chief of the Integrated DDR Section and from the UN. I retreated to the comfort of academia in Japan to recover, finding a new, welcoming world. The beleaguered DDR team, quite dysfunctional, imploded to some degree. The UN mission and UNDP took stock for some months before relaunching its community violence reduction program with a focus on community-based mass employment projects.

Although the election of President Préval had succeeded in bringing a popular government by mid-2006, optimism was not to bear fruit in an environment of continuing criminal chaos, *le marronnage*, continuing corrupt judiciary, and the protection of the exclusive interests of the elite.[21] With notable exceptions within the UN DDR program's senior staff, naivety reigned. We lacked a clear grasp on the revolving history of Haiti, and we underestimated the malignant nature of the continuing aspirations of the elite (the bourgeoisie) in their subjugation and exploitation of the marginalized masses of Haitians. The UN as a whole failed to realize that for those holding power and wealth, nothing has changed. The very tools that the UN community violence reduction approach espoused, the very language they used—conscientization, grassroots facilitation, community-based organizations, community empowerment—were anathema, a threat to the ascendancy of the elite and their death grip on the resources of Haiti.

Maybe they were not wrong. A Haitian nation conscientized to the instruments of their suppression, their unending poverty, would be a raging machine ripe for social revolution. If history can tell us anything, the revolution will be bloody. The terror of the teachings and the praxis of neighboring Cuba, directed by the charismatic Fidel Castro and the eulogized Ernesto Che Guevara, are probably not far from the minds of the "morally reprehensible elite" and their eternal ally and primary end-user beneficiary, the United States.[22] Perhaps another social revolution is the only hope for the people of Haiti.

Notes

1. The Border Consortium describes community security as "a people centered approach to addressing violence, conflict and abuse that integrates human security, development, peace building and state building paradigms." The Border Consortium, *Protection and Security Concerns in Southeast Burma/Myanmar* (Bangkok, Thailand: The Border Consortium, November 2014), 2, citing Saferworld, "The Community Security Handbook," April 2014, 4, http://www.saferworld.org.uk.

2. James Cockayne, "The Futility of Force? Strategic Lessons for Dealing with Unconventional Armed Groups from the UN's War on Haiti's Gangs," *Journal of Strategic Studies* 37, no. 5 (2014): 736–769, DOI:10.1080/01402390.3024.901911.

3. From Dean Piedmont's comments on an early draft of this chapter, May 5, 2013.

4. From my discussions with senior UN DDR staff, February 2015.

5. Robert Muggah, *Securing Haiti's Transition: Reviewing Human Insecurity and the Prospects for Disarmament, Demobilization, and Reintegration*, a report commissioned by the Firearms and Explosive Control Division (Geneva: Small Arms Survey, 2005). Robert was working closely with me during this period.

6. Ibid.

7. Ibid.

8. Tonton Macoutes were the brutal militia of thugs established as the personal enforcers of François "Papa Doc" Duvalier, president for life, who governed Haiti by fear and murder from 1957 to 1971.

9. Muggah, *Securing Haiti's Transition.*

10. *Politique du ventre* is a particularly popular term to describe the driving motivation of those seeking political power in Haiti. well described in Robert Fatton's analysis of Haiti's recent political past, *Haiti's Predatory Republic: The Unending Transition to Democracy* (Boulder, CO: Lynne Rienner, 2002).

11. Direct execution modality (DEX) is a UNDP financial mechanism that permits the resident representative of UNDP to have disbursement authority, within certain parameters, of centrally allocated or donor funds. This is as opposed to the national execution modality (NEX), in which the host government controls the funds. DEX is an exceptional financial mechanism used when the host government may not have the capacity to manage such funds.

12. There is a saying in Haiti that although 80 percent of Haitians are Catholic, 100 percent are voodoo.

13. I had considerable difficulty in justifying to UN management some aspects of the budget for this event (twelve cases of the best champagne, six dancing troupes, and so forth). As payments were delayed, I became quite apprehensive of supernatural consequences to be potentially meted out by angry *houngans.*

14. Bill is the founder and MD of Bill Brookman Foundation & Bill Brookman Productions Ltd., Leicestershire, UK.

15. Haitian Rara street music is associated with the festivities of Easter week, when groups of community youth parade, swaying and dancing through the streets, often in boisterous competition with neighboring community groups. They play homemade musical instruments, such as cylindrical bamboo or metal horns (*vaksen*) and various types of drums and maracas.

16. The Wunlit Accord was signed in 1998 between community leaders from the Nuer and Dinka tribes to stop cattle raiding and mutual atrocities.

17. Wiza Loutis, *Evaluation de la situation des femmes dans le cadre de la violence armée en Haïti,* trans. Natalie Mann (Port au Prince: MINUSTAH, 2006).

18. Commonly called the Cape Town Principles, this is the report of the 1997 working group on the Convention on the Rights of the Child, a collaboration between child-focused NGOs and UNICEF.

19. Cockayne, "The Futility of Force?" 762–763.

20. Ibid.

21. *Le marronnage,* originally referring to the escaped slaves hiding out in the hills, has come to represent a particularly Haitian characteristic of obscure and ambiguous narrative with which the Haitian takes pride in confusing the foreigner.

22. This reflects the broad thesis of Paul Farmer, *The Uses of Haiti* (Monroe, ME: Common Courage Press, [1994] 2005).

6

Theory Meets Practice?

Although the evolution of the theory of DDR might be seen as a linear progression, scholars may be forgiven for feeling frustrated at not witnessing a linear progression in how the theory is applied. In DDR, the lessons may be learned, but context dictates how those lessons might be applied. Adapting the theory to the reality of a given context, while also addressing the priorities, is the skill of the program planner and the implementer. A recent program in Nepal offering reintegration support to a small group of Maoist fighters who did not meet specific criteria for inclusion in plans for formal demobilization, offers an example of how some aspects of the evolved theory had to be sacrificed due to insurmountable constraints. But such a sacrifice meant that resources could then be focused on other achievable elements in order to reach some of the desired outcomes.

Although it met many obstacles, the UN Interagency Rehabilitation Programme (UNIRP) in Nepal (2010–2013) offered a small-scale DDR program—a laboratory—in which some aspects of the evolving theory could be tested in practice. Rather than applying the second-generation approach that would consider broader community security issues, this opportunity was able to address an array of topical crosscutting issues, such as effective information management, dynamic monitoring of evaluation and adjustment, the gender perspective, psychosocial issues, and improved job placement support. The situation involved a complex political environment with limited baseline data, inhospitable geographic conditions, and unrealistic expectations. The fragmented socioeconomic environment was compounded by an absence of national buy-in to the process, UN institutional risk averseness, and weak communications. In this adverse environment, though some evolved elements of the theory were well applied and offered examples of good practice, an effective community-based approach was not possible in this context. Even as excellent sustainable job placement was achieved, the regional influences, the absence of UN leverage, narrow political interests, and a poor local socioeconomic environment ensured that the

77

process failed to win the broader perceptions, attitudes, and trust of all the actors. The major failure of this program, however, was that the methodology was not selected for replication for the larger group of qualified Maoist combatants who had remained as pawns of the political process in cantonment. The majority of these combatants were ultimately treated to a quick fix by being bought off with a cash lump sum.

Nepal

The Context

Nepal is a highly fragmented, stratified society of twenty-nine million people, with more than sixty mixed ethnicities, casts, and subcasts and about seventy languages.[1] It has complex religious, animist, and cultural belief systems, steeped in feudal fatalism and widespread extreme poverty. The status quo is reinforced by the feudal and caste-dictated control of a small privileged elite supported by Indian patronage. The country had been wracked by ten years of low-level insurgency costing more than 13,000 lives, in which the Communist Party of Nepal (Maoists) mobilized significant numbers of disaffected youth in "a people's war" to confront the state. The Maoists attempted to address the injustice, inequality, and gross structural violence inherent in that society and the social, political, and economic exclusion. They aimed to abolish the feudal monarchy and establish a people's republic. This "war" was brought to a close in November 2006 with the signing of a so-called comprehensive peace accord. In fact, that peace accord was anything but comprehensive, with every conceivable contestable aspect of it subjected to protracted and intractable negotiation or standoff. Although the shooting war had stopped, little progress was made in bringing political stability and a termination of the basis for the conflict,[2] despite the abolition of the monarchy, UN monitoring of the implementation of the peace accord, the election of a broadly representative Constituent Assembly, and a short period of Maoist government. Certainly, little improvement has been seen in the quality of life for the masses in a period characterized by virtual government, during which time the government was present, but little governance was visible.

Both the Nepalese Army and the Maoist People's Liberation Army complied with the letter of the provisions of that comprehensive peace accord and the subsequent Agreement on Monitoring of the Management of Arms and Armies. They secured the requisite equal number of weapons in locked containers, and the Maoist army placed its cadres in seven main cantonments, each with three satellite cantonments, spread strategically (from a Maoist perspective) across the country. In December 2008, the UN registered the Maoists in cantonment as totaling more than 23,600 combatants.[3] In addition, the police reduced their presence to normal rule-of-law policing levels, and the Nepalese Army stopped offensive patrolling.

With their surprise electoral success in 2008, the Maoists found themselves in a stronger political position than they had anticipated, and they formed a government. Their bluff had been called, as they now had the people's imprimatur and an obligation to deliver on their promises. With the support of the UN Mission in Nepal (UNMIN), an interim Constituent Assembly was initially established for a period of two years with the task of drafting the national constitution and delivering the peace process through the integration of members of the Maoist army into the Nepalese Army or their rehabilitation into civilian society. The Maoists shunned the term DDR while still required to implement some of the steps involved. In mid-2009, in an environment of political stalemate and Indian pressure, Prachanda, the leader of the Maoist movement and by then president of Nepal, feeling that the Maoists would fare better in opposition, ceded political power back to the pro-Indian Seven Party Alliance after only nine months in power.

Seeking international legitimacy, including the removal of US travel restrictions and an end to their shaming by the UN as an organization that recruits child soldiers, the Maoists made a unilateral decision in December 2009: They quite suddenly agreed to discharge 4,008 of their cadres who had been deemed to be either children (under the age of eighteen) on the date of the cease-fire or late recruits to the Maoist army who had joined after the signing of the peace accord.[4] Close to 30 percent of these former combatants were female. In light of the "irregularity" of the recruitment, the government of Nepal under the Seven Party Alliance, considered both the underage and the late recruits to be ineligible for either integration or rehabilitation support. With the government disinterested in supporting the reintegration of this group, and UNMIN being a UN special political mission with limited capacity, the UN country team of development partners took responsibility, on humanitarian grounds, to develop and implement the provision of rehabilitation options for these 4,008, who were termed "verified minors and late recruits."[5] The aim of this support was to facilitate their rehabilitation into the community and assist in finding education, skills training, or entrepreneurial opportunities for sustainable livelihoods.

The verified minors and late recruits were officially termed "unqualified." Unfortunately, this term translated into Nepali as something closer to "inadequate," which contributed to an enduring sense of indignation and marginalization among the unqualified groups. The UN lumped both groups together and required the Maoists to remove all 4,008 from the cantonments. Although the Maoists did expel this group from the cantonment, Maoist leadership felt that the benefits proposed by the UN were insufficient to meet the kind of promises they had been making and the expectations that had been created among their cadres. Thus, both the government and the Maoists disowned the process of rehabilitation to some degree, leaving the UN pretty much on a solo run.

The UN Interagency Rehabilitation Programme in Nepal

A process to address this caseload had been on the cards for more than two years since the peace accord had been signed in late 2006, while the unqualified cadres remained in the cantonments. However, the Maoist leadership had not told them individually who was on the list until the time of departure. Generally, the former combatants were unhappy to be forced at short notice from the cantonment. This sense of dislocation is well illustrated in the documentary "The Disillusioned Soldier," produced by Al Jazeera,[6] which follows one underaged Maoist combatant's growing disillusionment with the revolution, through his departure from the cantonment to his rehabilitation in a remote rural community with the support of UNIRP.

Inside the cantonment, conditions were relatively good, with full board, a monthly stipend paid by the government, and basic infrastructural support and utilities. Educational and training support, including information technology, masonry, electrical, and plumbing, were offered in a systematic way by the German government's development agency, GTZ. Many had developed a purpose in life, a sense of community, and indeed a family in the cantonment. In Nepal's feudal, caste-based society, the poor youth and especially women are at the lower end of the pecking order. But during the "people's war," they had contributed to a successful revolution and had achieved a level of self-actualization. Having lived in a relatively egalitarian environment in the cantonment for up to five years, return to a society that had not progressed significantly in the meantime would be a retrograde move. Girls in particular would experience difficulty returning to their communities. In addition, mixed-caste marriages among the young cadres, which had been encouraged in the cantonment, were taboo in the conservative society, which perceived that they—especially girls—had been living in a relatively promiscuous environment. Further, many young girls returning with children resulting from those marriages would likely find some level of rejection from their own families and the new in-laws with whom it would be traditional practice to reside. These challenges were compounded by the high expectations that were, to some degree, purposefully created by the Maoist leadership in order to facilitate the exit from the cantonment. Cadres believed that, having sacrificed for the revolution, they were entitled to permanent high-level jobs.

Program planners experienced some sense of dilemma in removing the young Maoists from the relatively benign environment of the cantonments to the uncertainty of life in the depressed national economic conditions. It was especially daunting in the face of little evidence of economic recovery, the disadvantages of a fragmented feudal society without any broader political solution, and the continuing confusion of how the general body of Maoist cadres in the cantonment would be reintegrated into society or absorbed into the national army.

In March 2010, with collaboration and an intense consultative process among four UN agencies—UNDP, UN Children's Emergency Fund (UNICEF), International Labour Organization, and UN Population Fund—resources were combined to create the UNIRP to support the rehabilitation of verified minors and late recruits.[7] It was hoped that successful support for this relatively small group would encourage the 19,600 Maoist cadres remaining in the cantonments to embrace sensible options for reintegration by demonstrating to them that rehabilitation into the community with sustainable livelihoods was feasible. The UN Peace Fund for Nepal committed between US$9.4 million and US$14.0 million on a sliding scale, depending on levels of participation as the program progressed.[8] This multidonor funding mechanism, supported by Norway, the United Kingdom, and Switzerland, was established in 2007 to complement the funding mechanism led by the government of Nepal, especially in light of Nepal's transitional political environment. UNDP's core funding made additional contributions to cover specific aspects of UNIRP, including addressing the gender perspective.

I was initially hired as senior rehabilitation adviser to develop the program; I was then retained to support the technical staff, maintain a strategic overview, direct the program's innovative aspects, and lead the dynamic evolution of the program in a changing environment. I was also tasked with providing technical advice to the UN country team and, as required, to national stakeholders, particularly government and Maoist negotiators. This advice was primarily given in matters concerning rehabilitation of the verified minors and late recruits and was associated with planning the rehabilitation of the 19,600 Maoist cadres remaining in cantonment.

A core international management team guided the program and progressively developed the capacity of the predominantly national officers. The program staffing structure was designed to cater to the integrated multi-agency approach. According to the plan, the staffing structure must effectively provide the services necessary to contribute to the rehabilitation of verified minors and late recruits. This implied the following tasks: liaison with stakeholders; development of collaboration with parallel programs; security considerations; administration and logistics support; profiling of caseloads; counseling; designing and organizing rehabilitation options; dynamic monitoring, evaluation, and adjustment; database development, maintenance, and analysis; communications strategy; accompaniment of beneficiaries through the process; follow-up; and so on.

Further, it must focus on addressing areas of program delivery frequently neglected and noted in lessons learned in previous DDR programs throughout the world. This focus was to include an emphasis on developing excellence in integrated information management; database development and application; and monitoring, evaluation, and adjustment processes as aspects of dynamic management. It was to facilitate real-time decisionmaking to capture short-term opportunities and to adjust and improve in-progress program implementation. Contributing to the real-time information flow was a free call center, operating long hours, that could respond to beneficiaries' queries with initial information, log complaints, confirm entitlement, and record initial registration through online connection with the regional offices. All data would automatically feed into the program database, with exceptions flagged. The system would schedule the first referral consultation with the guidance counselor in the relevant regional office. The call center would also manage an innovative short messaging system (SMS) that could send short information in Nepali or local languages directly to the private mobile phones of specific groups of verified minors and late recruits. The prevalence of mobile phones among the caseload of beneficiaries would have an inordinate impact on aspects of how the program could be implemented, not only in disseminating program information but also in the beneficiaries' capacity to communicate and respond to program issues as a group.

In light of the high percentage of women in the caseload and the particularly difficult societal conditions for Nepalese women, together with the overarching issue of the impact of masculinities in former combatant reintegration, practical mainstreaming of gender sensitivity and the insurance of gender-responsive programming was led by a dedicated gender adviser.[9] Specific supports were developed to ensure the maximum participation in the program by eligible women. Such supports included the provision of additional allowances to permit women to attend courses away from home, with family accompaniment as necessary; child-care facilities; supplementary dietary support for lactating mothers; and mother and child health support. Further, gender-sensitive psychosocial counseling and support were offered to both men and women.

In anticipation of the psychosocial challenges facing the verified minors, late recruits, and their families upon their return to the feudal civil society and the transition from military to civilian, each regional office would have two professional psychosocial counselors, in addition to the usual rehabilitation counselors. The provision of these staff members by highly competent national NGOs, led by Transcultural Psychosocial Organization (TPO) Nepal and organized by UNICEF, initially proved somewhat controversial. In the briefings of Maoist commanders prior to the program's commencement, the mention of psychosocial counseling drew derision: "Our troops are not crazy," they said. However, the program persevered, and two female trained psychosocial counselors were deployed to each regional office, with one being present in the room when initial career counseling was offered. The counselors would make a preliminary assessment regarding each client's potential psychosocial support needs and would then refer as needed for clinical support. The services were offered to each client at the end of the initial counseling session irrespective of perceived need, and included tailored elements of family outreach and some follow-up mentoring. More than 30 percent of clients opted for this support, and the psychosocial counselors were kept very busy. Various independent evaluations and a scholarly longitudinal study of the impact of this psychosocial support showed highly positive results.[10]

Derision from Maoist commanders regarding program planning was not unusual. When the intention to provide for the option of animal husbandry training was mentioned, their response was also dismissive: "You want to turn our troops into pig farmers," they sneered. But such a career was a sustainable and lucrative option for any former combatant, especially considering that more than 80 percent of the verified minors and late recruits came from farming backgrounds.

The projected geographic spread of caseload, which would require up to two years of livelihood support and accompaniment, was to be addressed by five regional offices, each in a major regional center and each led by an experienced international UN volunteer. The rationale for using an international staff member in each regional office, despite the availability of highly capable national officers, was based on the security implications associated in dealing with a highly volatile caseload in an unpredictable environment. National staff and their families were more vulnerable to threat and intimidation, an issue that came to the fore early in the program.

The program staff's quality and competence proved exceptional and effective. Three international members of the core management team—the program manager; the regional office/reintegration coordinator; and the information, reporting, and monitoring and evaluation coordinator—were Afghani nationals who were veterans in implementing complex, challenging DDR efforts in conflict. Led by a highly adaptive vocational skills and career guidance counselor as senior rehabilitation officer, a man with decades of experience in the Nepali Chamber of Commerce, the national staff members were committed, fast learners who strove to absorb the spirit of the people-centered, human security–motivated approach to program development and delivery. Despite frightening experiences as a result of goading and threatening behavior by an initially disgruntled caseload, team members, including those in exposed regional offices, maintained patience and a demeanor of respect to verified minors and late recruits. This positive demeanor contributed to a progressively improving attitude by the caseload as the program developed. Many of these staff members continued to contribute to peacebuilding in Nepal and farther afield after the closure of the program.

Interagency Integration

This program's approach was developed as a hybrid to draw lessons from the difficulties of attempting an institutionally integrated approach to implementing a DDR program with diverse UN agencies, each with its own institutional culture, as was experienced in Haiti and Sudan. The challenge with UNDP taking the lead was in creating a structure that allowed each agency to contribute its strengths to the program in a consensual management mechanism, while retaining their integral institutional chains of command in a collaborative environment. This difficult task was achieved through painstaking consultation at all stages of program development with the senior rehabilitation adviser, the program management team, and heads of agencies at the UN country team table. These consultations were chaired by a supporting UN resident representative. It also required careful and trusting relationship building, both professional and personal, and continuous communications among the technical officers leading each agency's effort—not to mention copious amounts of good coffee. The goodwill and friendly relations developed, as well as the sharing of ideas and expectations in an environment of mutual respect, ensured that the representatives of the four collaborating UN agencies worked together to optimize the achievement of results.

This collaborative approach was also extended to third-party NGOs and organizations engaged in the peacebuilding process. Constructive and non-defensive relations were developed with Saferworld, International Alert, and the Carter Center, which were engaged in researching and publishing independent reports concerning the conditions of verified minors and late recruits and the impact of the UN program. UNIRP proactively supported that research by sharing information and ensured that their findings contributed to the dynamic monitoring, evaluation, and adjustment process, as well as to progressive improvement of implementation.

Constraints and Solutions

The Nepali Ministry of Finance limited program design in terms of unit cost. According to the ministry, the value of the package to each beneficiary was not to exceed the total value of compensation paid to the families of second-level martyrs, a classification devised in the context of postconflict compensation to bereaved families. The amount was valued at approximately US$1,300 per family. This limitation was a considerable constraint to offering an effective rehabilitation package to each unqualified individual. Although a unit cost of approximately $1,300 would be considered average in the context of the large-scale African reintegration programs of the classic DDR genre, costs for services, materials, and logistics support are much higher in Nepal than, for example, in Sierra Leone. This limitation was compounded by the relatively small number of beneficiaries being targeted, leading to a distinct absence of economy of scale. Further, Nepal's contrary geography and communications infrastructure and the wide geographical spread of beneficiaries contributed to increased costs. Even with five regional offices spread strategically, it was often necessary to cover the cost for local flights or for many days' worth of subsistence allowance when traveling on foot to permit beneficiaries living in remote Himalayan valleys to attend career or psychosocial counseling sessions. Further, accommodation had to be provided for such beneficiaries who chose to attend the rehabilitation training courses in the regional towns where the institutions tended to be.

Within these financial constraints, however, the program could offer transport support, monthly stipends, health support, and career counseling and guidance toward optimum personal livelihood sustainability. The options for the career counseling included choices between two years of formal education; health-related skills training, such as laboratory technician; various choices in technical skills training, of which mobile telephone repair technician was very popular; and microentrepreneurial support. The program also provided psychosocial counseling and support in addressing job placement support and gender-related constraints to program participation. A special reserve for emergency health support was also provided. In enhancing the services being offered, the program was able to manipulate some additional benefits beyond the government fixed financial limit, such as by providing daily hot food to participants while they were engaged in training. The hot food element proved to be a logistical nightmare, however, as it was exposed to fluctuating standards and manipulation by suppliers and service providers.

During the period from the identification of the unqualified caseload through the registration process, to the program's launch in June 2010, Maoist leadership did not permit UN staff adequate access to the caseload to record personal details through confidential interviews. Such interviews would have facilitated a process of personal socioeconomic profiling that would have disclosed education levels, work experience, domestic circumstance, health requirements, competencies, aspirations, desired location of resettlement, and expectations. Interviews supervised by the Maoist commanders provided some relevant, but limited, status information, such as age, gender, rank, unit, and home location. This information was compiled into a database that was entered into the program management information system. But much of even this limited information was found to be unreliable due to coached answers not necessarily reflecting the truth. These were the only data available to start planning the program and, not surprisingly, proved to be a far-from-sufficient baseline to assist in designing demand-driven rehabilitation options to address genuine needs, aspirations, and capacities.

Instead, the program had to be designed on an "educated guess" basis, relying on local staff knowledge and practitioner experience. Program implementation was supported by the mainstreaming into the routine management system of an effective dynamic monitoring and evaluation strategy incorporated into a custom-built comprehensive rehabilitation management information system. This system pulled together quantitative and qualitative program information to facilitate dynamic adjustment of implementation, manage expectations, and encourage improved levels of national ownership of the processes. The constant monitoring, evaluation, and adjustment involved gathering quantitative and qualitative information on a daily basis from all sources—regional offices, partner organizations, staff enquiry, extraction from the program dynamic database, media, and so forth. This information gathering occurred through routine cursory staff assessment and analysis, generally through a process of triangulation. The information was reviewed from different angles and sources, frequently informal meetings while standing in common space, with all staff members contributing. Such a regular participative approach allowed for immediate adjustment of program design and implementation, as well as correction of faulty information, practices, or unrealistic indicators of achievement; it gradually helped improve program delivery, with a priority on achieving results. From the perspective of the senior rehabilitation adviser, this practice of dynamic monitoring, evaluation, and adjustment, mainstreamed into all aspects of program implementation, was the key to achieving successful results, despite less-than-perfect initial program design. In practice, this tool was a gem that not only addressed programmatic needs but also contributed to the spirit of participation, mutual respect, and contribution among all staff members—a primary team builder.

From the program's launch in June 2010, early take-up from an eligible caseload of 4,008 was slower than expected. Subsequent investigation indicated that, fueling the broad doubt among caseload members that this program could meet their expectations, there was also active discouragement by some of the Maoist leadership in regional cantonments. In addition, of the 4,008 members, approximately 970 (24 percent) had already left the cantonment and, in fact, the country, ostensibly to secure remittance work in the Gulf States, Saudi Arabia, Malaysia, Indonesia, or Thailand, as was common for Nepalese youth and an essential contribution to Nepal's gross domestic product (GDP). Of the remaining 3,038 members, 90 percent would eventually contact the program and make enquiries about benefits, while 2,234 (73 percent of the available caseload) actually enrolled in one of the four rehabilitation options being offered.[11]

Because the dynamic monitoring indicated a weakness in job placement support, in early 2011, the program hired Dr. Richard Bowd, an expert in the field of optimizing human capital in DDR programs, to drive that aspect of the process. He got results. An aggressive job placement support campaign ensured that almost 75 percent of graduates remained in decent employment or were running their own businesses by July 2013,[12] in a country where approximately 15 percent of youth are employed. The provision of a comprehensive gender-sensitivity element and broadly available psychosocial counseling and support were additional elements of good practice. Despite considerable challenges, both national and institutional, the UNIRP has achieved extraordinary results and is recognized in the DDR community as offering many examples of good practice.[13]

In this volatile environment of a disgruntled group of young former combatants, the program needed to be rapidly responsive to early warnings of imminent difficulties associated with program delivery. This required the staff to have the capacity to make immediate press releases or to directly negotiate with former combatants, both of which offered elements of risk. Negotiations in an unpredictable environment were physically dangerous, and rapid press releases were politically dangerous. Whereas DDR practitioners are conditioned to accept elements of calculated risk, development program managers are not. With the resident coordinator of the UN ultimately responsible for the safety of UN staff members, in addition to walking a delicate line in his political and diplomatic relations with the government, UNDP's senior management was often cautious to the extent of being risk averse. On occasion, the relevant senior managers insisted on what program staff saw as unnecessary levels of micromanagement, implementing constraining approval procedures for some activities that offered only very short windows of opportunity and that would be missed if not grasped quickly. These constraints limited the program's capacity to respond to a dynamically evolving environment and gave rise to occasional frustrations within program management.

Lessons from the Implementation of UNIRP in Nepal

The Comprehensive Peace Accord: Only the beginning of the solution. The planning process for the integration and rehabilitation of former combatants was greatly complicated by the ambiguous political environment and the way in which national adversaries viewed the provisions of the comprehensive peace accord.[14] The provisions included the integration of members of the Maoist army into the Nepalese Army or reintegration into civilian society. The adversaries saw this as the starting point of negotiations for the details of the process, rather than as an agreed-to position.

An absence of UN political leverage in Nepal. The overarching influence of the geopolitical environment limited the levels of political leverage available to the UN, the UNMIN, and the development agencies. This undermined the capacity of the UN to insist on the application of international standards in planning and delivering an effective rehabilitation of former combatants or a credible SSR process. The UN underestimated the impact of this fact from the outset.

Using caution when undertaking the option for cantonment in the DDR processes. One lesson from the international practice of DDR relearned in Nepal is that challenges associated with operating cantonments for combatants—especially before formal disarmament—can outweigh the benefits. Cantonments can give rise to major security threats, as they offer a concentrated target; and an opportunity for the cantoned military groups to consolidate and to train. Such opportunities may delay or derail implementation of the peace process. Further, they are costly in terms of human resources, materials, and finance. As such, if they are essential, cantonment periods should be established after disarmament, for as short a time as possible, with security guaranteed by third parties. In Nepal, the existence of sustainable cantonments contributed to several years of political stalemate.

The international community's counterproductive investment in armed combatants inside the cantonments. International support for the sustainability of Maoist combatants through infrastructural and educational investment over an extended period inside the cantonments was contrary to international DDR principles and most bilateral funding rules. This investment may have helped lengthen the political stalemate by reducing the pressure on Maoists to address their cadres' needs and may have retarded the desire for a return to civilian life.

A UN-owned process. It was a radical move to launch the UNIRP in the absence of effective national ownership. Although doing so is contrary to international DDR principles, it did channel humanitarian commitment to a very vulnerable caseload and established a tenable moral position for the UN.

Absence of baseline data. The absence of sufficient baseline data on the former combatant caseload was a serious handicap for planning a reintegration and rehabilitation process. Such baseline data would have included socioeconomic profiling (a process that was obstructed by Maoist leadership), as well as an analysis of the local, national, and global labor market into which former combatants must reintegrate. This absence constrained the capacity to design training options and support systems that could have synchronized the demand of the labor market with the capacities and aspirations of the beneficiaries. It also led to a time lag in improving program delivery; this lag was addressed through the implementation of a dynamic monitoring, evaluation, and adjustment system. The omission of adequate baseline data remains a recurring failure in DDR programs globally.

A community-based approach. The UNIRP failed to develop a robust community-based approach, citing the wide geographical spread of participants, an absence of economy of scale, and budgetary constraints. This failing was somewhat addressed as the program progressed, through the inclusion of peacebuilding activities; engagement of verified minors and late recruits with community-based organizations, women's groups, and youth groups in collaborative social, cultural, and sporting activities; and improved outreach of necessary services to families of participants. Despite the constraints, this failure to emphasize the community-based approach at the outset was a shortcoming.

Intra-institutional tensions due to the clash of emergency and development approaches. DDR is usually an emergency program operating in a dynamic, evolving postconflict environment. Rapid response is required to exploit short windows of opportunity to capture short-term objectives. This environment favors some degree of substance over form—for example, moving rapidly with imperfect documentation to achieve results, rather than waiting to ensure perfect documentation. As such, it demands a level of political risk taking. Development agency prerogatives, on the other hand, must consider the longer-term political and diplomatic impact of actions and thus favor a nuanced, perfectly formed approach to interaction with political entities and the public of the host country. This is particularly so in terms of public information and relations with the host government. In Nepal's complex political environment, the constraints placed on DDR practitioners in the area of public information and in dealing with the government of Nepal in a risk-averse environment led to considerable response-time delays and frustration.

The importance of collaboration with parallel programs. Although tentative efforts were made to develop synergies through collaborations with parallel programs purporting to offer support to the war-affected communities or to support youth employment, as implemented by the government of Nepal and bilateral development partners, the initiation of such collaboration did not materialize. It will be wise to consider the impact of this omission; it is important to ensure that there is the political and institutional will for such collaboration, as it can optimize the outcomes of peacebuilding and development investment in the future.

The relevance of the integrated DDR standards. A primary lesson learned in the planning and delivery of the UNIRP is that the lessons learned in global practice concerning DDR and its crosscutting issues, and codified as a toolbox within the Integrated DDR Standards, were relevant to Nepal's integration (absorption into the Nepalese Army) and rehabilitation environment. However, the Integrated DDR Standards did not offer a template for application in Nepal. Innovation was necessary in addressing a unique environment with specific political, security, economic, and sociocultural facets. The UNIRP has lessons to offer international practice, particularly in the areas of dynamic monitoring and evaluation, gender-specific support, electronic information management and the innovative use of technology, psychosocial support, and job placement support.

Rehabilitation of Qualified Maoist Cadres: The Considerations

The 19,600 Maoist army cadre members who remained in cantonment were the main bargaining chip for the Maoist leadership in seeking a return to power. The main political sticking point in making progress was the expectation that a significant number of these would be integrated into the Nepalese Army as specific groups with high levels of rank harmonization. Those not to be integrated expected to receive handsome financial compensation and possibly the offer of rehabilitation packages that could include education or vocational training with guaranteed jobs. The Nepalese Army, however, had been opposed to the idea of absorbing a significant number of former Maoist guerrillas other than as individuals with lower-level rank harmonization. The political discussion about those who were not to be integrated into the Nepalese Army was almost exclusively focused on the cash value of a "golden handshake," rather than any serious consideration of options for sustainable socioeconomic reintegration.

In late 2011, it was becoming clear that the national actors were fully orientating toward offering a large cash lump sum as the most effective way of emptying the cantonments. Technical advisers called for caution. There are no hard-and-fast rules or even sound evidence-based guidelines regarding the wisdom or otherwise of cash payments in DDR. What are the pros and cons of the potential impact of cash payments as an option to support the rehabilitation and reintegration of former combatants?

Cash Elements in DDR

Drawing on two decades of practice, the Integrated DDR Standards advise:

> Direct cash payments should be the smallest part of any benefit package. Food and other goods and services (tools, seeds, counseling, etc.) are a better option. . . . Participation in community-based quick-impact projects for short-term livelihood support should be linked to the receipt of reinsertion assistance, particularly any cash payments.[15]

Although a wide range of opinions regarding the use of cash transfers in DDR exists both in practice and in theory, a small number of rigorous empirical studies actually address it, and nobody had seriously considered the implications for Nepal. The few studies most relevant to the circumstances in Nepal would indicate that although the case for and against the use of cash transfers for reintegration in DDR is reasonably well balanced, the simple answer is that it is possible, given appropriate circumstances, for such cash elements to contribute to the success of the DDR processes.[16] However, using such cash elements also offers specific challenges related to context, exposure to corruption and third-party rent taking, and weak institutions, not to mention when, where, and how cash elements should be applied. (See Table 6.1.) Despite these considerations, it may be supposed that a significant amount of global negative press for cash payments comes from a vested interest—that is, the development agencies whose raison d'être is the creation and maintenance of the delivery systems for in-kind support.[17]

Cash Payments: Pros and Cons

In offering advice to both the UN country team and the government of Nepal, I prepared the following brief review to provide an objective overview of the global pros and cons of using cash transfers in DDR and to permit the adaption of conclusions in the case of the rehabilitation of Maoist ex-combatants in Nepal.

Cash Benefits and Unit Cost

The UN country team further requested the development of a comparative table in order to offer some informed ideas regarding the type and level of

Table 6.1 Cash Elements in the Reintegration Processes: Pros and Cons

Potential Benefits of Cash in DDR	Potential Drawbacks of Cash in DDR
Can be attractive to former combatants, provided it is at a scale that meets their expectations in a timely manner.	Can fuel expectations and increase security risks, especially in the Nepali context. In light of political manipulation and hype, it will be difficult to meet the high expectations of former combatants without a significant public information campaign and proactive management of expectations.
With assured cash flows and effective delivery systems, cash elements can contribute to stabilization of the program and the broader peace process.	There is little margin for error regarding cash flows, timing, and delivery systems. Small problems such as delays in cash delivery can lead to spontaneous violence.
Provision of cash elements early in the demobilization phase of a DDR process can accelerate the demobilization process and the return of former combatants to civilian life.	It may be expected that party or local commanders might deduct a significant percentage of cash paid to former combatants on payment or at source, as has been alleged to be the practice with payments made to cadres inside the cantonments.
Cash payments can offset or delay political and civil unrest contributed to by former combatants when other in-kind elements of their rehabilitation package are delayed or do not meet their expectations.	Cash elements of rehabilitation/reintegration processes frequently contribute to community resentment. The community and most war-affected populations are not receiving significant cash transfers and could consider that former combatants are being unfairly privileged.
Cash elements can soften the burden of returning former combatants to the community through the capacity to spread benefits to the local economy.	Former combatants may have little experience in financial management and could miss the opportunity to optimize sustainable benefit (a view that is not sustained by empirical studies, which suggest that it may be attributable to Western orientalist and patronizing mind-sets).
Cash payments are easier and cheaper to administer and implement than material or in-kind support.	They can contribute to security risks associated with transporting and delivering cash, in addition to a heightening risk to those receiving payment, who will be broadly known to be in possession of cash in their communities.
Can stimulate institutional capacity building through local government or local peace committee administration of cash disbursements and so forth.	Cash payment procedures can be compromised by local institutions. For example, if local institutions, such as local peace committees, were engaged in delivery, could one expect full accountability and transparency? Further, it would be necessary to consider the security implications for Maoist former combatants where non-Maoist-dominated local peace committees operate.
Cash elements can stimulate local economies, particularly in the informal sector, over the broad geographical spread of former combatant resettlement.	Cash transfers without sustainable in-kind support—training, education, or entrepreneurial— will have a very short-term impact.

Table 6.1 Continued

Potential Benefits of Cash in DDR	Potential Drawbacks of Cash in DDR
The influx of significant regular cash payments can stimulate the development of community infrastructural capacity, such as cooperatives or local banking.	Significant resources in the hands of returning former combatants can undermine community social structures by offering coercive power to a volatile group with political aspirations.
A post-reintegration survey in Sierra Leone found that the transfer of a modest transitional security allowance ($300) had significant impact in contributing to long-term sustainability.	Cash transfers associated with disarmament may contribute to the perception of a program that offers cash for arms, which may enhance the marketability of small arms and can also stimulate the proliferation of armed gangs.
In the Nepali cultural and postconflict context, cash can allow former combatants to finance their return into the family and community, overcoming traditional and political prejudice. Such prejudices include the stigmatization of girls (in particular, those associated with mixed-cast marriages) and adverse familial/community perceptions of their characters as a result of their time in the cantonment.	Possession of cash by girls, in particular, returning to their traditional roles in feudal communities can seriously undermine their personal security. This is so when they are not deemed by the community as eligible to own significant personal resources.
Cash offers former combatants a flexible and dignified choice regarding the direction of their own futures.	Cash can become the main objective of the program in the minds of beneficiaries and associates, to the expense of sustainable inputs.
As above.	The sudden influx of cash to a community and the demand for local commodities and resources (e.g., property, local produce, etc.) can have a significant inflationary impact on the local economy.

Sources: In addition to my own work, I have drawn and adapted from Sigrid Willibald, "Does Money Work? Cash Transfers to Ex-combatants in DDR Processes," *Disasters* 30, no. 3 (2006); Albert Caramés, Vicenç Fisas, and Daniel Luz, *Analysis of Disarmament, Demobilisation, and Reintegration (DDR) Programmes Existing in the World During 2005* (Barcelona: Escola de Cultura de Pau, 2006); the monthly reports of the UNIRP in Nepal (2010); Sarah Dalrymple, *Common Ground: Gendered Assessment of the Needs and Concerns of Maoist Army Combatants for Rehabilitation and Integration* (Kathmandu, Nepal: Saferworld, November 2010). a. Isabela Leao, *Swimming Against the Stream: DDR in Sierra Leone* (PhD dissertation, State University of Milan, January 2011).

cash benefits that had been offered in previous DDR processes and to assist in estimating the potential costs of offering a rehabilitation package to the qualified Maoist combatants. They asked for this ostensibly in seeking a viable, attractive alternative to the "golden handshake." Table 6.2 offers a sample of levels and types of cash support offered to former combatants in key phases of a range of DDR programs, taking into consideration per capita GDP as a proxy

Table 6.2 Comparative Overview of Cash Element Benefits and Unit Costs in DDR

Country	GDP	Direct Cash Payment and In-Kind Benefit	Unit Cost
Afghanistan	$281	Daily pay of $3 for two to four months with integration or skills training	$2,750
Angola	$2,643	Payment of $100 once they reach their place of origin, with public-sector employment or skills training elements then offered	$1,800
Burundi	$121	From $515 to $586 according to rank, in ten installments, with integration, political positioning, or skills training offered	$1,000
Central African Republic	$353	$500 paid at the end of the disarmament and demobilization phases (PRAC); these funds reached few of the projected former combatants	$1,758
Colombia	$3,733	A monthly subsidy of $155 for eighteen months to facilitate social reintegration	$13,000 (to date)
Côte d'Ivoire	$883	A planned $924 to be paid in three installments, with support for social reintegration; the process was much delayed by ongoing conflict	$3,125
DR Congo	$141	$300 in two installments, with support for social reintegration (training/education)	$1,228
Eritrea	$277	$50 monthly for twelve months	$1,000
Haiti	$510	A stipend of $40 per month for former combatants for the duration of training and support of socioeconomic reintegration, with additional support to families	$7,420
Indonesia (Ache)	$810	$600 to each community for each former combatant returned and land share for direct beneficiaries	$2,666
Liberia	$176	$300 in two installments and skills training/education for six to eight months, with a stipend of $30 per month of training	$3,000
Mozambique	$332	Post-dated checks spread over 24 months	$1,000

Table 6.2 Continued

Country	GDP	Direct Cash Payment and In-Kind Benefit	Unit Cost
Nepal (UNIRP)	$427	Approximately $300 from the UN and $350 from the Maoist party immediately upon discharge and demobilization, coupled with in-kind rehabilitation support and a stipend of $40 per month for the duration of training (3–6 months) and a provision of three meals per day (valued at between $60 and $80 per month, depending on region and local prices)	$2,332
Rep. Congo	$2,218	Credits of $350 for each former combatant, together with community projects	$1,000
Rwanda	$338	$330 in two installments, together with community-based social reintegration; the provision of payments through individual bank accounts was a feature of this process	$800
Sierra Leone	$270	$300 in two installments and vocational training for up to six months, with a stipend of approximately $40 per month	$2,000
Average			$1,400

measure of average income and the average unit cost (including overheads and in-kind support) of DDR. The cash payments were not mutually exclusive of other in-kind support, including training; rather, they were an aspect of a more comprehensive reintegration support program. All GDP figures are drawn for the year 2006, with the exception of Nepal (2009).

Costing Rule of Thumb for DDR

In reviewing the ratio of per capita income compared to the unit cost of DDR, when the examples above are compared with the two extreme cases (Colombia and Rwanda) removed, the unit cost of DDR is on average equal to 3.4 times GDP. Despite a wide variation of the ratio of unit cost versus per capita income between DDR programs depending on context, such a ratio can offer a convenient rule of thumb for DDR planners in making a rough estimate of the potential unit cost of a DDR package. Informed contextualization can narrow the margin of error. Further, on estimating the potential unit cost, if the numbers of beneficiaries can be projected, an estimation of total budget can be considered. In the constant crisis management and unpredictability, not to mention chaos, of DDR implementation, such unscientific methodologies have legitimacy. An early capacity to project the total budget is critical in considering the realistic capacity to raise funds for necessary or desired cash transfers in DDR programs.

Cash and Case Studies

In light of the widely varying contexts, it was difficult for comparative purposes to identify the most similar DDR contexts to Nepal from among other international examples. The following are select examples of DDR programs that have applied cash elements in contributing to specific phases of the reintegration process. This section offers an encapsulated and selective overview of relevant facts and consideration of the general impact of the cash aspects of a DDR program.

Mozambique. The DDR process in Mozambique in the late 1990s went through various phases, with varying degrees of success and failure. An appropriate example of one innovative application of cash transfers is as follows.

Demobilized former combatants were issued a book of postdated checks offering monthly subsistence allowance, as agreed, for a period of twenty-four months. The former combatants could then return to their communities or disappear as they wished. They could use an established banking system to cash their checks, while totally dissociating from their former life as combatants, reasonably safe from access by former commanders. This solution offered certainty of paydays and personal financial security for a clearly defined period. Most commentators consider this process a success. Additional in-kind supports were offered on the basis of assessment and clearly defined needs.

Sierra Leone. The DDR process in Sierra Leone included cash benefits, taking specific care to ensure that they were not associated with "cash for arms."[18] An initial $300 was offered, estimated on the basis of six months of basic subsistence allowance for a family, considering that it could take up to six months to get former combatants into reintegration skills training or education options. Of this amount, 50 percent was granted on demobilization, and the remaining 50 percent upon reporting to the respective regional reintegration office (managed by the National Committee on DDR). Recent empirical analysis of the cash payments associated with this program found that the transitional security allowance payment, in particular, was frequently the most cash that a beneficiary had ever held, and it was often well used to create significant sustainability options for many beneficiaries.[19] Further subsistence allowances were paid associated with participation in education or skills training reintegration options. Late deliveries of subsistence payments due to cash flow and delivery system problems frequently led to a heightening of tensions and occasional threats to DDR staff.

Liberia. The DDR process in Liberia (2003–2009) featured a chaotic launch due to poor planning, loose eligibility criterion, and the attraction of easy money.[20] This resulted in the acceptance of 102,000 beneficiaries into the DDR program, after having initially estimated only 39,000 as the total number of combatants engaged in the civil war.

Under pressure by the United States to collect arms rapidly, the UN Mission in Liberia started the DDR process prematurely in December 2003, with an offer of $300 to Liberian former combatants as a transitional security allowance. Together with an extraordinarily lax preprocess identification and registration mechanism, this allowance was to serve as encouragement for rapid disarmament. With the sole eligibility criterion being to appear with 150 rounds of ammunition, all comers who produced this were permitted full entry to the program, with a unit value of $3,000. This lax registration process led to the arrival at Camp Schieffelin of a 13,000-strong unruly mob, many of whom were armed, all possessing the required ammunition and all claiming to be former combatants. The camp, however, had facilities prepared to receive and pay only 1,000 former combatants. Eight Liberians died in the subsequent riots, and UN headquarters in Monrovia came under armed siege, resulting in a panic-driven response of a rapid commitment to pay out to all comers. The result was that the program took six years to complete and was approximately 500 percent over the initial budget. On the positive side, it is subsequently considered that the resulting wide distribution of benefits, while leaving plenty for elite capture, contributed to broad acceptance of the DDR process. Further, the loose eligibility criterion is reputed to have sucked surplus ammunition, including the stock of some police ammunition stores, from Sierra Leone, probably contributing to the DDR process there.

Aceh. The DDR process in post-tsunami Aceh is notable in that it emphasized the sharing of benefits with the community, rather than individual cash benefits.[21] In the state-sponsored DDR process, the parties involved agreed that $600 would be contributed to community recovery and development projects for every former combatant returning to that community; there would also be a provision of land to returning combatants. In a distribution process controlled by rebel forces, however, material benefits were spread broadly beyond the planned direct beneficiaries, resulting in smaller individual receipts, and the land division did not occur at all. Despite this, the program is considered a successful example of facilitating ethical, community-based reintegration and strengthening of community security. Some further unofficial reintegration support was provided by the International Organization for Migration and was funded by Japan.

Central African Republic. Cash transfers associated with Central African Republic's two recent DDR efforts were particularly problematic.[22] In the 2004 PRAC program, a significant amount of the total program budget remains unaccounted for and is presumed misappropriated by national institutional actors, ostensibly in collusion with leaders of the opposing factions. In the 2009 DDR attempt, brokered during the inclusive political dialogue led by François Bozizé in 2008, the focus of all national actors, including institutional and faction leaders, was almost exclusively on opportunities for rent taking and the fungibility of funds. The "state" blatantly misappropriated US$16 million that was ostensibly donated by neighboring states and the Regional Bank exclusively for the DDR program.

Identification of genuine combatants was difficult, and delivery of benefits was almost impossible. Challenges included the sparse density of population distribution in a vast country; geographic, topographic, and security difficulties due to ongoing conflict; absence of rule of law; and extensive banditry. (While discussing this absence of rule of law with a local military commander in the northwest in 2009, he admonished me: "How dare you suggest this. Why, only last week I burned seven witches.") In addition to major challenges to implementing the delivery of cash benefits, an extraordinary absence of basic infrastructure (roads, communication, and power) and limited potential service providers confronted the delivery of in-kind support, including skills training. In late 2010, UNDP withdrew from all but limited technical support to this DDR program.

Rwanda. Aspects of the Rwandan DDR process, which is just one element of the complex regional Multi-country Demobilization and Reintegration Program, operated a system of individual bank accounts for former combatants. This element of the program was considered successful in ensuring a reliable and timely delivery system. It also contributed to bringing a new sector of the community into the banking system, which is deemed to aid personal financial management.

Rehabilitation of Maoist Cadres Remaining in Cantonment: Considerations in Late 2011

The political narrative that emphasized the provision of a substantial "golden handshake" for demobilizing Maoist combatants suggested that this process represented a voluntary force-downsizing effort through a retirement package, which is an element of SSR; it is essentially the DD without the R. The imperative that the sustainable livelihood capacity of the former combatants be strengthened to facilitate their reintegration into civil society was largely dropped. Nepal has weak institutions with a propensity toward corruption and rent taking. The Maoist army has a history of high levels of influence through the chain of command, even on former combatants. A focus on cash transfers alone in delivering rehabilitation support for former combatants could be expected to face many of the challenges observed in field experience and listed on the "drawback" side of the argument.

However, cash elements pitched at the appropriate levels and delivered under the overarching theoretical framework of human security could have achieved desired outcomes. Such outcomes would be in line with average per capita incomes, would meet the well-managed expectations of the beneficiaries, and would be delivered with efficiency and transparency in an environment of national ownership and full political buy-in. In the complex and unique socioeconomic context in Nepal, cash transfers should have been combined with well-planned in-kind facilitation of market-oriented livelihood sustainability skills training, tailored to individual beneficiary capacity and aspirations. Those livelihood options would include education and innovative entrepreneurial support, as well as access to microcredit support focusing on Nepal's main bread earners—tourism and agriculture—in both the private and the informal sectors. Such facilitation could have included targeted support for critical crosscutting issues, such as psychosocial support, gender-specific needs, and health requirements, together with a community-focused holistic approach. What did happen?

Rehabilitation of Maoist Ex-combatants in Nepal, 2012 and Beyond

Early in 2012, the indications were that the politicians negotiating the rehabilitation process for the qualified Maoists would lean toward an expensive option, much higher than the international average, for the following reasons:

1. The nature and value of the package was based on political decisions. The Maoists maintained a strong bargaining position, and it was in their interests to ensure a high-value monetary package.

2. The Maoists, not being a defeated force, maintained a position of strong leverage, especially when considering that the political environment was one of continuous "spoiler appeasement," in seeking short-term peace.

3. The high expectation of combatants in the cantonment was a major consideration when assessing the level at which the package must be pitched to ensure a voluntary process.

4. The relatively good conditions in cantonment, including the educational and vocational opportunities, as compared with the quality of life that could be expected upon reintegration into civil society, dictated that a strong incentive was needed to encourage combatants to leave the cantonment.

5. The process of disarmament, demobilization, and reintegration being pursued in Nepal—integration and rehabilitation—lacked the level of credible deterrent that, in many international DDR processes, provides the "stick" element of a "carrot and stick" approach to incentivizing a voluntary reintegration process.

6. The evidence of the UNIRP indicated a significant effort on the part of the Maoist political machine to retain the chain of command and services of former combatants. This suggested an absence of political will to release the impact or leverage offered by the ability to remobilize a fighting force.

In Nepal, UN engagement in and influence on ensuring a human security approach to the rehabilitation of the 19,600 combatants who remained in Maoist cantonment had been constrained by geopolitical influences and the assertion of a brand of national ownership that addressed narrow political interests. When the UN has little leverage, the benefit of experience-based advice is often rejected and the theory ignored. As the dust settled on brash politically driven processes, three options were given for rehabilitating the qualified Maoists: (1) an attractive cash lump sum of between US$5,100 and US$8,200, depending on rank; (2) the option to join the Nepalese Army; or (3) the option to undergo an education, entrepreneurial, or skills training course. Of the 19,600 former combatants, 15,602 opted for the cash, 1,444 expressed interest in joining the army, and six opted for livelihood training.[23] Although the choice of the remaining approximately 2,600 is not explained, it can be expected that the number includes those remaining engaged in the Maoist political party or its youth wing; the bulk may have left the country prior to accepting an option or may have chosen to self-reintegrate.

Thus, the majority of Maoist cadres walked out of the cantonment with a large (by Nepali standards) cash lump sum and no other support systems. According to D. B. Subedi, with a few exceptions, most of them spent the cash on important domestic issues, such as building a house, educating their children, or paying off debts, rather than on nefarious activities.[24] However, the money is now spent, and the majority cannot find jobs, as they do not have the skills to enter the competitive job market. There is a perception among civil society in Nepal that some have reverted to criminal activities or political violence. Thus, in their absence of capacity to secure sustainable livelihoods, the former combatants remain perceived as a threat to the nation's peace and stability.[25] Yet, the government of Nepal has claimed that the job is done. Although a substantive academic study has not yet been completed to offer evidence for conclusions regarding the success or otherwise of the reintegration of qualified cadres of the Maoist army, the early indications are not good. The UN, together with other international organizations, may yet be landed with the role of picking up the resulting human debris of an arrogantly developed, politically driven, technically flawed process of reintegration of former combatants in the polarized communities of Nepal. Cash pay-outs, inappropriately politically motivated and poorly managed in the absence of consideration of sustainable livelihoods, may indeed be a recipe for disaster.

Additional Lessons Learned from the Broader Integration and Rehabilitation Process in Nepal

Regional Politics and the Loss of the Human Security Approach

In addition to the Maoist leadership, the regional powers in both India and China supported the idea of a lump sum cash payment to combatants in the cantonments, presumably concluding that it would contribute to their own differing interests. Ostensibly for India, in light of their internal difficulties with the Maoist Naxals, these interests may have been that cash payment would rapidly dissipate the numbers of Maoist combatants in the cantonment. For the Maoists and perhaps also for China, such payments would strengthen the Maoist political position, while moving the political process in a direction that the international community would support. A people-centered approach under the overarching philosophy of human security was abandoned when encouraging the qualified Maoist combatants to leave the cantonment. Although bilateral and diplomatic partners focused on short-term political progress, it was essential for the UN to advocate a rights/needs-based approach to the reintegration of former combatants to be in compliance with the provisions of the UN Charter, as expressed within the human security concept. And yet, UN efforts in this direction failed. In addition to considering the rights and needs of the individual former combatants, a broader community-based approach would have been appropriate.

Shift DDR from a Narrow Focus on Former Combatants

Ever since the signing of a comprehensive peace accord, the Maoist leadership had manipulated the combatants in the cantonments as pawns in a political power play. The rehabilitation of verified minors and late recruits was an exceptional obligation to a specific group—the minors—that fell to the UN, which dealt with it as a benchmark on the path to peace. Following the payments of lump sums to former combatants or the absorption of a number of them into the Nepalese Army, the exceptional treatment of Maoist former combatants can no longer be justified as a critical element of stabilizing the peace process. Any further benefits to former combatants must be in the context of contributing to broader community development.

DDR in Mindanao, Philippines: Mission Almost Accomplished, 2016

On January 24, 2014, the government of the Philippines and the Moro Islamic Liberation Front (MILF) signed the final agreement on Normalization and Bangsamoro Waters. This agreement covered the final elements of a peace accord ending forty years of guerrilla warfare that had seen more than 100,000 people killed in the southern island group of Mindanao and the Sulu Archipelago. However, it was not the end of the peace process. Public and political reaction to the death of forty-four police officers in an extraordinary antiterrorist operation led by the police Special Action Force in MILF territory on January 25, 2015, torpedoed—or at least delayed—parliamentary ratification of the accord, which remained unratified as of November 2016. This delay/failure perpetuates the despondency generated by the lingering specter of a series of inconclusive DDR attempts over the past decade.

In early January 2015, it had looked as if the peace accord was going to stick. From a DDR perspective, it seemed to reflect convergence in the application of many elements of the evolved theory, including a perception of political will and apparent conflict sensitivity on the part of prime stakeholders. Stakeholders in the peace process demonstrated a willingness to listen to expert advice, accept neighborly support and mediation, apply lessons learned from global experience, judiciously use confidence-building measures, moderate language in applying culturally sensitive nonconflict communications, and show a willingness to compromise. But the positive impact of these investments was then derailed by a failure to address the complexity of the environment and by direct sabotage of the process. In Patricio Abinales's opinion, the process was derailed by a misplacement of orthodox narrative that set a "high premium on minority-majority tensions, religion as an inspirational force for armed change and the omnipresence of a capable state and its coercive apparatuses."[26] In applying DDR theory, however, consider what could have been a successful peace process and what might still be so, should the tensions between the government of the Philippines and MILF be resolved.

The Context

The island group of Mindanao covers six regions and twenty-six provinces, with a population in 2010 of more than twenty-one million, of which approximately 32 percent are Muslim. The struggle for independence, or at least higher levels of autonomy, by the indigenous Islamic population of Mindanao and the Sulu Archipelago has stretched from the sixteenth century through Spanish and US colonial eras to the resistance of the "pacifying and Christianizing" policies of the post–World War II government of the Philippines. The latter efforts created a multicultural "tri-people" environment of the indigenous Islamic Moro people, the indigenous animist Lumad people (totaling approximately 10 percent), and the resettled Christians. By 1970, the settlers outnumbered the indigenous population by 74 percent.[27] For the Muslims, who have a cultural affinity to carrying guns, the gun restrictions being imposed by the Ferdinand Marcos government during the 1970s, coupled with the dilution of their majority, land grabbing, and perceived social and political inequity, were taken as an existential threat. Intensification of bloody rebellion ensued. A heavy government security presence did not reduce the proliferation of unregistered small arms, which were easily imported or locally manufactured and which raised the stakes in the conflict.

Initially seeking independence and moderated to autonomy in the mid-1970s, the Moro National Liberation Front and its armed wing, the Bangsa Moro Army of approximately 30,000 fighters, perpetrated an insurgency that saw approximately 60,000 people killed between 1971 and 1976. Government action and incentives to the population led to a reduction in the Moro National Liberation Front's influence and capacities, resulting in more sporadic insurgency and the fragmentation of the movement, including the splitting off of the Moro Islamic Liberation Front in 1983.[28] The Corazon Aquino presidency made greater efforts at delivering a peace process; with the welcome mediation of the Organisation of Islamic Cooperation in 1987, the Moro National Liberation Front officially agreed to accept autonomy rather than independence. With the Moro National Liberation Front subsequently sidelined due to political setbacks and renewed fighting, thirteen of twenty-three provinces in the disputed region, together with a less than 20 percent Muslim population, voted in a government-run plebiscite. To the chagrin of the Moro National Liberation Front, only four provinces—two in Mindanao and two in the Sulu Archipelago—accepted autonomy. The government proceeded with the creation of the Autonomous Region in Muslim Mindanao. The Moro National Liberation Front found this unacceptable and resumed fighting.

The government continued talks with the Moro National Liberation Front with the view of signing a comprehensive peace accord, which was eventually achieved in 1996. An aspect of this peace accord was the integration of Moro National Liberation Front forces into the national army or police force. In addressing possible sensitivities, this integration did not include any element of disarmament or demobilization, and the capacity of disgruntled elements of the Moro National Liberation Front to regroup and relaunch the insurgency was not addressed. This accord was not a DDR process, though it did have some levels of success in reducing violence. In integrating Moro National Liberation Front members into the army and police, normal educational and physical entrance requirements were waived, with some intensive training courses, including basic literacy, created to bring cadres up to an acceptable standard, as necessary.[29] An uneasy calm ensued, with frayed levels of trust between government forces and the integrated units. Limited resettlement assistance was available to those who did not opt for integration; others moved into other armed groups, such as MILF, or criminal gangs. Many Moro National Liberation Front cadres were dissatisfied with their lot and with what they considered as excessive compromise in accepting the autonomy.

Moro National Liberation Front communities saw little sustainable impact of the peace process. The effort at pacification of the Moro National Liberation Front is often assessed by scholars as having been more concerned with achieving rapid peace, so that issues of terrorism could be addressed post-9/11,[30] and with opening Mindanao to commercial exploitation, rather than bringing a community through a postconflict environment to development. With noted exceptions, especially in terms of community-based participative aspects of the process, perceptions of poor planning, rushed implementation, failed unmonitored projects, clientelist benefit, local corruption, and exploitation as regards commercial investment abounded. The capacity of the fundamentalist Abu Sayyaf armed group was greatly reduced by the US-supported army operations. However, MILF kept up their struggle.

Although the aftermath of the 1996 peace accord and the related investment and community capacity building certainly contributed to diminishing the MILF's fighting capacity, the accord did not resolve the root sense of injustice and inequity among the Muslim community. Ultimately, the accord did not stop the fighting. In the ongoing conflict, it was not easy to achieve development results. Armed groups splintered into factions with various motivations, further complicating future efforts. In recent years, the armed groups that continue to battle the government, some in response to the government's military aggressiveness, have included MILF and the balance of the Moro National Liberation Front (combined to about 17,000), both fighting on issues of sovereignty; the Communist Party (approximately 5,000), fighting on ideological issues; Abu Sayyaf and associates who claim to be affiliated with al-Qaeda (approximately 500); and various smaller groups (totaling about 25,000)—all of whom may eventually require DDR.[31]

With regional support to the peace process being provided by Indonesia, Malaysia, and the Organisation of Islamic Cooperation and with international support from the UN and Japan, a tentative plan for DDR was developed pending a comprehensive peace accord. The plan, which was pitched at a cost of approximately US$80 million, is now in limbo pending the implementation of the "normalization" agreement in the context of the peace accord ratification of January 24, 2014.

Normalization 2014

The Normalization Agreement of 2014 appeared to reflect high levels of conflict sensitivity and political will on the part of both MILF and the government of the Philippines. The primary ace held by the government under President Benigno Aquino was that it had been willing to grant autonomy at a level with which the government was confident, after decades of negotiation, MILF would find acceptable. The government was prepared to be innovative and to take some political risks in offering confidence-building and interim stabilization measures.

MILF's sensitivities to the language to be used arose from Islamic religious, cultural, and interpretational concerns. In 2013, I facilitated a course on gender-sensitive programming in DDR in Manila that was attended by government peace negotiators, the Moro National Liberation Front, and MILF. The course was hosted by the Norwegian Defence University College, with UN support. The word *gender* posed a particular problem for MILF, as they perceived that it implied a Western development theory committed to gender equality and universal human rights, which was incompatible with Islam. Further, they saw the term *DDR* as a

Western idea that implied the surrender of nonstate armed groups. So, instead, we called the course "Addressing the Needs of Men and Women in the Transition from Military to Civilian," and concerns were calmed. In the peace negotiations, the government's and MILF's acceptance of the conflict-sensitive term *normalization* to describe the processes was a major confidence builder.

The Annex on Normalization to the Framework Agreement on the Bangsamoro addressed the essential conflict elements, including the following:

- The way forward for law enforcement, including accountability to local communities
- Transitional components of normalization that ensure that the transition to autonomy will be undertaken in a spirit of partnership, with the necessary supporting institutional structures—both security and political—and with international monitoring
- The mechanics of the process of decommissioning weapons to "place them beyond use," drawing from the Irish Good Friday Agreement lexicon and including associated dispute resolution and support for the smooth transition of former combatants from military to civilian life
- The redeployment and behavior of the government armed forces
- The handling of unexploded ordnance and mines
- The disbanding of private armed groups
- Support for socioeconomic development
- Cooperation in developing the appropriate transitional justice provisions to correct historical injustices and human rights violations, including the creation of a Truth and Reconciliation Commission
- Support for resource mobilization
- The development of confidence-building measures as rapid gestures of goodwill

The associated schedule of implementation was provided in a separate annex.[32]

In moving toward the Final Comprehensive Agreement on the Bangsamoro, MILF had further concerns arising from the fact that some of the provinces being granted autonomy under the agreement—in particular, the islands stretching down the archipelago—were not connected by any land bridge but by broad expanses of sea. Those islands might, in the event of disagreement, become politically inaccessible. This issue was resolved by the extension of the autonomy to the waters joining the autonomous provinces, an innovative caveat that took the agreement beyond normal jurisdictional arrangements in the context of the Law of the Sea. An agreement addressing this issue was signed on March 27, 2014.

The major lessons to be learned, or relearned, from the progress so far, including its DDR aspects, must be that the primary element of mutual trust is essential. This trust can be created by a clear demonstration of mutual political will for achieving agreement through compromise, mutual sensitivity, linguistic dexterity and flexibility, respect, the provision of confidence building, and interim stabilization measures.

The police Special Action Force operation that set out to capture terrorist bombers in MILF territory on January 25, 2015, succeeded in killing one of the targets but it also lost forty-four policemen. The action demonstrated not only operational ineptitude but also extraordinarily bad timing—unless the purpose of the operation was to derail the peace process. Increased violent Islamic extremism in Mindanao associated with the splintering of MILF, as well as increased activities of other smaller Islamic armed groups, has contributed to increasing tensions since then. Some groups are claiming affiliations to al-Qaeda or, more recently, to the Islamic State; for them, anything less than full independence is unacceptable. As a comprehensive peace accord draws closer, many in the Philippine majority conservative elite are concerned that ratification of the peace accord would undermine their war against this violent Islamic extremism. Speculation that the accord was effectively sabotaged by the Special Action Force's botched operation is not so farfetched in the context of Abinales's assertion of the prevailing orthodox narrative. Deliberations in efforts to ratify the accord of January 2014, granting levels of autonomy to Mindanao in the context of the Bangsamoro Basic Law, have been ongoing at various levels of parliament since May 2015. The hope that such a peace could be achieved during the term of President Benigno Aquino, which expired on June 30, 2016, was dashed. However, hope reemerges under the new president, Rodrigo Duterte, who has launched his unconventional popular rule as "a tough man" in prioritizing the search for solutions to the Philippines' several conflicts.

Can the Theory of DDR Be Applied?

Nepal offers a complex polarized and intransigent political environment, a suppressed socioeconomic condition, and a fragmented feudal cast-based society. From an operational perspective, limited baseline data, an absence of UN leverage, and the absence of unambiguous national buy-in to the process all combined to obstruct progress. The lack of scope for a concerted community-based approach to programming that would focus on broader community rehabilitation, rather than purely on the subject caseload, further contributed to the challenge. The plan also failed to develop an effective integrated communications strategy that would sell a unified message from national stakeholders and international organizations to win the positive perceptions, attitudes, and trust of the full caseload of former combatants and the community. Despite all of this, the program's success in supporting unqualified former combatants, which was represented by achieving sustained livelihood placement of almost 75 percent of the UNIRP's caseload of verified minors and late recruits, suggests that the theory can be applied to some degree. The small scale of this program and the marginalized nature of the caseload, considered as somewhat outside the peace process, permitted a level of experimentation in drawing from the evolving theory. The incremental scale-up and responsive improvement were a result of an effective and dynamic monitoring, evaluation, and adjustment system, which would have been difficult to implement in a larger program with more immediate strategic implications for a peace process.

The DDR community of practice identifies lessons drawn from the program as examples of good practice.[33] These included gender-responsive programming, management information systems, information and data management, monitoring and evaluation, psychosocial support, career counseling, and job placement support. The example in Nepal contributes to the perception that the key to applying the theory of DDR appears to be careful adaption to the specific context and prioritization of the essentials that must be achieved to deliver acceptable outcomes in a dynamic, evolving environment.

The jury is still out regarding the success of the support offered to qualified former combatants of the Maoist army. It deliberates the wisdom, or otherwise, of buying off combatants with substantial cash incentives—in this case, in the absence of elements contributing to livelihood sustainability or, indeed, in the absence of any significant element of trust. The preliminary feedback coming from the field in Nepal is not optimistic that the cash lump sum was effective in supporting sustainable reintegration.

The resolution of the protracted and multifaceted conflict in Mindanao, despite the current suspension, may eventually offer another opportunity to determine whether the application of DDR theory actually works. The 2014 Framework Agreement between the government of the Philippines and MILF reflected a conflict-sensitive approach in absorbing many aspects of the evolving theory of DDR, as seen in the Annex on Normalization. Implementations of previous DDR processes in the Philippines have been severely lacking. However, early evidence of political will, mutual trust, and commitment of the parties to the current comprehensive agreement was apparent and generated optimism, though the recent suspension is another setback. Although it may take decades to achieve the cessation of violence, the prime position of trust in every phase of the Mindanao peace process is clear.

Second-generation DDR has envisaged practice with strengthened community-based approaches and DDR in other than postconflict environments. Here dynamic approaches allowed adaption in accordance with context. However, even bigger stakes are being played for in DDR during war, where trust cannot be built and entry points for a human security approach to violence reduction are limited. The next chapter considers the extraordinary efforts to implement DDR in support of counterinsurgency operations in the ongoing conflicts in Afghanistan, Colombia, and Somalia.

Notes

1. Drawn from my experience as senior rehabilitation advisor to the UN in Nepal from 2010 to 2012.

2. Adapted from Simon Ryan and Owen Greene, "Disarmament, Demobilization, and Reintegration in Nepal: A Mini-study," Saferworld and Centre for International Co-operation and Security, University of Bradford, UK, July 2008, as well as from personal observation.

3. As recorded in the DREAM DDR Database System (a specific DDR database system designed over the previous decade by UNDP) and held in the custody of UN Development Programme, Nepal.

4. Child soldiers are defined in accordance with the Paris Commitments of 2006 (adapted from the Cape Town Principles of 1997) on the prevention of the recruitment of children to armed factions.

5. The UN country team is the committee of heads of UN development agencies in country, led by the resident coordinator, who is also the country representative of the UNDP—in this case, Robert Piper.

6. Subina Sherestha, "The Disillusioned Soldier," *Witness Report,* Al Jazeera, December 31, 2012, http://www.aljazeera.com/programmes/witness/2011/11/2011112813233689170.html.

7. The official launch, in accordance with the funding period, was in June 2010.

8. I drafted the program document and budgets in broad consultation.

9. The issues of masculinities often associated with male former combatants include a deterioration of self-esteem during the effort to reintegrate into civil society, a sense of frustration at the distancing from the fraternity and camaraderie of the armed group, and a propensity toward gender-based violence.

10. Irma Specht, *Independent Evaluation of the UNIRP* (Kathmandu, Nepal: Transition International, February 2013); and the Transcultural Psychosocial Organization (TPO), *A Longitudinal Psychosocial Assessment Among VLMRs During Reintegration* (Kathmandu: TPO, 2012).

11. These figures are from UNDP, *Post-rehabilitation Participant Satisfaction Report* (Kathmandu, Nepal: UNIRP, September 2013).

12. Ibid.

13. Specht, *Independent Evaluation of the UNIRP.*

14. Adapted from my observations in contemporaneous notes as submitted to the UN resident coordinator in March 2012.

15. UN, "Level 4, Operations, Programs and Support," in *Operational Guide to the IDDRS,* 154 UNDP/DPKO, New York, December 2006.

16. Sigrid Willibald, "Does Money Work? Cash Transfers to Ex-combatants in Disarmament, Demobilisation, and Reintegration Processes," *Disasters* 30, no. 3 (2006).

17. Ibid.

18. Molloy "The Gender Perspective in DDR: Lessons from Sierra Leone" 2004; *The Qualitative Quantitative Dilemma* (Master's thesis, Tokyo University of Foreign Studies, 2009).

19. Isabela Leao, *Swimming Against the Stream: DDR in Sierra Leone* (PhD dissertation, State University of Milan, Italy, January 2011).

20. Drawn from Molloy, *The Qualitative Quantitative Dilemma.*

21. Adapted from *Indonesia: DDR in Ache 2005–2009* (Barcelona: Agència Catalana de Cooperació al Desenvolupament and Spanish Agency for International Development Cooperation, 2009).

22. Drawn directly from my experience as senior adviser DDR, UNDP, Central African Republic, in early 2009.

23. Figures adapted from D. B. Subedi, "War to Peace Transition in Nepal: Success and Challenges Ahead," *Small Wars Journal,* November 9, 2013.

24. Ibid.

25. Ibid. This assertion is also corroborated (if not yet rigorously supported by empirical evidence) by the preliminary findings of a cursory review by members of the International Research Group on Reintegration, Tromsø University, October 2014.

26. Patricio Abinales, "Missing the Peace in Muslim Mindanao," *East Asia Forum*, May 6, 2015, http://eastasiaforum.org/2015/05/06/missing-the-peace-in -muslim-mindanao.

27. Drawn from Ceasar Villanueva, George Aguilar, and Niall O'Brien Center, *The Reintegration of the Moro National Liberation Front in Mindanao* (Bradford, UK: Centre for International Security, University of Bradford, July 2008), 3.

28. Ibid., 5.

29. Ibid., 8. Eventually, the integrated cadres were formed into ten engineering companies, thirty-nine rifle companies, and a support group of 1,500 police officers.

30. The Abu Sayyaf faction, having split from MNLF, had allegedly affiliated with al-Qaeda.

31. Drawn from a presentation on the DDR process in the Philippines by Folke Bernadotte Academy, Stockholm, at the DDR Course held at the Barcelona International Peace Resource Center (BIPRC), Spain 2010.

32. Drawn directly from the Annex document to the agreement, 2014.

33. Relevant evaluations include Specht, *Independent Evaluation of the UNIRP*; UNDP, *Post-Rehabilitation Participant Satisfaction Report*; Paul Bonard and Yvan Conoir, *Evaluation of UNDP Reintegration Programmes,* vol. I, eds. Sabine Cornieti and Jon Grosh (New York: UNDP, February 2013).

7

DDR in War

Classic DDR insists on the necessity of rarely all-present prerequisites: a cessation of violence, a comprehensive peace accord, a secure environment, political will on the part of all parties, and voluntary participation. Second-generation DDR considers two further angles: DDR in other-than-postconflict environments, excluding outright war, and the necessity for a holistic approach to DDR beyond combatant-centricity. This new generation aspires to achieve conflict-sensitive community security and sustainability derived from broader community engagement.

A third category is DDR during war, which involves extraordinary challenges, with the security perspective remaining dominant in the absence of a cessation of violence. Power plays and maneuvers are in full swing. DDR in war is an aspect of the war strategy and, as such, is driven by one side of the conflict posing a threat to the other. Soft power imperatives of DDR are tempered and complicated by offensive operations. A human security approach is confused by the imperatives of security. The level of risk for all involved is high. DDR during war offers a special dilemma for peace enforcement, peacekeeping, or peacebuilding international initiatives, except for those led by bilateral actors who have vested interests. While wishing to support the return of legitimate use of armed force to the state and an end to hostilities, DDR in war is a premature environment for DDR implementation using the skills and experience possessed by the international humanitarian or peacekeeping organizations. Afghanistan and Colombia offer contrasting examples that exude the complexity and frustration of such efforts. DDR in the ongoing conflict in Somalia, with both UN and regional organization engagement, offers similar challenges.

In March 2013, the UN Security Council created a hybrid offensive UN force, the Force Intervention Brigade, to deal with the scourge of incorrigible armed militias ravaging eastern Democratic Republic of Congo. This peace enforcement unit of the peacekeeping mission raised complex legal questions and challenged the UN's role in implementing DDR during war.

Afghanistan

The Context

The US-led coalition of the willing intervention in Afghanistan, after the Bonn Agreement of 2001, threw up major challenges for the classic DDR approach, causing the UN to retain a low profile. Afghanistan was far from a postconflict environment. After the initial rout of the Taliban, the United States strove to change the security dynamic that impeded the influence of the Hamid Karzai government in areas controlled by the dominant warlords of the Northern Alliance. They used a process of SSR that included elements of DDR in an attempt to remove surplus fighters and their weapons (those who had fought against the Taliban) from the national security payroll. It was to be a process of conversion, bringing the monopoly in the use of armed force to the state through the Afghan National Army and bringing the rule of law under the control of the police. Unfortunately, what actually occurred was a confused approach to a disputed counterinsurgency doctrine that pitted the traditional approach of mass and firepower against the application of soft influencing (shaping) activities, together with kinetics, to "win" the people. The counterinsurgency approach would "separate the fishes from the water" by protecting the people from the insurgency threat and by offering a normative environment.[1]

David Petraeus's new counterinsurgency doctrine of 2006 claimed that the US Army and Marine Corps must be "nation builders as well as warriors."[2] This doctrine focuses on populations needing protection; establishing and expanding secure areas; isolating insurgents; conducting effective, persuasive, and continuous information operations; and offering amnesties and rehabilitation to those insurgents willing to support the new government. Civil police were to take the lead with the host nation as soon as possible. DDR was seen as an essential element of this state building. Yet, few DDR practitioners would believe that soldiers are qualified to undertake such ambitious state-building tasks. Historically, US agencies have projected an orientalist approach in light of pervasive cultural relativity and moral absolutism. The Canadian counterinsurgency manual of 2008, on the other hand, admonishes practitioners to avoid moral relativism, recognizing that in complex sociocultural contexts, specific facets of morality are not universal, and "no absolute right or wrong exists." Relativism can confuse culture with morality. Thus, counterinsurgency must be cognizant of local custom and culture, giving rise to an understanding that values may be different from Western norms. Likewise, it is critical to avoid cultural absolutism in attempting to impose inappropriate social constructs to the host culture and society.[3]

The reservations of DDR practitioners that soldiers are properly trained for such sensitivity were compounded as the practice of the counterinsurgency doctrine came tumbling down in 2010. To the glee of the traditional "shock and awe" proponents in the military industrial complex, General Stanley McChrystal lost the confidence of both his superiors and his troops.

He had enthusiastically attempted to enforce a soft approach to "win" the people during the counterinsurgency campaign in Afghanistan. This occurred long after US attempts at implementing a security-focused DDR process with the Northern Alliance in the relatively Taliban-free window of opportunity soon after the Bonn Agreement. How did that initial DDR go, and did the subsequent DDR efforts, led by the UN and the government of Afghanistan, fare any better?

DDR in Afghanistan

Even prior to the Bonn Agreement of 2001, international actors had considered that demobilization and reintegration of former combatants would be a critical process in stabilizing the security environment and in demonstrating the peace dividend in Afghanistan. For success, it would be necessary to ensure Afghan ownership, as well as leadership and political will for a voluntary demobilization process that would target young fighters, deserters, and vulnerable groups, including female-headed households, and offer viable alternative livelihoods.[4] The Afghan Interim Administration adopted these DDR recommendations in its security, demobilization, and reintegration framework. This was an aspect of a broader SSR process to break command structures of illicit armed groups and armies and to establish new, legitimate, ethnically balanced professional armed forces that were answerable to the state.

According to T. X. Hammes, the Bonn Agreement was nothing close to a comprehensive peace accord, as it did not include the Taliban and other Pashtun factions.[5] Instead, it was an agreement among the victors. Michael Vinay Bhatia and Robert Muggah stated that it was more a power-sharing agreement than a peace treaty.[6] The complexity of the environment into which the United States, NATO, the International Security Assistance Force, Operation Enduring Freedom, and UN security and state-building interventions had stumbled after the Bonn Agreement has been a conundrum stumping security analysts and scholars for more than a decade. This chapter focuses on the main DDR elements of those operations—how they evolved, what they achieved, and what has been relearned from them in implementing DDR in the context of ongoing counterinsurgency or counterterrorism operations.[7]

Bhatia and Muggah noted the UN preoccupation with "national ownership, comprehensive frameworks and community inclusiveness"; the UN approached DDR as a "short-term, stand-alone initiative rather than a long-term strategic interaction." It did this even as the UN Integrated DDR Standards emphasized "enabling frameworks and bureaucratic structures rather than the dynamics of demobilization or the often dynamic requirements of peace-building."[8] The UN's role in Afghanistan illustrates the core of the struggle in which both practitioners and scholars are currently gingerly engaged, as they tweak the evolution of DDR theory.

Afghanistan's DDR programs were "intertwined with the dynamics of state-building and the state's effort to monopolize the use of legitimate force."[9] The current efforts in Afghanistan have challenged some of the basic assumptions governing conventional DDR programming. Prime among the failures in the Afghan New Beginning Program (ANBP) (2003–2006) and the Disbandment of Illegal Armed Groups (DIAG) (2005–), both of which target the disarmament of the friendly Afghan Armed Forces, are the "common conceptualization of commanders and combatants as homogeneous actors [and] the failure to recognize the complex relationships between former combatants and their communities . . . an essential factor in shaping mobilization."[10] If DDR is to generate positive dividends, it needs to extend its "perspective beyond rational choice and combatant-centric approach and better accommodate factors relating to real and perceived legitimacy, outreach and community peace-building."[11] Bahia and Muggah insist that the DDR must be pursued not as a narrow "economic process of reintegration, but rather . . . as symbolic, diplomatic, political and legal processes linked to local, national and international conceptions of legitimacy," necessitating the "ascendance of state armed forces and their acquisition of a monopoly over the legitimate use of force."[12] In addition to the structural flaws in the programs, Bhatia and Muggah assert that the inability of the international community or the government of Afghanistan to articulate a coherent plan to promote security and minimize security dilemmas was critical.

George Ferks, Geert Gompelman, and Stefan van Laar explained that nominally, at least, the Afghan government administered both the Afghan New Beginning Program and the Disbandment of Illegal Armed Groups with UN support.[13] The former focused on the heavy weapons of the main Northern Alliance armed groups and was led and funded by Japan, whereas the latter focused on the more resistant elements of the smaller Northern Alliance armed groups and was led by UNDP. Continuously threatened by the Taliban, these DDR processes represented aspects of foreign strategy that involved military interventions and the re-establishment of state structures. A hybrid approach, initially tested in Iraq, fused (or confused) security and human security considerations, local social service/utility, and infrastructural projects and established Provincial Reconstruction Teams (PRTs). These teams were ostensibly to support the government in extending its authority and in addressing essential community needs in terms of social infrastructure.[14] However, in the absence of institutional or conceptual unity, US commanders saw them, to a large degree, as contributors to force protection, rather than as a community peacebuilding/development tool; they saw the PRTs as an aspect of the counterinsurgency that could contribute to human intelligence gathering for accurate targeting and for addressing the "hearts and minds" aspects of the war.[15] Kenji Isezaki, chief of the Afghan New Beginning Program, which was the initial post-Bonn DDR process in Afghanistan, stated that the success of PRTs was critically important to the

DDR effort in extending local government reach—and, thereby, security and scope for development—into rural areas. This would, in turn, facilitate reintegration of former combatants. NATO considered PRTs as the successful aspect of the comprehensive approach,[16] an integrated cross-government and civilian-military approach to counterinsurgency devised to maximize collaboration and to develop synergies in achieving objectives. However, the co-option of the PRTs by local warlords, their frequent inappropriate mechanisms of implementation, and the targeting opportunity that they provided all militated against them making any contribution to successful DDR in terms of the reintegration of former combatants.[17]

Diverse regional concerns, reflected in the debatably nefarious interests of foreign state intelligence agencies—particularly, the Inter-services Intelligence of Pakistan—through their diverse interference and spoiling activities, compounded the complexity of the DDR efforts. These efforts were designed to address those "friendly" militias that had been engaged against the Taliban, had been co-opted into the Afghan Armed Forces, and would collaborate in the international plan for stabilization and state building in Afghanistan. However, incorrigible insurgents, including the Taliban, al-Qaeda, and criminal groups, were to be faced with military means. Concurrently, the aim of the national reconciliation program was to encourage moderate individuals to leave those incorrigible armed groups and reintegrate into civilian life.

Multiple local leaders and regional warlords, with forces ranging from a few combatants influencing local villages to full-scale armies controlling regions in clientelist relations, prevailed in a cauldron of ethnic, power, criminal, fundamentalist, and identity challenges. These warlords were often espoused with state authority and were referred to as government officials linked to illegal armed groups. This was all in an environment awash with arms, both light and heavy. The US/NATO/International Security Assistance Forces chose to face their "war on terror," dragging a reticent UN into a post-Taliban Afghanistan to support the establishment and stabilization of the state toward an acceptable humanitarian environment. In this complexity, the initial focus of DDR—the Afghan New Beginning Program—was on what was considered the lower-hanging fruit, those warlords of the Northern Alliance who had built relations with NATO while fighting the Taliban and who were already on the national payroll.

Afghan New Beginning Program

Progress on implementing the Afghan New Beginnings Program was slow, finally pushed forward by the results of the Tokyo donor conference in February 2003, when US$141 million was made available by eight nations—mainly Japan, but also the United Kingdom, Canada, the United States, the European Commission, Norway, Switzerland, and the Netherlands. Japan was appointed as lead nation in the DDR process, primarily offering advocacy, funding, and administration of ANBP. Implementation was to be handled by the UN Assistance Mission in Afghanistan (UNAMA), the small UN political mission, rather than a peacekeeping operation. UNAMA was under the special representative of the Secretary-General, Lakhdar Brahimi, of Brahimi Report 2000 fame and former foreign minister of Algeria, who worked closely with the Interim Administration's Demobilization and Reintegration Commission. ANBP was administered through a central office in Kabul and eight regional offices, each with civilian and military staff and a mobile disarmament unit.

An international observer group, including representation from UNAMA and donors, offered impartial oversight.[18] Isezaki was particularly proud, having persuaded Brahimi to provide his own military advisers as the core of the military observer team, while also persuading other national diplomatic missions in Kabul to provide their military attachés as observers to monitor the DDR process. This was the "first international observer group based on bilateral aid."[19]

Isezaki noted that, at the time, UNAMA, in pursuing its "light-footprint approach," was maintaining a passive posture in avoiding association with the heavy hand of the United States.[20] The UN highlighted special circumstances in Afghanistan—the weakness of the interim authority, the absence of political leverage, and the total dependence on the cooperation of the warlords; as such, it initially recommended offering the incentives associated with DDR prior to disarmament. In this proposed reintegration, disarmament, and demobilization—that is, RDD—the "carrot," or benefits, came before the "stick" of disarmament, rather than the usual DDR. Isezaki saw this as offering an opportunity to warlords to take advantage of the interim authority and the international community's intentions by off-loading their nonoperational (aged, disabled) cadres, while retaining effective cadres and their weapons as leverage for future demands. Isezaki successfully opposed this idea to the extent that at the February 2003 donor conference in Tokyo, Karzai stated that the disarmament and demobilization must be completed before the elections and that those phases of DDR must be completed within a year.

Confirming the numbers of actual combatants in the field was difficult. Although preliminary estimates had been between 40,000 and 50,000, the combined warlords claimed up to 250,000. Concerned at containing the program's budget and scope, Isezaki forced the government to accept a total figure of 100,000 combatants that he deemed to be closer to the truth. Isezaki further reasoned that by focusing on the main and most influential warlords of the Northern Alliance—particularly, the two biggest groups that had been warring between themselves—the bulk of combatants would be included. The easiest way to grab the lowest-hanging fruit was to focus on their heavy weapons—tanks, artillery, and so on.

Isezaki also drew attention to further complications in Afghanistan. Irrespective of the much-lauded benefits of national ownership, the DDR was implemented by the government of Afghanistan and thus could not be deemed neutral or international, especially as the strongest Panjshiri warlord, Marshal Mohammad Fahim, was the minister for defense. In an attempt to mitigate the potential for resulting conflict and concerned with the commitments of its own pacifist constitution, Japan insisted on parameters regarding the ethnic balance within the recruitment of the Afghan National Army and of defense officials. Although this insistence amounted to a controversial use of conditional overseas development aid as leverage,[21] it offered an element of equity that allowed the US-led SSR process to move forward.

In the meantime, in an environment of insurgency in an ethnically and regionally fragmented society, the United States was struggling to lead the establishment of a national Afghan army. In the new government, key ministries were distributed among the most influential warlords, including the Panjshiri faction, with their clients serving as officials. Isezaki talked of "the simultaneous execution by the United States of a 'war process' led by the Department of Defense, intended to eliminate terrorism, and a 'peace process' led by the State Department, the US embassy, that seeks to build a country."[22] The two are incompatible.

Local militias and tribal leaders, who often received salaries and equipment from coalition forces, were masters in manipulating the US effort to their own ends, overstating local threats and disrupting the DDR process. However, the United States, with its left hand not concerned with what its right was doing, continued to pump large stocks of weapons to its favorite warlords. These warlords were often rivals of those who had agreed to disarm, thus totally undermining the impact of DDR and contributing to the security dilemma. Isezaki had limited impact in pressuring the United States to reduce this activity. In pragmatically acknowledging the United States as the only game town, Isezaki deviated from his rulebook and agreed to remove some militias—those needed to support the counterterrorism effort—from the list of militia factions to be disarmed. His caveat was that this was to be done only until the new restructured and retrained Afghan National Army could develop the capacity to address the relevant security concerns. The US government independently chose 5,000 former army or militia members and called them the Afghan Guard Force, agreeing that this force would take responsibility for the eventual disarmament.[23] From 2005, ANBP also undertook the destruction of antipersonnel mines and ammunition and cantoned and deactivated 12,248 heavy weapons across the country, representing approximately 98 percent of the total estimated stock.[24]

The method of cantonment in Kabul, where the example was to be set, undermined the cantonment process. The International Security Assistance Force, without taking any professional guidance, cut an independent deal with the factions, effectively dividing the city of Kabul among factions and contributing to rearmament.[25] This mistake probably resulted from a convoluted and uncoordinated command structure involving the United States, NATO, International Security Assistance Force, and the UN, with a mix of military and civilians, all with competing philosophies and egos.

Further, NATO/International Security Assistance Force was not significantly deployed outside of Kabul and could not provide the level of deterrence that would support a DDR program. US airpower only offered the image of deterrence, giving the resurgent Taliban scope for maneuvering in the rural areas. As the elections of October 2004 approached, there were high expectations, not least from Isezaki, of the PRT activities offering infrastructural and socioeconomic support to communities in unstable areas. The PRTs were operating under NATO control in the north and under International Security Assistance Force in the south and had the goal of "winning" the people, with a nod toward counterinsurgency doctrine.[26] They held these high expectations even as the bulk of resources remained concentrated on the traditional kinetic operations of counterterrorism. Thus, the expectations for a positive impact from the PRT were largely wishful thinking.

Ferks, Gompelman, and van Laar noted that with ANBP addressing only the Northern Alliance and with the new Afghan National Army made up exclusively by the Northern Alliance, other major groups in Afghanistan—especially, the Pashtun in the south—experienced a significant security dilemma. The exclusion of the Taliban from the process was also considered by many to be counterproductive. Still, the listed achievement of the ANBP is significant.[27]

Those opting for reintegration support initially received a cash grant that was later suspended and factored into a stipend to reduce rent taking by commanders. They also received career counseling and support in finding employment or self-employment. The livelihood options included those traditional sectors common to other DDR processes—education, agriculture, skills training, and entrepreneurial support. They also included innovative ideas, such as creating teams to undertake local infrastructural contracts in a cooperative arrangement, teacher training, and demining teams. This was in addition to the option for selected former combatants to engage in the SSR process through integration into the Afghan National Army or the police. Approximately 50 percent opted for agriculture support, 25 percent for entrepreneurial support, and about 20 percent for skills training.[28] A commander's incentive program that included management and some foreign training was offered to about 500 senior generals and local commanders to encourage compliance with and support for the program.

By June 2005, UNDP claimed that the Afghan New Beginning Program had effectively disarmed all Afghan militia forces and that it would therefore end the program. However, total disarmament was not reflected by the facts on the ground. The Tajik-dominated units in Kabul and Panjshir remained active. Many had, in fact, reinvented themselves as police units.[29] As Hammes commented, although ANBP was certainly efficient in that it removed a great deal of hardware from the field and took significant numbers off the state recurring defense budget, it was not effective in demobilizing the armed groups, which maintained their core structures and significant numbers of weapons. Isezaki contended that the ANBP as a stand-alone DDR process that was designed to downsize the Afghan Defense Forces as an aspect of SSR, without considering a coherent comprehensive security strategy including a focus on the strengthening of the rule of law, actually created a security vacuum that permitted the return of the Taliban.[30]

Disbandment of Illegal Armed Groups

The Disbandment of Illegal Armed Groups was designed to pick up those informal factions of the Afghan Armed Forces that were under the control of individual warlords; engaged in various activities, such as local security and power plays; supported drug trafficking and terrorist activities; and deemed a threat to the integrity of the state. They were estimated to comprise about 120,000 armed elements. It was hoped that DIAG would broaden the government's span of control through the country, bring the monopoly of the legitimate use of force back to the state, and gain the support of the people. A supporting legal framework was enacted that covered the control of private security companies and gun control. A management institution was established as the Disarmament and Reintegration Commission; its executive body was called the Disarmament of Illegally Armed Groups Forum, which was supported by an executive secretary with decentralized implementation by provincial committees using local knowledge. Ferks, Gompelman, and van Laar commented, however, that no role was considered for local NGOs or civil society.

Launched in June 2005, this program immediately entered controversy, with the Disarmament and Reintegration Commission being tasked to vet candidates for the National Assembly and provincial council elections in order to identify who might be ineligible due to associations with armed groups. Much pressure was placed on the commission from all sides of government for maximum accommodation in the interests of short-term security. Of 6,000 candidates, 1,108 were initially identified as suspected to have links with armed groups. However, only thirty-four were finally disqualified.[31]

DIAG had at its disposal a broad range of the "tools and levers available to the government: political, social and economic instruments, information and law enforcement."[32] With weapons collections points established in each province, DIAG was not offering individual benefits; rather, it offered development resources that were to be distributed at a community level with the inclusion of stabilized areas into broad national recovery programs. It was obvious that sound provincial government management and central government resourcing would be crucial to such a program.

By mid-2006, DIAG yielded almost 17,000 heavy and light weapons with about 86,000 pieces of ammunition; however, this did not reflect a significant level of disbandment of illegally armed groups, a problem compounded by the continuous distribution of weapons by foreign intelligence agencies. By mid-2007, the numbers of weapons collected had risen to 26,000 light weapons and 3,900 heavy weapons, which was also deemed a disappointing yield.[33]

Programmatic aspects of DIAG were not the greatest problems. The political complexity, and its impact on security, was the major crux. The absence of a comprehensive peace accord, the exclusion of southern armed groups, the absence of genuine political will for the process, the positioning and influence of the northern warlords, and, not least, the ongoing conflict all militated against successful outcomes—that is, the stabilization of Afghanistan and the expansion of the authority of the state.

Despite widespread pessimism, Bhatia and Muggah took a more pragmatic view of the result of the two DDR efforts—ANBP and DIAG. Although the statistics of weapons collected, cantoned, or destroyed and the numbers of combatants demobilized do not necessarily equate to a reduction in armed violence, there is "some evidence that the various DDR programs served an important role in shifting the 'balance of power' away from regional warlords towards the Karzai government."[34] They identified the determinants of DDR success in Afghanistan as investment in both diplomatic coordination and local outreach. According to Bhatia and Muggah, "Enhancing state legitimacy and its monopoly in the use of legitimate force is a *sine qua non* of DDR effectiveness."[35] As such, it will require a "better understanding of the dynamics shaping combatant mobilization and the formation of armed groups."[36] However, both ANBP and DIAG were seen as entry-points for addressing spoilers. The overarching challenge remains in achieving real and perceived legitimacy.

Afghanistan Peace and Reintegration Program[37]

As DIAG wound down, the government of Afghanistan developed a follow-on program to address moderate opposition fighters, including from the Taliban and the hostile groups, that could be encouraged to reintegrate into civil society through the Afghanistan Peace and Reintegration Program (APRP). However, this effort was not linked with any of the tentative negotiations that were occurring in a second track or even more discreetly, and thus the results were limited. The International Research Group on Reintegration considered this program from the perspective that, according to Bhatia and Muggah, the UN often neglected—that is, the dynamics of demobilization and the dynamic requirements of peace-building.[38] Their study was designed to offer policy insights and distill broader lessons on reintegration from the Afghan processes that might contribute to the research-based evidence often lacking when assessing reintegration processes.[39] It used four main concepts:

First is the concept of trajectories, or the direction taken by combatants as they leave the armed group. The second concept is the multicentric notion of community, looking beyond the sociogeographic locus of family or lived space to a broader consideration of community, such as believers and comrades. The third is disengagement, or changes in behavior during the exit processes. Twinned to engagement, this concept is driven by push and pull factors, or negative and positive forces that contribute to decisionmaking. The final concept considers reintegration from its three-dimensional social, economic, and political perspectives. The authors' primary methodology was interviews of APRP participants, including former combatants and commanders.

Many fighters were deeply disillusioned with the Taliban and the direction of jihad. However, APRP failed to address their needs and, at worse, undermined their security in society, with those former combatants becoming targets of their former colleagues. Despite the community's widespread exhaustion with war, APRP did not provide significant encouragement for fighters to leave the Taliban. Along with the criticism of the program, however, there was some praise for limited successes, such as the provision of urban safe houses to participants under threat.

APRP was at the heart of Afghan politics in furthering the counterinsurgency effort. It drew moderates from the resistance and helped spread the legitimacy of the government of Afghanistan, contributing to the military effort and creating conditions to encourage negotiations with the Taliban. Thus, the program was highly contested, as reflected in the attacks on and killings of senior officers associated with the program.[40] Such threats undermined the capacity of the APRP, just as they had also contributed to the poor track record of both Afghan New Beginning Program and Disbandment of Illegal Armed Groups.

By July 2010, APRP had processed 2,320 individuals, with a further 1,845 in the pipeline. This was a relatively meager result considering the investment in both human and material resources.[41] The program was implemented in three stages that reflected an assimilation of the global lessons of DDR, the evolution of the theory, or a nod in the direction of Bhatia and Muggah's concerns: (1) social outreach, confidence building, and negotiation, with provincial and district leaders reaching out to individuals and communities; (2) demobilization, which includes registration and hand-over of weapons, issuance of identification papers, and amnesty from arrest, with consideration given to former combatants' security needs; and (3) consolidation of peace through the associated reduction in armed violence and strengthening of rule of law, focused on the community and recovery from conflict.[42]

Findings from a series of interviews indicate that the push factors for demobilization—that is, disillusionment with the Taliban, exhaustion with war, needs to be with family, and so forth—were reasonably strong. However, the pull factors of the APRP that could be offered to former combatants—in particular, their post-demobilization security—were weak. Former combatants often found it safer to remain in urban areas than to return to their rural communities. In general, this double disillusionment experienced by Taliban former combatants in the APRP did not bode well for positive outcomes. However, it may well have contributed to the spread of the government of Afghanistan's legitimacy, which was a major counterinsurgency objective. It may also have formed a foundation for the reintegration of former combatants due to a potential softened attitude of the Taliban in considering participation in government after the US withdrawal.[43]

Mike Martin's study of the history of conflict in Helmand Province and the impact of British counterinsurgency operations there is damning.[44] He attributed failure to a combination of factors. Primarily it was due to the propensity to oversimplify the nature of the conflict to an environment in which the new government is struggling to impose its sway, the Taliban is opposing them, and the people are in the middle. It is the failure to recognize the complexity of dynamics and fluctuating relations among tribes and clans at a subdistrict level. Martin claims, as is the theme throughout his book, that the human terrain is not just an aspect of the counterinsurgency; the human terrain is the counterinsurgency.[45]

The appraisal of the impact of the decade-long US and allied intervention in Afghanistan, including multiple DDR processes, will rest on an assessment of the legitimacy and capacity of the government of Afghanistan in offering rule of law and stability in the aftermath of the withdrawal of US and allied troops. The indications are not good. The US-led counterinsurgency and counterterrorism campaigns, even with ten years to consider the implications, have failed to win over Afghan grassroots perceptions and attitudes. According to Rubin, "Afghans at a more grass-roots level have little faith in either the Afghan government or the Americans."[46] Between a rock and a hard place, the Afghan administration must face this ultimate security dilemma of how to survive after the departure of its protectors, having failed to protect the people against either the Taliban or oppressive, corrupt warlords. It has also failed to improve human security in sustainable ways. The international efforts, including DDR, alienated the people, losing their positive perceptions, attitudes, and trust. In short, those efforts did not work.

Post-2014: A Broader Commitment to Normalization

After the withdrawal of most foreign forces in 2015, the conditions for an effective DDR process—that is, a postconflict end of hostilities with agreement on the way forward to peacebuilding—still do not exist. In fact, rearmament of the formerly disarmed warlords is currently occurring. Neither the foreign intervention nor the government of Afghanistan has managed to gain the positive perceptions, attitudes, or trust of the people. Their failure to grasp local solutions soon after 9/11 was decisive.[47] After the withdrawal of foreign troops, "Talibanization"—predominantly of the south and central areas, with expanding northern pockets—is inevitable and indeed well underway. The best that can be hoped is that it will be delayed and controlled, leading to a functioning state with which the world might do business—a process of "normalization." The future for DDR in Afghanistan must be considered in the context of an eventual overarching SSR and in bringing the rule of law to all Afghanistan. This process must be combined with the adaption of emerging ideas on implementing DDR in the context of violent extremism.

A major challenge for DDR in Afghanistan has been the treacherous security and political environment, compounded by conflicting objectives of security and human security. The conundrum of attempting to emphasize a people-centered human security approach when the predominant focus of the military intervention effort has been on security has not yet found a solution. How can one offer reintegration options to former combatants when their safety cannot be guaranteed once they leave the mutual protection of the armed group? Even in the unlikely event of a best-scenario outcome in Afghanistan—that is, a moderated Taliban seeking interaction with the world and accepting a degree of inclusive government in the interests of stability and normalization—a large-scale effective DDR will be required to demobilize and reintegrate masses of combatants and associates (security companies and so on).[48] For Afghanis, the hope must be that, whoever takes power in the coming years, conditions can be created in which the population can have a degree of predictability and live in peace—that is, live in a normative environment.

Colombia

The Context

Originating in the political turmoil of the early 1950s and the US-backed suppression of the people in the war against communism in the 1960s, Colombia, through La Violencia, has moved through evolving and regressing phases of popular revolution, complicated by the dimension of organized cocaine trafficking.[49] Popularized initially by the quest for social justice, the Marxist revolution saw the launch of an ongoing, sixty-year, asymmetric civil war between the government of Colombia and its right-wing paramilitary groups and left-wing movements, such as the predominantly rural-supported Revolutionary Armed Forces of Colombia (FARC) and their competition for popular influence, the more urban National Liberation Army. In the beginning, the leftist revolution was strengthened by collaboration with the liberation theology of dissident elements of the Catholic Church, driving a process of *conscientization* of the masses through praxis with the poor. This guerrilla war has seen approximately 300,000 killed, with about 75 percent of those noncombatants, and approximately five million people displaced.[50]

From the mid-1960s through the 1980s, the CIA mobilized cocaine trafficking to the United States and Europe to fund its antiguerrilla activities in

Colombia. They used this same practice concurrently with opium trafficking in the Golden Triangle of Asia to fund anticommunist activities in the region around Vietnam. The resources involved in the cocaine trade have swamped the social aspects of the revolution and have largely criminalized the activities of both left and right guerrilla movements, diminishing the capacity for political solutions. Under effective government pressure, reduced popular support, and the concurrent waning of Soviet influence and proxy war support in the mid-1980s, Communist guerrilla movement attempts to enter legitimate politics were met by whole-scale assassination of their representatives by right-wing paramilitaries and undercover military "black operations." This drove them back to the remote regions and underground, where they maintained their levels of guerrilla capacity through the cocaine trade.

The emergence of a strong urban guerrilla movement in the mid-1970s was met, under Julio Turbay's presidency, with brutal counterinsurgency methods that drew strong condemnation, nationally and internationally, for human rights abuses. It also led to a political backlash and electoral rejection of the governing party, encouraging the negotiation of an initial, if short-lived, cease-fire by the subsequent administration in 1984. The initial cease-fire drew in most guerrilla groups other than the National Liberation Army, which continued its campaign. The revolution morphed partially into a drug war, with a confusion of dominant family-led cartels driving the violence in protection of their interests through mass murder, assassination, intimidation, or the buy-off of their political opposition, using the quasi-politically motivated armed movements. Through the 1980s, amid faltering peace efforts, La Violencia continued with noted audacious attacks on the administration that were mostly perpetrated by the urban guerrilla 19th of April Movement (M-19), which captured the Supreme Court in 1985 with bloody outcomes. In the early 1990s, FARC's movement toward political legitimacy was once again met with mass assassinations, reputedly by drug cartels, though military black operations were the more likely perpetrator. FARC stepped up its cocaine-funded activities through the mid-1990s, with mixed levels of competition and collusion with the cartels, to the extent that growing coca had become the prime livelihood for a large percentage of the rural poor. The US-backed government's war on drugs was losing political capital for the government. Meanwhile, high-profile FARC attacks on government positions near the turn of the millennium, during which time large numbers of troops and police officers were killed or taken prisoner, increased the political imperative for a negotiated solution and concessions. Right-wing paramilitary groups responded by coalescing into the drug-funded United Self-Defense Forces of Colombia and attacking FARC, the National Liberation Army, and their perceived social base. The bloody civil war has continued, with indiscriminate casualties resulting from the huge numbers of antipersonnel mines deployed by the leftist movements and remaining in the ground in rural areas.

DDR in Colombia

From 2002 to 2010, President Álvaro Uribe viewed the DDR of Colombia's leftist movements as one aspect of a robust counterinsurgency campaign. He was mixing "the carrot," encouragement to defect, a pull factor, with "the stick" of offensive operations, a push factor—a combatant-centric approach. The aim of the concurrent focus on about 30,000 members of the right-wing paramilitary groups was to hit the lowest-hanging fruit in an effort to reduce levels of armed violence and crime. Since 2002 the state has launched four major DDR processes to address the conflict. These efforts through 2006 included catering for the collective demobilization of paramilitary groups, primarily focused on the United Self-Defense Forces of Colombia, and offering support for short-term socioeconomic reinsertion. Since 2006, these efforts focused more on offering individuals the opportunity to disassociate from the leftist guerrilla groups and to enter a process of longer-term socioeconomic reintegration.

The chosen "soft" aspect of the campaign to draw off members from the guerrilla movement was to offer incentives and a level of refuge in the state to reticent and more pliable members willing to return to civil society. This process was also designed to improve intelligence for targeting incorrigible guerrillas through interrogation of the deserters. Due to the confusion over the ideological and criminal motivations for guerrilla activities in Colombia, the resources at stake, the national reach, and the brutality in response to dissidence, progress has been slow and costly, with limited success. Structural weaknesses include the intractability of inadequate compromise in peace negotiations, the absence of a facilitating legal framework until 2005, and an ineffective national communications strategy to support a decentralized commitment to support the reintegration of former combatants.

The program was energized in 2006 when responsibility for its management passed to the newly established presidential High Council for Reintegration under the high-profile commissioner, Frank Pearl. The council had a commitment to develop a maximalist approach to DDR that would not only address the needs of former combatants but also more widely contribute to victim justice and communities benefiting from the reduction in violence. Since 2011, President Juan Manuel Santos directed that, in addition to military solutions, a more holistic and integrated perspective to conflict resolution must be considered. Santos saw the need for a community security approach in engaging bottom-up, community-based contribution by linking the DDR effort to the wider socioeconomic environment—a community-centric approach. This was designed to harness a transformational outcome from DDR, as an instrument for peacebuilding. This process involved a decentralized approach that incorporated improved legislation to offer redress and reparations to victims and restoration of land to the dispossessed, thus creating the perception of a caring state to diminish the conflict's root social causes.

Uribe had been very proud of his DDR efforts. In managing the media spin, he conceived and hosted the first International DDR Congress in Cartagena de Indias, in May 2009, bringing neighboring heads of state, international practitioners, and scholars, including myself, to present on the cutting edge of DDR. As part of the congress, Colombia's program was well grandstanded. However, many international participants had reservations that, at that stage, the Colombian program was still more an aspect of Uribe's counterinsurgency security strategy of destroying the guerrillas than it was about human security or the reintegration of former combatants. In 2010, that weighting shifted more toward human security under the new president Santos.

From 2003 to late 2012, approximately 23,500 of the leftist guerrilla groups (FARC, National Liberation Army, and others) were deemed demobilized in the individual focused process, while approximately 31,900 of the paramilitary United Self-Defense Forces of Colombia were demobilized through the collective approach.[51] A comprehensive reintegration process, reflecting the maximalist approach, considers eight essential dimensions of life in support of demobilization: personal psychosocial needs, the family, home ownership, livelihood/career, education, health, citizenship obligations and rights, and security. The High Council for Reintegration's commitment to support the rehabilitation of former combatants saw a shift from short-term reinsertion into the community to support for a broader socioeconomic reintegration over a longer term.

Maria Derks, Hans Rouw, and Ivan Briscoe suggested that the High Council for Reintegration's strategy, which envisages a long-term commitment to supporting reintegration (until 2020), is unclear in how it will avoid creating dependency of former combatants on its support, considering the inadequate socioeconomic absorptive capacity in most of the communities of resettlement.[52] They also advised that a strengthened communications strategy can help reduce the stigmatization of former combatants, while an increased community violence reduction strategy, as opposed to policing, can help encourage better participation. The authors highlighted a level of disconnect between central and local government and the need for the empowerment of greater local initiative in ensuring that local support for reintegration is optimized.[53]

Despite the Colombian government's capacity, in terms of resources and expertise, to lead the delivery of DDR programs, the crux remained in encouraging take-up of the supports offered and drawing combatants away from the guerrilla movement while the war continues. Success of the current round of peace talks between the government of Colombia and FARC could greatly invigorate the program; thus, there is optimism. In August 2014, for the first time in fifty years, the Colombian Army, represented by its second in command, sat down with FARC in Havana, Cuba, to talk "warrior to warrior." In another achievement for this current round of talks, victims were represented, and issues of transitional justice discussed.[54] Despite setbacks and skirmishes during the four years of negotiation in Havana, two of them in secret, "full, final, and definite" agreement was achieved in August 2016. This promises to address social exclusion, deliver justice to victims, and to build an enduring peace. Ratification is subject to a plebiscite with the main opposition to the accord rallying around Uribe and the issue of a perception of justice denied.

Somalia

Disengagement During Offensive Operations?

Before 2008, the UNDP in Somalia had attempted various types of small arms interventions, violence reduction, and support for the reduction of armed forces in one or more of the three entities of that dysfunctional country—Somaliland, Puntland, and South/Central Somalia.[55] Following my evaluation, conflict analysis, and recommendations as a consultant for UNDP in 2008, which drew directly on my experience in Haiti, UNDP shifted from its support of de facto governments in order to remove surplus fighters from militias (which is really an SSR function) to a community-based approach. This new approach was to contribute to a normative system by placing weapons beyond use in order to strengthen community security and reduce community violence as an aspect of its support to rule of law and governance programs in Somalia. Daniel Ladouceur, who had designed Haiti's Community Violence Reduction program, developed and managed the resulting program in Somalia. In the most difficult areas of South/Central Somalia—particularly in Mogadishu, in the post–Islamic Courts Union era of 2009, when the more radical Al Shabaab took control of large areas—the community security approach required a carefully considered and very discreet "do no harm" implementation. Building on the experience of such grassroots initiatives and efforts to entice youth from piracy by NGOs, such as Norwegian Church Aid's Alternative Livelihood to Piracy,[56] this approach assisted established local NGOs and community-based organizations in developing and implementing their own community-based social and economic projects. The approach mobilized local influential opinion and religious leaders, involving a very "light foot" or even invisible support of external actors. It was designed to encourage a deradicalization of youth, who were the primary recruitment base for Al Shabaab, through community, family, and peer pressure and to contribute to a reduction of violence in the community.[57] It facilitated local solutions to local problems by offering locally led, and therefore culturally and religiously sensitive, approaches to violence reduction during the conflict.

In 2016 the initiative against Al Shabaab in South/Central Somalia is constantly shifting, depending on the impact of the latest atrocity, under the offensive operations led by the new government of Somalia (2014–) and supported by the African Union and the UN.[58] Although they are hugely controversial, it is worth reviewing the processes associated with the disengagement of violent extremists during conflict that is currently being piloted by the government of Somalia.[59] The government is building on the earlier multiagency approach, after effectively taking control of most operations, ostensibly to support the disengagement of youth at risk, pirates, and disillusioned members of Al Shabaab. Can aspects of this process offer a replicable or adaptable model that can reconcile some of the incompatibilities between security and human security in delivering DDR concurrent with offensive operations? Serious controversy persists regarding matters of access, transparency, human rights, the rights of the child, the voluntary participation of combatants, and the relationship of the program to offensive operations in what is being projected by the government of Somalia as a type of integrated DDR programming conducted alongside robust offensive operations. The government seeks the collaboration of diversely managed camps, including the Serendi Project Disengagement Centers in the cities of South/Central Somalia, managed by the International Organization for Migration, and the National Programme for Disengaged Combatants.[60] However, in the dysfunction and opaqueness of war, humanitarian and human rights sectors of the UN are expressing great concern. Their concern over the absence of access to the caseload and persistent rumors of abuses is that the processes have been co-opted and are being controlled by the intelligence resources of either state or federal governments to contribute to security objectives, rather than focusing on deradicalization and reintegration. In such an environment, the UN Assistance Mission in Somalia, unable to guarantee a people-centered approach or even the maintenance of basic human rights for those participating, remains cautiously aloof from the processes.

As they currently operate, these disengagement processes in Somalia, other than confirming lessons learned in other attempts at DDR during offensive operations, offer little that can be adapted to designing functional DDR programs during offensive operations. The recurring challenges in attempting to reconcile security-driven objectives with a human security agenda persist. If a successful disengagement process of radicalized youth is to be implemented in Somalia during offensive operations, while also maintaining basic UN principles of DDR as expressed in the Integrated DDR Standards, it is likely that the process will need to be removed physically and operationally from security considerations. Collaboration is needed between the government of Somalia and the UN over the protection of DDR beneficiaries. To maintain the confidence and trust of all stakeholders regarding the protection of basic human rights and the maintenance of a people-centered approach, general oversight by a respected third party—perhaps the UN—is necessary.

Democratic Republic of Congo

The Hybrid UN Force Intervention Brigade

In March 2013, UN Security Council Resolution 2098 controversially added a potential new dimension to DDR in the context of a peacekeeping operation when it created the hybrid peace enforcement mechanism, the UN Force

Intervention Brigade. Established within the UN Organization Stabilization Mission in the Democratic Republic of Congo (MONUSCO) and nominally under the control of the special representative of the Secretary-General and the UN force commander, working in close collaboration with the Armed Forces of the Democratic Republic of Congo, its creation is deemed to be context specific and is not meant to set a precedent for UN peacekeeping missions.[61] The Intervention Brigade was deployed to destroy the incorrigible perpetrators of a continued defiance to the international mandate to end the conflict in eastern Democratic Republic of Congo. These perpetrators used brutal violence, particularly against civilian populations, and repeated humanitarian outrages. A review of the challenges, particularly those of legitimacy, facing operation of the Intervention Brigade underscores the challenges facing DDR during offensive operations.

The UN Force Intervention Brigade has offensive capacity beyond that normally maintained by a UN peacekeeping force, which normally involves light mechanized infantry with limited support weapons. Such a peacekeeping force usually operates under the agreed principles for UN armed intervention of "consent, impartiality and non-use of force except in self-defense."[62] In pursuing a policy of peace enforcement, however, this new force in Democratic Republic of Congo is tasked to neutralize and disarm illegal armed groups, in collaboration with the Armed Forces of the Democratic Republic of Congo, applying the use of assets such as attack helicopters, field artillery, special forces, snipers, and even drones.

The force's rules of engagement appear stretched beyond those usually used during UN peacekeeping missions in order to permit offensive action. The rules of engagement are the carefully stated policy of a military force, offering clear guidance to an individual soldier regarding the use of live ammunition and the various levels of force permissible. This robust tasking of the UN Force Intervention Brigade, however, seems to go beyond UN Charter Chapter VII provisions and obligations to protect civilians, constraints and duties that are already mandatory within UN missions. In addition to stretching the interpretation of the legal provisions legitimizing UN armed interventions in the context of the UN Charter and international humanitarian law, some see the force as making the UN party to the fight, rather than an unbiased peace intervener. This situation, among the obvious political disadvantages, creates increased risks for the mission and any associated civilian staff and humanitarian workers.[63] Further, it may diminish the roles of the core mission force—that is, the troops of the remainder of MONUSCO—to defensive roles, constrained by the less robust conditions of service dictated by their troop-contributing countries (TCCs). It may also create a perception of foreign agency among host populations, thus undermining the intervention's perceived legitimacy, creating a crisis of legitimacy. Through a dependency syndrome, it might also contribute to a diminishing capacity of national troops to address the conflict. The legalities associated with the deployment of the UN Force Intervention Brigade in the context of international humanitarian law and the protection that it offers to UN peacekeepers are complex and potentially far reaching. However, Scott Sheeran and Stephanie Case claimed that those issues have been inadequately considered.[64]

Bruce Oswald conceded that the activities of the UN Force Intervention Brigade may have, at times, crossed the threshold between self-defense and offensive action and that the legal implications of such actions remain unclear.[65] He took a contrary view to Sheeran and Case concerning the negative implications of this innovation for either UN staff or international law. According to Oswald, the idea is not so "revolutionary," as it simply expands the role of the UN force. It represents a natural progression of the evolution of UN peacekeeping in addressing an intractable situation of violence by sending a clear message of UN commitment to incorrigible nonstate armed groups.[66]

The UN Force Intervention Brigade, which primarily operates in North Kivu, initially focused on the reputedly Rwandan-backed Mouvement du 23-Mars (M23) rebels who had recently captured Goma. Following M23's defeat and capitulation, the focus was expected to move on to other nonstate armed militias operating in eastern Democratic Republic of Congo. However, with deteriorating relations between the mission and the host government, as well as the applied influence of the regional TCCs in pursuing their own shifting political interests, the capacity of the UN Force Intervention Brigade has been controversially constrained. The ongoing UN-driven DDR program in North Kivu is likewise constrained by noncooperation by the Armed Forces of the Democratic Republic of Congo. Security corridors, designed to facilitate disengaging members of illegal armed groups in reaching the demobilization centers, are being blocked, and those captured are being held as prisoners of war, rather than being forwarded to the DDR program.[67] The lessons being learned from the experience of the UN Force Intervention Brigade—particularly its incapacity to act independently in the interests of the mandate—calls into question the viability of the UN engaging in offensive operations using ad hoc formations provided by multiple TCCs.

DDR in War: Considerations

The US- and NATO-led post-9/11 invasion of Afghanistan, which had the objective of establishing a stable, pro-Western government operating along democratic lines, was never going to present easy solutions. Following the initial routing of the Taliban, the Bonn Agreement offered an operating platform through the Karzai government that was an arrangement among victors. In a fragmented country with multiple semi-independent regional warlords, their armies co-opted onto the national payroll, an environment of continuing conflict awash with arms, and an ongoing counterinsurgency operation, DDR was seen as a mechanism to assist in stabilizing the situation and in spreading the reach of the government. To some degree, it was envisaged as a precursor to political solutions. Supported and assisted by the UN, the government of Afghanistan's Afghan New Beginning Program focused on the armies of the Northern Alliance warlords. It cherry-picked heavy weapons and managed to remove significant numbers of combatants from the national defense budget. Again with UN support, the government of Afghanistan's Disbandment of Illegal Armed Groups program tried to pick up selected remaining illegal armed groups not covered by ANBP, but with limited success. The Afghanistan Peace and Reintegration Program, also led by the government of Afghanistan, is a follow-on program to the Disbandment of Illegal Armed Groups that, in ongoing conflict and with obscured accountability and transparency regarding the application of finance and benefits, is having limited results.

Scholars consider that both ANBP and the Disbandment of Illegal Armed Groups, which both focused on "friendly" forces, did contribute to spreading the government's reach and legitimacy. However, the inability of the government of Afghanistan, DDR implementers, or counterinsurgency and counterterrorism forces to protect either the communities or former combatants undermined greater achievement. This failure limited the perceptions of the communities and the combatants that the processes were in their interests. The Afghanistan Peace and Reintegration Program, which focused on potential moderates among the hostiles, had even fewer results to show. However, it may offer a functional framework for DDR if a normalized environment can be achieved after 2016.

DDR in Afghanistan was always implemented and manipulated as an aspect of a Western agency–driven SSR process. It attempted to bring the monopoly in the use of armed force to the Karzai government through the capacity of a professional Afghan National Army, all while reducing unsustainable recurring budgets. Concurrently, it attempted to extend rule of law through a functioning police force. The intended security structures reflected those of a functioning Western state. Yet, these security aspirations failed to draw on repeated history in recognizing the reality of Afghanistan's complex informal governance structures and power relations. Any considerations of human security were peripheral and purely in the context of "winning the people" as an aspect of a counterinsurgency operation. Little thought was given to the potential for an appropriate culturally and religiously sensitive people-centered normative environment that could contribute to sustainable stability. As a result, both human security and security were lost.

Dealing with fifty years of a protracted left-wing guerrilla war, right-wing armed opposition, and organized armed cartels engaged in narco-trafficking, Colombia, drawing on the evolution of DDR theory, has devised an integrated community security approach to delivering DDR. It encourages individual guerrillas to disassociate from the armed movement, while concurrently entering peace negotiations with the guerrilla movements. The crux has predominantly been the complexity of doing DDR during war. Even following the successful negotiations with FARC in Havana, incremental, though diminishing, constraints will still remain in addressing the organized crime of cocaine-trafficking cartels. In recent years, Colombia's effort to deliver DDR to address social injustice and security has been bearing fruit. The indicator of its success or otherwise will be seen in the level of sustainable reintegration achieved by participants in the DDR program in the longer term.

From the perspective of DDR in war, Afghanistan and Colombia offer contrasting conditions of conflict but similar levels of complexity. Afghanistan was perceived, post-9/11, as an opium-fueled radicalized Islamic threat to international stability in its potential to harbor the spawning of international terrorism in a close-to-failed state with low capacity. This issue was to be addressed by Western international intervention in capacitating a functioning, West-leaning legitimate government. DDR in Afghanistan was seen as a precursor contributing to political solutions. Yet, the various attempts at DDR in Afghanistan have failed to deliver the desired results.

Colombia is a protracted conflict originating in post–World War II bipolarity and the Soviet spread of support for Marxist revolution. This was fueled by gross social injustice and inequity that was exposed in the process of liberationist social *conscientization*. Through the late 1960s to mid-1980s, popular revolution was opposed robustly by a US-supported hardening anticommunist drive by the government. The legacy of diminished bipolarity after the demise of Soviet influence and the social enlightenment after the legacy of multiple Central and South American peace processes changed the conflict dynamics. It gradually morphed into cocaine trafficking–driven organized criminal armed violence, which was impervious to political solutions. Cocaine-funded right-wing militias combined to fight the leftists for control of the business. The government's carrot-and-stick approaches to contain the conflict and DDR offering the softer option drew limited results. In the early part of the new millennium, with the new political realities associated with a functioning constitutional democracy with indigenous capacity, electoral pressure necessitated a supporting legal framework that would address a broader community security approach to DDR regarding social injustice, inequity, and victim reparations.

Although the war in Colombia has barely ended, the community security approach to demobilization and long-term reintegration has drawn off members from the guerrillas and reduced the recruitment base. Intolerance of corruption, together with robust police and military action to reduce the benefits of the cocaine trade, has brought FARC to the negotiating table in Havana. The cessation of hostilities with the main guerrilla movement may now be achieved. The national commitment to longer-term reintegration, together with the application of necessary resources and expertise, may well see successful outcomes in a postconflict environment.

In Somalia, in the evolving environment of violent extremist mobilized conflict, a community-based, peer group approach to encouraging disengagement—that is, a human security approach supported with a light footprint by the international community—has been co-opted by the security apparatus of the state in developing human intelligence. As access to the disengaging combatants closed, the space for the human security approach has receded.

The use of the UN Force Intervention Brigade in the Democratic Republic of Congo with a robust mandate appears to be a suspension of an overarching human security approach to UN programming—that is, in a major change to UN programming, security has precedence over human security. The implementation of human security–motivated projects to support security outcomes—such as the PRTs in Afghanistan in the context of the comprehensive approach—failed. DDR is about contributing to armed violence reduction through the "civilianizing" of former combatants; as such, it falls within the parameters of the human security agenda. DDR cannot be successfully implemented in a purely security context in which the UN, through robust actions, has become a party to the conflict, where the targets of those robust actions have not decided to disengage from the violence.

Reviewing attempts at DDR in ongoing conflict, whether in Haiti, Afghanistan, Colombia, Somalia, or the Democratic Republic of Congo, points toward one striking commonality. The overarching prerequisite, even in war, is of a government striving to develop the capacity to project a legitimate rule of law, justice, and equity to all of its citizens. In this matter, convergence exists in the implementation of both counterinsurgency and DDR. This convergence rests in the primary importance of more people-centric approaches.[68] Addressing the attitudes, perceptions, and levels of trust of the people, in mirroring the doctrine of insurgency, the criticality of winning the people is central to successful implementation of counterinsurgency and of DDR. Although this fact has been an aspect of DDR theory from the outset, it has been neglected in practice. The common decisive deficit in both counterinsurgency and DDR has been the failure to address a range of shared security dilemmas, including the complex contradictions and trade-offs that exist between a human security agenda approach and a security-driven approach in both DDR and counterinsurgency. In attempting DDR in a complex security-driven counterinsurgency environment, the general incompatibility between the human security agenda and a security-driven approach becomes evident. For the disarmament and demobilization planner and practitioner, this poses the primary dilemma. Political and economic interests prevalent in an ongoing conflict, and the related unstable landscape, further complicate the impact of the security dilemmas. The question remains whether a human security approach to DDR programming is possible in a conflict environment where security is prioritized through offensive action.

This question represents added levels of complexity in planning for next-generation DDR. The UN is still struggling with the conundrums that have permeated the evolution of the practice and the theory for decades through classic and second-generation DDR. Now is the time to consider these enduring conundrums and pursue how some answers may currently be evolving.

Notes

1. *Mao Tse-tung on* Yu Chi Chan *(Guerrilla Warfare),* trans. Samuel B. Griffith (Quantico, VA: US Marine Corps, 1961). Mao compared the guerrillas to fish that swim in the water of the people. If the political temperature is right, the fish will thrive.

2. David H. Petraeus and James A. Amos, *FM3-24 MCWP 3-33.3 COIN: Manual of Offensive, Defensive and Stability Operations* (Washington, DC: Headquarters, Department of the Army, December 2006).

3. Canadian Army, Land Force, *B-GL-323-004/FP-003 Counter Insurgency Operations (English),* Chief of Staff, Canadian Forces Headquarters, Ottawa, Canada, December 13, 2008.

4. UNDP, Asian Development Bank and WB Afghanistan, *Demobilisation: Toward a Programme for Reintegration of Ex-combatants* (draft sector report), Kabul, Afghanistan: UNDP, December 2001.

5. T. X. Hammes, "Attempting Disarmament Without Peace," in *Disarmament, Demobilization and Reintegration (DDR): Case Studies of Partial Success and Enduring Dilemmas,* ed. Richard Millet (Fort Leavenworth, KS: Combat Studies Institute Press, forthcoming 2017).

6. Michael Vinay Bhatia and Robert Muggah, "The Politics of Demobilization in Afghanistan," in *Security and Post-conflict Reconstruction: Dealing with Fighters in the Aftermath of War,* ed. Robert Muggah (Oxon, UK: Routledge, 2009), 126–164.

7. This chapter reviews the three most important of the five DDR processes in Afghanistan since 2001.

8. Bhatia and Muggah, "The Politics of Demobilization in Afghanistan," 126.

9. Ibid.

10. Ibid.

11. Ibid.

12. Ibid., 127.

13. George Ferks, Geert Gompelman, and Stefan van Laar, with Bart Klem, *The Struggle After Combat: The Role of NGOs in DDR Processes,* Afghanistan Case Study (The Hague, Netherlands: Cordaid, 2008). Bart Klem and Pyt Douma completed the associated synthesis study.

14. Robert J. Bebber, "The Role of Provincial Reconstruction Teams (PRTs) in Counterinsurgency Operations: Khost Province, Afghanistan," *Small Wars Journal,* accessed April 1, 2012, http://www.smallwarsjournal.com/blogs/journal/docs -temp/131-bebber.pdf.

15. Lucy Morgan Edwards, *The Afghan Solution: The Inside Story of Abdul Haq, the CIA, and How Western Hubris Lost Afghanistan,* chapter 17, "Return to Kandahar," (London: Bactria Press, 2011); Barbara Stapleton, "A Means to What End? Why PRTs Are Peripheral to Bigger Political Challenges in Afghanistan," *Journal of Military and Strategic Studies* 10, no. 1 (2007), www.jmss.org, accessed July 26, 2016.

16. Adapted from Philipp Rotmann, "Built on Shaky Ground: The Comprehensive Approach in Practice" (research paper, NATO Defense College, no. 63, December 2010).

17. From my discussions with Kenji Isezaki, May 2013.

18. Ferks, Gompelman, and van Laar, *The Struggle After Combat,* 16.

19. Kenji Isezaki, *Disarmament: The World Through the Eyes of a Conflict Buster,* Kodansha Gendhi Shinho, (Tokyo, 2004), translated into English by Shindho, Tokyo, 2011, 96–97. Isezaki led the Japanese contribution to ANBP.

20. My discussions with Isezaki, May 2013.

21. Ibid.

22. Ibid.

23. Isezaki, *Disarmament,* 123.

24. Ferks, Gompelman, and van Laar, *The Struggle After Combat,* 16. More than

5,000 tons of ammunition and mines were destroyed during that year. Further, it surveyed 722 ammunition caches containing more than 20,000 tons of ordnance.

25. Isezaki, *Disarmament,* 111.

26. Ibid., 114.

27. The names of 93,000 Afghan militia forces were removed from the Ministry of Defence payroll, saving recurring budget of US$120 million. Of those, 63,380 were disarmed, with lists of those to be demobilized compiled by regional teams and verified by demobilization verification committees. Individual demobilization packages included food, a *shalwar kamiz* (traditional Afghan men's clothing), a medal of honor, and a certificate of good conduct. Two hundred sixty units were decommissioned; 57,431 chose a reintegration support option; 57,629 small arms and light weapons were collected; the Afghan militia forces were demobilized; conditions were created to facilitate the national deployment of the Afghan National Army; and additional associated benefits were distributed to 13,312 former combatants. Ferks, Gompelman, and van Laar, *The Struggle After Combat.*

28. Ibid.

29. Hammes, "Attempting Disarmament Without Peace," citing an International Crisis Group report of February 2005.

30. Discussion with Isezaki, May 2013.

31. Ferks, Gompelman, and van Laar, *The Struggle After Combat,* 30.

32. Ibid.

33. Ibid.

34. Bhatia and Muggah, "The Politics of Demobilization in Afghanistan," 152.

35. Ibid., 154.

36. Ibid.

37. Although two reintegration programs were initiated by the government of Afghanistan in 2005—the APRP and the Program Tahkim Sulh (Strengthening Peace Program, PTS)—both targeting the moderates of the hostile groups, I address them both under APRP.

38. I am a core member of the International Research Group on Reintegration, which is based at the Center for Peace Studies, Tromsø University, Norway.

39. Zuhra Bahman and Stina Torjesen, *Double Disillusionment: Disengaging from the Insurgency in Afghanistan* (Tromsø, Norway: International Research Group on Reintegration, 2012).

40. Ibid., 11.

41. Ibid., 13.

42. Ibid., 13.

43. Matthew Rosenberg and Taimoor Shah, "Taliban Hint at Softer Line in Talks with Afghan Leaders," *New York Times,* December 22, 2012.

44. Mike Martin, *An Intimate War: An Oral History of the Helmand Conflict, 1978–2012* (London: C. Hurst & Co., 2014).

45. Martin, *An Intimate War.*

46. Alissa J. Rubin, "Karzai Bets on Vilifying US to Shed His Image as a Lackey," *New York Times,* March 13, 2013.

47. Morgan Edwards, *The Afghan Solution.*

48. Partly adapted from Deedee Derksen, "Reintegrating Armed Groups in Afghanistan: Lessons from the Past," USIP Peace Brief, March 7, 2014, accessed August 19, 2014, http://www.usip.org/publications/reintegrating-armed-groups-in-afghanistan.

49. From a composite of desk review, discussions, and contemporaneous notes while attending the First International DDR Congress in Cartagena de Indias, Colombia, in May 2009.

50. From discussions with staff of the Colombian Reintegration Agency (ACR) at the Gender Perspective in DDR Course, hosted by the Norwegian Defence International Centre, in Manila, Philippines, in 2013.

51. Ibid.

52. Maria Derks, Hans Rouw, and Ivan Briscoe, *A Community Dilemma: DDR and the Changing Face of Violence in Colombia*, Peace Security and Development Network, (Clinendael and IKV Pax Christi) Netherlands, July 18, 2011.

53. Ibid., 5.

54. Drawn from "Colombia's Peace Process: The Moment of Truth," *The Economist,* August 30, 2014.

55. I was consultant to UNDP in Somalia in 2009, tasked with assessing DDR efforts to date and with designing a way forward.

56. Ingvild Magnaes Gjelsvik and Tore Bjørgo, *Ex-pirates in Somalia: Disengagement Processes and Reintegration Programming* (Tromsø, Norway: University of Tromsø, Centre for Peace Studies, 2011).

57. UNDP, "Community Security Through Engaging with Youth at Risk: A Partnership Between UNDP, UNICEF and ILO," UNDP Somalia, Nairobi, December 2010.

58. The massacre of 147 students at a university in eastern Kenya in early April 2015 and multiple additional atrocities, including bombings of hotels in Mogadishu and the murder of government officials in 2016, attested to the resurgent capacity of Al Shabaab to counterattack on alternate fronts.

59. Much of this is drawn from Venda Felbab-Brown, "DDR, a Bridge Not Too Far: A Field Report from Somalia," in *UN DDR in an Era of Violent Extremism* (New York: United Nations University–Centre for Policy Research, June 2015).

60. See Report of the Secretary-General to the UN Security Council, on Somalia, Document S/2014/699, Para 34, UN, NewYork, September 25, 2014.

61. Much is drawn and adapted from "The UN Intervention Brigade in the DRC," *IPI Issue Brief* (July 2013), accessed November 5, 2014, http://www.reliefweb.int, and Scott Sheeran and Stephanie Case, *The Intervention Brigade: Legal Issues for the UN in the Democratic Republic of the Congo* (New York: International Peace Institute, November 2014).

62. Consent, impartiality, and nonuse of force except in self-defense. Agreed, but not legally binding. These issues are considered in Sheeran and Case, *The Intervention Brigade.*

63. Sheeran and Case, *The Intervention Brigade,* 9–12.

64. Convention on the Safety of UN and Associated Personnel through the relevant Status of Forces Agreement (SOFA) and the Rome Statute of the International Criminal Court. Drawn from Sheeran and Case, *The Intervention Brigade,* 1.

65. Bruce Oswald, "The UN Security Council and the Force Intervention Brigade: Some Legal Issues," chapter 17 in *Strengthening the Rule of Law Through the UN Security Council,* Challenges to Globalization Series (New York: Routledge, 2016).

66. Ibid., 20–21.

67. Drawn from my discussions with senior staff of MONUSCO, March 2015.

68. Desmond Molloy, *An Unlikely Convergence: Evolving DDR Theory and Counterinsurgency Doctrine* (PhD dissertation, Tokyo University of Foreign Studies, July 2013).

8

The UN Approach to Reintegration

DDR remains a theory and practice under continuous scrutiny. In this chapter, I review how the theory has dynamically evolved in light of that scrutiny and how it has responded to changing and diverse contexts and perspectives. No two contexts are ever the same. In this flux, can integrated DDR standards keep pace with theory in both UN- and non-UN-implemented DDR? In what direction is UN DDR policy developing?

What are the new complementary mechanisms and concepts of DDR? Some recent ideas such as interim stabilization mechanisms, the value of former combatant cohesiveness, and consideration of the reality of the UN's commitment to the gender perspective in DDR will inform practice. Richard Bowd considered the role of reintegration in transforming social capital and contributing to reconciliation in the community as an aspect of social reintegration.[1] The International Research Group on Reintegration has developed key organizing concepts to facilitate the study of reintegration, including political economy, context, separation trajectories, a multicentric notion of community, the concepts of engagement and disengagement, and a maximalist interpretation of reintegration with socioeconomic and political dimensions. The International Labour Organization offers guidance on how to approach the livelihoods aspect of socioeconomic reintegration.

What are the main intellectual and operational challenges facing the scholar and the practitioner of DDR? The scholar continues to struggle with the conundrum of devising criteria to permit evidence-based analysis of the achievements of DDR practice. The practitioner's dilemma remains the failure to identify the agreed metrics for planning and evaluation purposes. A new school of DDR scholars, including Richard Millett and Eric Shibuya, have realized that we have been asking the wrong questions. The functional metrics are not the quantitative ones that have been the subject of focus; rather, they are the qualitative ones—the perceptions, attitudes, and trust of the people that DDR is contributing to their interests in creating normative systems.

135

The DDR practitioner's conviction that reintegration support works, based on intangible qualitative indicators and common wisdom, is no longer sufficient. Where is the evidence? A key question that continues to be debated is simply, What is reintegration? The answer appears to be complex and context specific. Are the Integrated DDR Standards (IDDRS), as they relate to the reintegration of former combatants and to UN-integrated programming, still relevant and sufficiently responsive in dynamic postconflict environments? Do those standards address the increasing number of second-generation situations and DDR in ongoing conflict and radicalized environments? Ten years after their initial publication, are the standards contributing to the foundation for next-generation DDR? What is the return on investment in reintegrating former combatants, and is that return sufficient? What new approaches to reintegration will improve outcomes?

DDR: The Evolution of the Theory

According to Walt Kilroy, in 2007, nineteen DDR processes were underway in the world involving 1.1 million combatants with a total budget of $1.599 billion.[2] Despite this, the questioning of the common wisdom, as reflected in successive UN Secretary-General Reports, that DDR (including the associated reintegration support) is a vital contributor to peacebuilding in a postconflict environment is not new. Considering their proximity to the cessation of armed violence and their obvious immediate impact, the disarmament and demobilization phases of DDR come under little scrutiny. However, scholars such as Robert Muggah, Macartan Humphreys, and Jeremy Weinstein, through the application of rigorous quantitative methodologies, in studies reviewed in this book, have been unable to confirm tangible evidence of the positive causal impact of reintegration support in DDR. They have been unable to segregate the impacts of DDR from the impacts of multiple other postconflict peacebuilding interventions and circumstances. Thus, they have been calling for reevaluation of the DDR processes and the development of functional evaluation metrics.

Humphreys and Weinstein used rigorous scholarly methodology to launch the first serious questioning of DDR proponents' assertions. Their efforts involved identifying evidence of the benefits of reintegration support through a large-N survey of more than a thousand former combatants engaged in the Sierra Leone DDR process in 2003.[3] Their methodology of analysis was the application of refined regression analysis. They did not find conclusive evidence. Their subsequent series of papers based on their 2003 data set have emphasized this fact, sometimes to the chagrin and confusion of DDR proponents, whether donor, practitioner, or theorist.[4] Practitioners were initially astonished at Humphreys and Weinstein's null findings, considering their convictions, which were based on qualitative deduction from observation. However, practitioners also could not support their conviction with the required evidence.[5] In 2007, Pugel used a methodology similar to that of Humphreys and Weinstein, with some adjustments in the operationalization of variables, to test the DDR process in Liberia. He found that reintegration support in the context of DDR in Liberia did contribute to supporting the sustainable reintegration of former combatants.[6] Further, in 2011, a longitudinal study, conducted over two years by Isabela Leao, of a small group of the respondents to the 2003 survey found that the Humphreys and Weinstein survey may not have received the respondents' honest opinions, as there had not been an attempt to build any relationship with them; Leao also pointed out that participants had been paid money to engage in the initial survey.[7]

Despite numerous new reintegration programs in multiple contexts and the application of various methods of analysis, practitioners have been unable to present consistent quantitative evidence that reintegration support in the context of DDR works. However, do practitioners and scholars agree from the outset on exactly what those expected outcomes should be for the investment being made? Is DDR about ending hostilities? Is it about providing sustainable livelihoods for former combatants? Is it about creating normative environments for communities? Is it about building peace in order to facilitate development? Can desired outcomes be adjusted in a dynamic way as the postconflict environment evolves? Different stakeholders have different perspectives in attempting to answer these questions. A review of the UN institutional approach to the reintegration of former combatants, with or without DDR, in considering these questions is timely in light of the rapidly evolving dynamic of global violence that is requiring innovative approaches. This evolving dynamic is evident in the collapsed Arab Spring and the broadening conflicts focused on Afghanistan, Iraq, and Syria, as well as in the associated spread of radicalization through the Middle East and North Africa.

Positive progress in the global dynamic will demand innovative thinking to develop the appropriate context-specific supports. Such contexts may include the tentative and torturous journey toward democracy in Myanmar; eventual local solutions to the causes of armed violence in Afghanistan, Sri Lanka, and Colombia; and the vague possibility of a refocus on human security in Haiti. Increasing demand for security and human security facilitation, support, or intervention is arising in the reality of constricting global economic resources and the realignment of global order.

From early in the new millennium, DDR planners and practitioners were aware of the weakness of many aspects of DDR design and implementation. Repeatedly applying the practice of previous programs in various contexts did not offer the elements of success expected. The variables of each context were heterogeneous, and even a minor shift on the specific critical path offered a significantly different trajectory. In light of that heterogeneity, a body of directing doctrine—that is, a classified body of well-analyzed guidance that is widely used and accepted as best practice—cannot bind DDR.

Following the enlightenment of the UN Brahimi Report of 2000, an enabling environment for innovation existed within the UN.[8] This was led within the UN Department of Peacekeeping Operations by its energetic and visionary head, Jean-Marie Guéhenno. This innovation and movement toward an integrated "UN working as one" necessitated the continuing development of theory and the operationalization of mutually agreed guidelines that would establish foundational principles to capitalize on institutional strengths and avoid waste of resources in achieving desired outcomes. Thus, the collaborative UN Integrated DDR Standards project was launched, drawing on agency representatives, practitioners, and scholars and resulting in a body of agreed-upon and dynamically evolving guidance, initially published in December 2006.

Since the publication of IDDRS, the idea of the evolving character of DDR has changed from a predominantly technical logistical set of processes focused on former combatants or a technical aspect of a peace process in support of other confidence-building measures that address political and security concerns (that is, Muggah's minimalist approach). Indeed, it has shifted toward a more holistic community-centric attempt to contribute to positive peace through strengthening human capital, while also addressing development concerns (that is, Muggah's maximalist approach). The evolution of the scope of DDR toward the maximalist model has been partially tracked by the dynamic adjustment of IDDRS through the continuous review and development of modules, as overseen by the UN Inter-agency Working Group on DDR. This group includes representation by twenty-two UN and partner agencies, including the World Bank. The group's operation is coordinated by a secretariat, to date located within UNDP headquarters in New York; it is comanaged by the UN Department of Peacekeeping Operations, UNDP, and a management team of main agency representatives. The energy and effectiveness of this working group has been dependent not only on the support of donors and the collaborating agencies but also, probably to the greatest degree, on the enthusiasm, capacity, and commitment of individual agency representatives and on the coordinating capacity of the secretariat.

The process of reviewing DDR processes and evolving contexts has been cumbersome. It is debatable whether, in facilitating the interests of twenty-two agencies in a collaborative system, it has been possible to focus on the vital essentials or on the timely delivery of necessary guidance. In late 2013, there was a sense of flux within the UN system regarding the future direction of DDR. This sense was accentuated by movement of knowledgeable personnel, whether through promotion, rotation, or departure; funding concerns for the Inter-agency Working Group secretariat; and questioning by management of the justifiability of the level of investment in DDR. In considering the relatively low visibility of the tangible return on that investment, there is an emerging view that the system of IDDRS administration and review may have outlived its use. With agencies now seen to be planning DDR engagement in a more independent way, the continuing relevancy of the roles and tasking as outlined in IDDRS is in question, particularly after taking into consideration the tensions between security and development outcomes.

A review of UN approaches to DDR is also timely in light of the recommendations in the *Report on Civilian Capacity in the Aftermath of Conflict Within the UN System* (March 4, 2011), from the Secretary-General's Senior Advisory Group chaired by Guéhenno, the former under-secretary-general for peacekeeping operations.[9] This report was a forerunner to the broader High-Level Independent Panel on Peace Operations Report (HIPPO), chaired by José Ramos-Horta and delivered to the Secretary-General in June 2015, the implications of which are addressed in Chapter 9. The Guéhenno report considers the need for a planned development of the professionalization and reprofiling of the UN system's capacity to support global postconflict intervention and peacebuilding into the future in an evolving and dynamic global environment. It envisages continuing resource constraints and working more closely with host countries and the community, as directed by appropriate policy. The guiding principles espoused by this report are the development of national ownership of intervention processes, increased global partnership, delivery with the appropriate expertise, and nimbleness in addressing dynamic postconflict environments (OPEN). The principles suggest a new way for the UN to do business. The report recognizes the increasing resource constraints that require the UN to rationalize intervention approaches that capitalize on its genuine capacities. Further, it tacitly acknowledges the inappropriateness of the UN continuing to field massive, costly missions with foreign expertise, without always considering the regional and national political and cultural sensitivities, to deliver postconflict stabilization and peacebuilding interventions in a paternalistic, directive manner. Perhaps this realization comes in light of glaring examples of the contracting levels of the UN's political leverage in certain regional interventions. One such example is the nonrenewal of the UN Special Political Mission in Nepal's mandate in 2011, a mission undermined by significant regional hostility to the UN presence.[10] Additional examples of the UN's limited influence on conflicts occurred in Syria, Gaza, eastern Congo, Mali, and Ukraine.

The attitude of UN agencies regarding the various experiments at institutional integration in delivering DDR illustrates general agreement that independent and stove-piped parallel operations in delivering massive crosscutting postconflict interventions, such as DDR, are a poor use of resources.[11] However, even when there is a shared vision of outcomes, full institutional integration that attempts to fully merge financial, budgetary, and administrative staff and systems into a single corporate vision has proved a painful failure that wasn't so practical from the outset. In fact, corporate resistance and the inability to harmonize systems were decisive in altering the approach. It has since been confirmed through successful practice that an appropriate mechanism for the "UN working as one" is through the development of collaborative processes that fully harness and complement agency institutional strengths and corporate capacities and that address relevant weaknesses, all in an environment of mutual respect and sound professional relationships. The design of successful interagency collaboration must be context specific in order to create the most appropriate functional integration to address the program's common objectives. This design is preferable and more functional than attempting full institutional integration by merging systems of UN agencies, programs, or funds with different corporate cultures and systems.

The thrust of the second-generation approach to DDR is in harmony with the recommendations of the Guéhenno report.[12] Second-generation DDR's emphasis on the stabilizing impact of the reinsertion of former combatants into the community, supported by bottom-up approaches, has gained ascendancy and continues to establish its place in the UN system. However, contexts continue to evolve, and the planners and scholar/practitioners are thinking beyond second-generation into next-generation DDR. The UN Department of Peacekeeping Operations is clearly adding impetus to its second-generation approach to DDR, going beyond support to disarmament through the inclusion of a reinsertion phase associated with demobilization. This step takes its engagement, together with the development agencies, into the community. The Department of Peacekeeping Operations is now seen to be maneuvering the appropriate staff at the headquarters level; it is also developing constructive collaboration throughout the organization and beyond, most notably with the UN Department of Political Affairs and the World Bank.

In 2010, approximately US$265 million of voluntary funding was channeled through UNDP in support of the reintegration of former combatants. Over the past twenty years, UNDP has gained considerable experience in DDR, developing good practice and contributing strongly to the establishment and implementation of the IDDRS. This experience has seen a progressive evolution of the DDR paradigm within UNDP's early recovery concept to include community security and community violence reduction, to greater collaboration with the Department of Peacekeeping Operations' second-generation approach to DDR. This is specifically relevant from the early phase of demobilization, when a deficit of confidence in the peace process may exist among the former combatants and civil society, to the evolution of the reintegration phase and the progressive stabilization of the peace process in a transition from a postconflict context toward development. UNDP has been tasked with ensuring that reintegration efforts are aligned with peace, recovery, and development programming.[13] In late 2012, in an attempt to review this capacity and being concerned with institutional coherence, UNDP's now-defunct Bureau for Crisis Prevention and Recovery called for a multicountry research study that would direct the recalibration of UNDP's approach to DDR. The scope of this study and the questions being addressed appeared to offer an indication that current questioning had moved toward the maximalist approach to

DDR, beyond combatant-centric programming, and that perhaps there was a place for the qualitative indicators of perceptions and trust that the DDR is contributing to the peace. In particular, it was expected to consider the sustainability of DDR initiatives in the context of their political, sociocultural, and economic livelihood dimensions.

The findings were to contribute to the development of UNDP policy and strategies in support of the reintegration of former combatants. The study proposed to define or redefine the theory of change implicit in the design of reintegration programs. The goal was to identify the relationship, convergence, or integration with other parallel programs being implemented in country and to review lessons learned and best practices in the context of sustainable and relevant political, social, and economic reintegration. The study expected to identify the evidence of benefits, consider the socioeconomic impacts at the national and local levels, and to identify direct supports and social benefits to both individuals and community. It was meant to review the levels of community participation in the process through "mechanisms of community-based reintegration and community security" and to identify aspects of a national mechanism for sustainability, all through a process of deconstructing DDR and reexamining approaches.

The specific research questions of the study were posed under the headings of effectiveness, efficiency, sustainability, relevance, and impact, which went beyond the traditional quantitative metrics and delved into qualitative results, such as synergies at a national and community level. The study used strengths, weaknesses, opportunities, and threats (SWOT) analysis to question UNDP's institutional comparative advantage in delivering its responsibilities in such programs. They considered the efficacy of UNDP's monitoring and evaluation systems, the sustainability of impacts, the effective operationalization of appropriate partnerships, the relevancy of program design to the national and local context, the identification of broad impacts, and the establishment of appropriate knowledge management systems.

Completed in February 2013,[14] the Bureau for Crisis Prevention and Recovery study reviewed DDR programs in eight countries, largely through desk review and short visits to five of the chosen countries.[15] Findings fell under three headings: (1) agency function and role, (2) coordination and partnerships, and (3) reintegration approaches. Under the first heading, it highlights the importance of monitoring and evaluation, citing the UN Interagency Rehabilitation Programme in Nepal for its dynamic monitoring and evaluation process, which they found exemplary and systematic. For the second heading, it recommends a system of respectful, close collaboration with shared objectives rather than structural integration when organizing multiple agencies to effectively facilitate the "UN working as one," as proved effective in Nepal and as has been demonstrated in twenty-two agencies collaborating in the DDR Interagency Working Group. In considering partnerships, the study stresses that local ownership through community-based participative processes in DDR, though difficult to implement, is a major contributor to successful outcomes. In terms of the third heading, although classic DDR is still relevant and occasionally necessary, innovative community-based approaches toward local conflict sensitivity that take into consideration community security offer new directions in developing effective reintegration. There is also a need for a focus on special needs groups and gender responsive programming. Finally, the report noted that the projected costs of reintegration are often underestimated.

Lessons learned in this study can be summarily reflected as follows:

- The measurement of impact matters.
- Conflict analysis is important.
- Interagency cooperation is a good idea.
- Local ownership and participation are smart.
- Gender-responsive programming "rocks."
- Customized assistance near the end of reintegration support is a multiplier.
- A mix of former combatant-centric support with community-focused initiatives is effective.
- Community security structures that encourage the community to devise local solutions to the conflict complement traditional DDR, but do not replace it.
- The number of former combatants being resettled has a proportional impact on the community.
- Demand-driven training for jobs is essential.
- Training is only one aspect of reintegration.

Considering the level of navel gazing that was in progress in UNDP headquarters concerning DDR prior to the study and the philosophical level of questions posed, these findings are something of an anticlimax; they are pretty much no-brainers. Perhaps, the surprise, from the perspective of the observing practitioner eagerly awaiting this report and anticipating a mandate for directional change for UNDP, is that there are no surprises. Although the study could have been expected to generate a level of institutional imprimatur, it offered nothing that practitioners had not already realized and were already addressing. The theory remained intact; it could have been expected that no news was good news. What is a surprise, however, despite the apparent affirmation of UNDP's appropriateness and effectiveness in its role in DDR, is the speed at which UNDP has run away from DDR. This includes the demise of its Bureau for Crisis Prevention and Recovery and the loss of most, if not all, of that bureau's DDR expertise and institutional memory.

Concurrently, the DDR Unit of the Department of Peacekeeping Operations has been building on methodologies painfully tested in Haiti and elsewhere since 2006, with a focus on second-generation approaches to DDR, to develop policies for moving into next-generation DDR. This move is supported by the development of appropriate multidisciplinary practical and scholarly capacity and collaboration in such areas as transitional justice and legal frameworks, deradicalization, DDR in counterinsurgency and counterterrorism, DDR in the context of violent extremism, Islamic-led DDR, and DDR in criminalized environments. This progression into next-generation DDR is considered in Chapter 11.

The International Labour Organization and the Evolution of Reintegration Theory

Focusing on economic reintegration, the UN International Labour Organization (ILO) published the 160-page *Socio-economic Reintegration of Ex-combatants: Guidelines* in 2009. This document offers a consolidation of lessons learned regarding the importance of sustainable employment in contributing to a positive outcome in the economic reintegration aspects of DDR, while not underestimating the impact of decent livelihood options on social reintegration.[16] The guidelines lose some credibility with practitioners, however, as they were launched as a solo run and appeared to grandstand ILO's institutional position, rather than contributing genuinely to development of the multiagency IDDRS and the "UN working as one."[17] ILO has a reputation among DDR practitioners for offering considerable technical advice for elaborate and long-term labor-enhancement strategies in postconflict environments and DDR contexts, without having the resources or the capacity to support implementation of the advice. This leaves DDR practitioners somewhat perplexed and unimpressed, perhaps with a tendency to underestimate the value of the advice.

The following information is cherry-picked from the opening stages of the document in order to highlight some of the useful guidance offered. The ILO guidelines acknowledge the complexity of the postconflict socioeconomic context, particularly in relation to employment. Seeing DDR as a priority in peacebuilding, the guidelines consider employment to be a critical aspect of the "R"—specifically, socioeconomic reintegration. Employment creation is therefore central to the postconflict effort. It goes beyond DDR and must be linked to all aspects of national socioeconomic recovery, for which strategic planning should have started early in the postconflict planning. The guidelines recommend that sustainable reintegration should consist of "both up-streaming conditions for creating an enabling environment in three programmatic tracks at macro, meso and micro levels for boosting job creation . . . [and] down-streaming more specific and targeted supply-driven measures for reintegrating former combatants."

As guiding principles for sustainable reintegration of former combatants, the guidelines cite the following:

1. Make employment central to the response.
2. Start early, and phase the interventions.
3. Ensure inclusion of specific former combatant groups in program design. (Despite the preference for community-focused approaches, especially among DDR scholars, former combatants need special attention.)
4. Ensure sustainability.

In following the common wisdom, the guidelines advocate greater emphasis on demand-driven training of former combatants in reintegration programs—that is, rather than just offering training options to former combatants because of the availability of training facilities, which is a supply-driven approach, they should be trained for jobs that actually exist and that contribute to a demand-driven market. The guidelines also call for a community-based approach to reintegration in order to contribute to a holistic approach to socioeconomic reintegration.

In general, these guidelines have not received the attention they require from DDR planners and practitioners, perhaps because of the effort required to develop the degree of integration and collaboration at the international and national level to contribute to the achievement of the strategic objectives outlined. Although highly desirable, preparing the data sets to support the appropriate labor market surveys would require a level of preplanning and broad coordination that is usually beyond the scope of a discrete, time-bound, budgetary-constrained, pressured DDR program operating in a volatile security environment. However, in preparing for a postconflict environment, these strategic considerations should be sufficiently pre-planned to ensure their inclusion in the relevant comprehensive peace accord so that they can receive the level of integrated attention required.

Although the guidelines mention the informal employment economy as a target area for former combatant livelihoods, it is not sufficiently addressed. According to Guy Lamb, "International Labor Organization has estimated that the informal income generation comprises 48% of non-agricultural employment in North Africa, 51% in Latin America, 65% in Asia, and 72% in sub-Saharan Africa."[18] Given these enormous figures, consideration of the potential for employment in the informal sector is clearly inadequate. Lamb did make a strong effort to collate relevant information on the rationale and potential for better harnessing of the informal economy for former combatant reintegration, as in Central African Republic, Democratic Republic of Congo, and South Sudan (the latter, in the context of the Transitional Demobilization and Reintegration Program). Building on Lamb's analysis, the DDR sector needs to take on board the implications of seeing the informal economy as a legitimate objective for stimulation in the context of enhancing postconflict livelihoods.

What Is the Status of the UN Approach to DDR?

Walt Kilroy, looking back to the foundational theory collated by early scholars such as Mats Berdal, Nat Colletta, and Kees Kingma, reviewed the many challenges in applying DDR effectively in dynamic contexts. He predicted the continuing need for DDR in postconflict environments.[19] He cited the UNDP Practice Note on DDR of 2005, which stated that the main beneficiaries of the program should ultimately be the wider community rather than former combatants. In reviewing the success or failure attributed to DDR programs, Kilroy claimed that although there is a positive perception of their impact, recurrent shortcomings are noted.[20] Such shortcomings often include a neglected gender perspective, difficulty in setting entry criteria, and problems caused by interrupted cash flows. However, the main difficulty is usually associated with socioeconomic reintegration and the capacity of former combatants to find sustainable decent livelihoods, which is closely linked to the macro-socioeconomic recovery of the postconflict state.

Although the policy recommendations drafted by those earlier scholars remain relevant, the variety of contexts and the complexity of the theory are evolving. The IDDRS offer a useful best practice tool in the five overarching principles, which advise that DDR programs must be "people-centered, flexible, transparent and accountable, nationally owned, integrated and well planned." These principles offer a framework within which a DDR program can be planned and a set of parameters by which to design or evaluate indicators of achievement. Regarding Humphreys and Weinstein's failure to find evidence that reintegration support was useful in Sierra Leone, Kilroy cited Molloy, who contended that skewing factors and difficulties with the operationalization of variables may have concealed positive results that are perceived by the practitioner in qualitative indicators. He also cited Edward Bell and Charlotte Watson in "recognizing that [in the implementation of DDR] the 'how' is often more important than the 'what.'"

In reviewing the DDR literature of the new millennium, Muggah detected a shift from the security-first (minimalist) approach, focused on military and policing priorities, to a broader development (maximalist) approach that considers the holistic human security aspects of DDR.[21] Further, he stated that his review of literature detects the progressive professionalization and standardization of DDR practice. Whereas early researchers were preoccupied with the "process and practice of DDR as a spatially, temporally and socially bounded activity . . . [they] seldom considered more fundamental issues of causality and correlation, actor agency or intervention outcomes."[22] More recently, researchers are broadening their research areas and analysis to include comparative case studies and statistical assessments, seeking more evidenced-based data on what works. These modern researchers are also testing the relationships between DDR and pertinent issues, such as the "combatant agency, peace agreements, transitional justice, SSR and state-building." According to Muggah, more than sixty DDR processes have taken place around the world since the early 1990s, most in postconflict environments of various contexts. The preoccupation with such processes has progressively broadened from the minimalist approach toward the maximalist approach. As DDR is an "inherently political and politicizing process, [designed to] reinforce and extend the reach and legitimacy of state authority," it has increasingly come under the scrutiny of political and social scientists.

Muggah further said that, in its contribution to development in postconflict environments, DDR is "designed to stem war recurrence, reduce military expenditure, stimulate spending on social welfare, prevent spoilers from disrupting peace processes, disrupt command control of armed groups and prevent resort to weapons of war."[23] In identifying the trends progressively evolving through trial and frequent error during the implementation of the many DDR processes since the early 1990s, Muggah noted a consensus settling on the importance of national ownership. He saw that DDR is no longer viewed simply as a technical program; rather, it is seen as "a technology of stabilization and state-building"[24] that is replete with political, economic, institutional, infrastructural, and social complexity and limitations. Muggah expressed hope that the complexity and context specificity of DDR interventions are being recognized. In considering the evolution of policy, he noted the UN initiative in producing the IDDRS and how this prescriptive policy reflects the tensions between the UN approach to DDR and national ownership, which is often a difficult concept to maintain while insisting on international standards. He also highlighted the danger of such a collection of good-practice guidance contributing to template-thinking, thus inhibiting flexibility.

While acknowledging the struggle for results, Muggah contended that practitioners need to support their work with an improved regime of evidence-based analysis and evaluation, using appropriate metrics to ensure that impacts and outcomes are achieved and are seen to have been achieved. He considered the eternal implementation dilemmas of budget, resources, and time versus clear best practice toward more sustainable outcomes and of targeting the former combatant versus the broader community. He discussed the approach of second-generation peacekeeping and stabilization missions and felt that the jury is still out regarding their efficiency. In relation to theoretical innovation, Muggah contended that the imperatives of practice are driving research. Moving beyond the first-generation focus on the institutional aspects and rational agency models, the second wave of theoretical enquiry is testing assumptions, comparative analysis, and the application of rigorous empirical methodologies of political and social science. This includes an attempt to refine appropriate metrics of reintegration success and failure. Muggah reiterated the need for humility and effective communications in considering what can be realistically achieved by DDR.

Drawing from the recommendations of the Stockholm Initiative on DDR in 2006, Nat Colletta, Jens Schjörlien, and Hannes Berts considered the value of providing interim stabilization measures, in the appropriate circumstances, in the context of armed groups in the volatile immediate postconflict period.[25] Interim stabilization measures are confidence-building measures that offer a breathing space, permitting the maturation of the peace process at both the state level and the community level. Such measures, adapted to specific contexts, while creating options for negotiators, will also encourage participation in the process by the armed group, while maintaining the benefits of the de facto community; relative security, camaraderie, cohesiveness, and the mutual support of the group.[26] Interim stabilization measures may permit a period of orientation and adjustment, perhaps in a holding pattern, during the changing political and social postconflict environment. This may allow the state, the former combatants, and the broader community to be engaged in DDR or SSR, thus facilitating the transition from a prioritization on security to one on development. Case studies considered by Colletta include, among others, Hun Sen's pragmatic "Win-Win Approach" in taming the Khmer Rouge in Cambodia in the mid-1990s, the agricultural engagement option offered to members of the Lord's Resistance Army in Uganda, and the prolonged cantonments of the Maoist army while maintaining the army's structural integrity after the 2006 comprehensive peace accord in Nepal.

Although the concept of interim stabilization measures makes sense, the reality is more complex. The tendency is for the disarming and demobilizing forces to avail themselves of interim stabilization measures in order to seek strategic security and political benefits from the opportunities. The Cambodian example was highly successful in ending the war, albeit with reservations regarding humanitarian issues, human rights, and justice. In Uganda, however, the Lord's Resistance Army used that time to consolidate and relaunch their campaign of terror, spreading across Central Africa in the "cockroach effect." In Nepal, the Maoists remained six years in cantonment, forging their Maoist People's Liberation Army into a better-trained, more cohesive, and determined force, leveraging the political environment so that, over time, they achieved most of their original goals.

According to Dean Piedmont, interim stabilization measures in Afghanistan and South Sudan contributed to an "enabling environment [while] the peace dividend can take root."[27] In a structural approach in Afghanistan (2004–2006), former combatants remained under military command but were retasked as civilian de-miners. In South Sudan (2006–2010), a strategic approach was adopted through the launch of an interim DDR process focusing on specific special needs groups. The hope was that this would lay the groundwork for what would be recognized as a phased process eventually leading to a more comprehensive DDR program.

Vanessa Prinz looked at the cohesiveness of armed groups, focusing on nonstate armed groups, and saw it as an angle that is worth factoring into

UN DDR program design.[28] DDR practitioners' anxiety about disassociating former combatants from their armed group underestimates the value of the cohesiveness that those combatants retained from their camaraderie in and commitment to the armed group. This cohesiveness offers a significant coping mechanism in retaining elements of the supportive camaraderie associated with the group; if harnessed appropriately, it could contribute to socioeconomic reintegration. Program implementers have, on occasion, seen this cohesiveness as an asset in relation to the reintegration of female former combatants due to the particular constraints they experience in certain contexts (for example, in Sierra Leone, Liberia, and Nepal). Prinz, noting the reticence to apply the same logic to male former combatants, suggested that this reticence seems to reflect an issue of distorted masculinities on the part of the practitioner.

The gender perspective in DDR has been the focus of much attention and mainstreaming in the evolution of UN DDR theory, including in the IDDRS. It is a perspective that planners and practitioners are perceived to have been grappling with in a reasonably successful manner. However, drawing from her poststructural analysis to "read between the lines" of the UN institutional discourse reflected in the IDDRS language regarding the gender perspective, Elizabeth Molloy suggested that the attention given to gender represents only an awareness of the complex issues that include power structures, identities, and norms.[29] Considering the passivity of the language used in the IDDRS in offering guidance on addressing the gender perspective during DDR, she contended that it does not represent a genuine attempt to instigate "action for social transformation." Rather, it is "seen to walk the difficult gendered tightrope between addressing traditional imbalance of power and preventing further conflict." In the prioritization of achieving peace, the gender perspective can be seen as a tangential issue that can put that objective at risk. From my perspective, what a poststructural analysis of the IDDRS language does not reflect is the determination of practitioners to deliver the spirit of the commitment to the gender perspective in DDR, as in the UN Interagency Rehabilitation Programme in Nepal.

As an aspect of DDR in Rwanda, Bowd applied rigorous scholarship to analyze social reintegration of former combatants into war-affected communities, as opposed to economic and political reintegration.[30] Somewhat in the genre of Humphreys and Weinstein, Bowd drew largely from a series of informal interviews with the actors, elite, community members, and former combatants and from an ethnographic perspective of communities. He took into consideration the impact of reintegration on social capital and reconciliation in the context of peacebuilding. He examined the obstacles faced by former combatants in their social reintegration and how they overcame them. In so doing, he considered the impact of their reintegration on reconciliation "by applying the concept of social capital as a bridge between former combatant social reintegration and reconciliation."[31] Bowd found that successful reintegration does contribute to positive social capital; likewise, if reintegration is not adequately supported and achieved, it has a negative impact on social capital. He urged that there be a greater focus on social reintegration in consideration of the transformation of social capital.

Bowd cited Robert Putnam's definition of social capital: "the features of social organization, such as networks, norms and trust, that facilitate coordination and cooperation for mutual benefit."[32] Drawing from a broad range of literature, Bowd used a model proposed by D. Halpern to offer a composite three-dimensional picture of social capital as a complex system.[33] This system comprises networks, norms, and sanctions at the level of individuals, communities, and nations through the functions of bonding, bridging, and linking, all of which have an impact on social cohesion. Social capital, which is influenced greatly by the security, political, and economic environment, reflects perceptions and attitudes at its different levels and is a dynamic qualitative phenomenon; it is a construct measured by case-specific proxy indicators. Bowd, concerned with how reintegration could affect social capital and reconciliation, adapted his work to consider how attention to social capital and, specifically, to perceptions and attitudes could contribute to successful DDR. Trust, communication, cooperation, and coordination are critical aspects of both reintegration and social capital. Focusing on these elements in a conflict-sensitive manner permits interventions to influence social capital and to contribute, through "positive transformations in social capital," to acceptable longer-term outcomes in the context of DDR.[34]

A recently published four study series of related case studies by the International Research Group on Reintegration delves deeper into reintegration in the context of DDR.[35] The first three studies review reintegration in Nepal, Afghanistan, and Somalia, seeking evidence of impact by going beyond the traditional program-focused quantitative metrics and attempting to come at the problems from innovative angles.

The fourth study reviews the gender perspective in DDR.[36] It asserts that the UN "overlooked the critical historical, geopolitical and domestic dynamics for mobilization" of combatants and underestimated the meagerness of its own leverage; therefore, it inadequately responded to the local environment. This led to the early termination of the UN Mission in Nepal's mandate. The study's innovative framework is reflected in the key organizing concepts, which led it to ask the right questions in planning, designing, implementing, and evaluating reintegration aspects of DDR. That framework considers the following:

1. Nepal's general political economy.
2. An explanatory framework of DDR in the specific context.
3. The concept of trajectories, or the paths that former combatants follow after separation from the armed group, and the related variables.
4. A multicentric notion of community—community is not just that to

which former combatants return. Within the armed group, combatants formed a supporting community.

5. The concept of engagement and disengagement, which permits a focus on the complexity of the decisions addressed by an individual undertaking a reintegration process.

6. The concept of reintegration in its maximalist interpretation with social, economic, and political dimensions.

The Afghan study reviews the current Afghanistan Peace and Reintegration Program through the lens of the same key organizing concepts as was used in the Nepal study.[37] The prognosis predicted through this analysis is not optimistic and sees a moment lost in contributing to peace in Afghanistan, as weary fighters, disillusioned about the Taliban, have failed to receive the expected social, economic, and security benefits of the reintegration process. The Somali study focuses on the social reintegration of former pirates through the lens of disengagement and the process of deradicalization. It primarily considers the social, cultural, and religious influence in contributing to former pirate disengagement.[38]

Taken as an innovative lens offering a focus on heretofore neglected elements of critical importance regarding the success or failure of reintegration, after considering specific qualitative metrics, these three studies contribute to identifying the right questions in planning, designing, implementing, and evaluating reintegration as an aspect of DDR.

The DDR Practitioner's Dilemma

Muggah did not provide answers to the practitioner's dilemma of advising on the development of appropriate metrics for DDR planning or evaluation.[39] This question is driving the current navel gazing, redistribution of resources, and rethinking of the DDR paradigm within the UN. If practitioners believe that the implementation of DDR programs has a positive impact on peacebuilding outcomes, then why is it so difficult for them to provide the metrics to measure the clear unequivocal evidence of the impact of their efforts or the successful application of donors' funds? I have suggested that the problem is too great a focus on quantitative indicators of achievement, whereas DDR's primary contributions to peacebuilding outcomes are qualitative.[40] Those quantitative indicators of achievement dictated in each program document tend to be static and reflect neither the reality of the dynamic postconflict environment nor the changing DDR context. I recommend the establishment of a system of mainstreamed dynamic monitoring and evaluation within all aspects of program implementation. Such a system involves the progressive reflection on both quantitative and qualitative outputs, weighting them appropriately in accordance with their perceived impact on the program, evaluating in a process of triangulation, and progressively adjusting the program indicators of achievement to reflect the reality of the program's developing priorities and achievable results. Kees Kingma, at an October 2012 International Research Group on Reintegration conference in Tromsø, suggested that such mainstreamed dynamic monitoring and evaluation is otherwise called "management."

This methodology, as piloted in the UN Interagency Rehabilitation Programme in Nepal (2010–2013), demonstrated extraordinary results in a very adverse environment. Frequent informal management meetings drew from the verbal and routine written reports of the regional offices and prioritized actions, making the required changes immediately. The informal and formal reporting systems were supported by an integrated management information system called Comprehensive Reintegration Information Management System, which was designed and created by the program's information technology and reporting staff. Dynamic monitoring and evaluation was a management tool rather than purely an evaluation tool; it facilitated a more proactive approach to program innovation, effectiveness, and efficiency. Routine analysis of feedback and adjustment resulted in the development of a highly innovative and effective gender approach addressing the specific Nepali contextual gender constraints; this led to Maoist female former combatants enjoying the benefits of full participation in their reintegration support options. Further, the system facilitated the address of difficulties associated with masculinities by bringing to program management's immediate attention the reported psychosocial stresses and frustrations being expressed by male former combatants and their spouses and families, allowing for a systematic response that included counseling.

The mainstreaming of a conflict-sensitive approach to program implementation supported by dynamic monitoring and evaluation facilitated rapid identification of "dividers and connectors" between the community and the program. This led to the adaption of a "do no harm" approach to program delivery, the adaption of health support, identification of the need for strengthened psychosocial counseling, the design of effective career counseling and job placement, and microenterprise support systems.[41]

Shibuya also came close to answering the question of those practitioner dilemmas.[42] The majority of his book, *Demobilizing Irregular Forces*, describes a systematic movement through the DDR processes, extracting the major issues as highlighted in a broad range of literature. The final chapter of his book focuses on his personal analysis, in which he reminds us that Muggah pointed out that there is little evidence that DDR works. If Muggah was right, then there are three possibilities. First, DDR may be a chimera offering only an illusion of achievement; second, DDR may be being consistently oversold; and third, researchers and practitioners may not have been looking at the right things. Shibuya suggested that in considering the relationship between DDR and peace, there are enough points of success in DDR to indicate that perhaps the latter two conclusions are the more likely. The most important element in DDR is the perception of progress, growing confidence within the population. The greatest challenge to DDR, according to Shibuya, is the unrealistic expectations that are frequently generated and exploited for political purposes. He suggested that planners and implementers invest greater effort in managing expectations.

Shibuya cited Anders Themnér's catch-22 question: if reintegration does not work, why do most former combatants not return to violence, and why do we keep doing it?[43] Themnér suggested two answers: The reintegration phase buys time and permits a cooling-off period for combatants. Or, savvy former combatants have started to consider reintegration assistance as a right; therefore, governments and international agencies are forced to offer it, even if it does not work. Shibuya again cited Muggah's reference to the Humphreys and Weinstein survey—despite finding no evidence that reintegration assistance contributed to sustainable peace, there was an increased *perception* of security after implementation of the DDR process. According to Shibuya, this "extremely important insight suggests a need for more subjective measures of performance." It isn't about the quantifiable metrics; it is about the perceptions and their impact on confidence and trust.

What is DDR supposed to achieve? Shibuya concluded that there is not a universal answer that can be slotted into theory. It is case specific, and the balance depends on circumstance. What is clear is that DDR planners and practitioners need to be ready to take risks. The level of those risks deemed as acceptable must be calculated based on good information and sound analysis of the expected return, particularly in relation to its impact on trust and perception.

Shibuya cited Melanne Civic and Michael Miklaucic in suggesting that the development of the acronym DDR has perpetuated the misleading perception of a "singular character" of D, D, and R.[44] Perhaps not all phases of DDR need to be implemented at all, especially if doing so would be counterproductive. Stakeholders in DDR must be ready to see an acceptable level of failure in any phase of the program, where the return on investment in achieving success in that particular facet of the program in terms of peace and security is negative. Thus, Shibuya advocated substance over form.

Drawing on his experience of the civil-military collaboration in Iraq and Afghanistan, Shibuya asserted that the focus should be on maintaining good relations rather than on following best practices. An environment of trust among actors that contributes to a collaborative environment based on shared motivation is vital. Such an environment includes macrolevel collaboration between the citizens and their communities and beyond, between the communities and the government. Shibuya derided the penchant for large organizations and practitioners to "template successful practices . . . to mechanize success," irrespective of the idiosyncratic contexts of DDR environments. With a focus on the underlying rationale, practitioners must remain aware that perfection will not be achieved in success and that "certain levels of failure may be acceptable." To a great extent, security, like community or nationalism, is imagined; it is a local construct. DDR is about creating that perception of security, which implies that the key to DDR is communications and management of perceptions, particularly regarding the levels of failure that are acceptable. In considering the challenges in the evaluation of DDR programs, a revealing statement by Shibuya is that due to the difficulty in measuring the real impact of the processes, "agencies tend to fall into the trap of using measures of effort rather than measures of effectiveness. . . . The things that can be measured are not the things that matter." He cited David Kilcullen in equating the required flexibility in the field of DDR with that of counterinsurgency: "The challenge for commanders and assessment staffs is . . . not to template previously developed metrics, but rather constantly develop and apply new indicators, based on a shared diagnosis of what the conflict is, and what is driving it."[45] From a practitioner's perspective, Shibuya gets it!

Millett, in the conclusion of his forthcoming work, *Demobilization, Disarmament and Reintegration (DDR): Case Studies of Partial Success and Enduring Dilemmas,* which offers nine case studies, also focused on the difficulties of measuring the impact of DDR programs.[46] He reflected some of the views expressed by Shibuya that perhaps scholars have been looking in the wrong place and must look beyond the quantitative metrics. Like Shibuya, he mentioned the tendency to attempt to replicate success, often with disastrous results. He also referred to the exaggeration of expectations of what DDR can deliver. DDR needs to "strike a balance between what should be done and what could be done."

In terms of disarmament, Millett mentioned the US penchant for gathering weapons and, with reservations, raised a flag regarding the value of arms buy-backs. He also considered the necessity to support disarmament with improved controls on the trafficking of small arms, border controls, organized crime, weapons legislation, and so on. Reintegration is the vital "carrot" that has drawn the mass of former combatants into the process. Despite doubts and misgivings regarding its impact, this step is indispensable. A point of consideration is that although economic regeneration is critical to offer absorption capacity for former combatants into sustainable livelihoods, "economic recovery itself does not guarantee successful reintegration."

The relationship among SSR, rule of law, and DDR permeates several of the nine case studies reviewed in Millett's book. The critical factors are the existence of a political will for DDR to work and the professional competence of those charged with administering it. In this case, nothing succeeds like success. Clear progress in these areas is the foundation for building continuing political will. The case studies draw attention to the disturbing and growing trend of the increasing privatization of security. In a poorly regulated sector, companies and individuals are of dubious provenance, often contributing more to problems than to solutions.

In his sum up, Millett noted the lack of consensus regarding where DDR is going. The problem, in light of the heterogeneity and complexity of DDR contexts, is not just to learn from the past but to know which lessons to draw.

As with Shibuya, Millett saw the necessity for the right personality at the spot at the right time. Local knowledge and sensitivity are vital attributes. Because "success is hard to measure and failure hard to conceal," quantitative metrics are dangerous and are open to misinterpretation or even spin. Therefore, qualitative indicators are equally important. Measuring the success of DDR while a conflict is continuing is meaningless; measuring is a postconflict process. We do not know where DDR is going until "the fat lady sings." Millett, mirroring Shibuya's analysis, explained that if the wrong questions are asked, the answers are irrelevant. Is violence decreasing? Are reintegration beneficiaries employed? Is community security improved? Is public confidence improving? Such questions are the key; they emphasize the continuing nature of the DDR program. As such, national ownership, linkages between the international intervention and follow-on government programming, and potential sustainability of the program are critical. The vital human qualities contributing to successful DDR are commitment, patience, caution, and especially humility. We will only know for sure how DDR went decades after a conflict has not returned.

Review

Despite broad supporting common wisdom, DDR remains a theory and a practice under scrutiny due to the inability to identify agreed-upon, evidenced-based metrics that will contribute to the planning and evaluation of progress or achievement. Even after tracing the evolution of the theory, the scholarly questioning and the efforts to develop appropriate metrics to facilitate evidenced-based analysis persist. Despite two decades of searching, there is still not an agreed answer. The UN is now undertaking a search of its own. There is a movement toward a broad maximalist approach to DDR, beyond the former combatant-centric focus to community-based approaches. A rethink of IDDRS beyond a UN-driven concept may be timely due to the increasing demand for support in an environment of tightening resources and capacity and more assertive regional and cultural sensitivities. UN agencies are recalibrating their positions regarding DDR. The Department of Peacekeeping Operations is developing its concept of second-generation DDR, along with appropriate collaboration, to lay the foundations for expected demand for support of reducing armed violence in contexts other than postconflict environments. UNDP acknowledges its accumulated experience in supporting various aspects of DDR over the past decades. However, in hindsight, it sees its institutional strengths and mandates within the less contentious and less risky elements of broader community-focused socioeconomic development in postconflict environments, rather than direct support exclusively to former combatants.

In considering complementary mechanisms and midterm evolving concepts, I reviewed ideas on interim stabilization mechanisms, the value of former combatant cohesiveness, and the reality of UN commitment to the gender perspective in DDR. Bowd considered how the role of reintegration is transforming social capital and contributing to reconciliation in the community. The International Research Group on Reintegration has developed key organizing concepts to facilitate the study of reintegration; these concepts include political economy, context, separation trajectories, a multicentric notion of community, engagement and disengagement, and a maximalist interpretation of reintegration with socioeconomic and political dimensions.

The practitioner's biggest dilemma is the failure to identify agreed-upon metrics for planning and evaluation purposes. A new school of scholars and practitioner/scholars suggests that we have been asking the wrong questions. The functional metrics are not the quantitative metrics that have been the subject of focus; rather, they are qualitative ones—peoples' perceptions and attitudes that DDR is contributing to their interests.

The next chapter considers important crosscutting issues in DDR and previews the threats and opportunities that abound as we move toward next-generation DDR.

Notes

1. Richard Bowd, *From Combatant to Civilian: The Social Reintegration of Ex-combatants in Rwanda and the Implications for Social Capital and Reconciliation* (PhD dissertation, York, UK: Post-war Reconstruction and Development Unit, University of York, September 2008).

2. Walt Kilroy, "Disarmament, Demobilisation and Reintegration: The Co-evolution of Concepts, Practices, and Understanding" (Program on States and Security, Ralph Bunche Institute for International Studies, The Graduate Center, City University of New York, 2009).

3. Macartan Humphreys and Jeremy Weinstein, "What the Fighters Say: A Survey of Ex-combatants in Sierra Leone" (CGSD Working Paper No. 20, Columbia University, Center on Globalization and Sustainable Development, with PRIDE-Salone, 2004).

4. Subsequent studies by Humphreys and Weinstein include "Disentangling the Determinant of Successful DDR," Columbia University and Stanford University, presented at meeting of the American Political Science Association, Washington, DC, 2005; "Demobilization and Reintegration," *Journal of Conflict Resolution* 51, no. 4 (August 2007); "Demobilization and Reintegration in Sierra Leone: Assessing Progress," in *Security and Post-Conflict Reconstruction*, ed. Robert Muggah (London: Routledge, 2009).

5. Desmond Molloy, *The Qualitative Quantitative Dilemma: An Analysis of Indicators of Achievement as Used in DDR Programmes* (Master's thesis. Tokyo: Tokyo University of Foreign Studies, 2009).

6. James Pugel, *What the Fighters Say: A Survey of Ex-combatants in Liberia, February–March 2006* (New York: UNDP and African Network for the Prevention and Protection Against Child Abuse and Neglect, April 2007).

7. Isabela Leao, *Swimming Against the Stream: DDR in Sierra Leone* (PhD dissertation, State University of Milan, January 2011).

8. *The Report of the Panel on UN Peace Operations* (Brahimi Report) (New York: United Nations, 2000).

9. Secretary-General's Senior Advisory Group, *Report on Civilian Capacity in*

the Aftermath of Conflict Within the UN System (The Guéhenno Report), (New York: UNHQ, March 4, 2011).

10. This was a UN Special Political Mission (SPM), rather than a UN Peacekeeping Mission (PKO). No military force was included. On the Special Political Mission in Nepal, see Tone Bleie and Ramesh Shrestha, *DDR in Nepal: Stakeholder Politics and the Implications for Reintegration as a Process of Disengagement* (Tromsø, Norway: International Research Group on Reintegration, Centre for Peace Studies, Tromsø University, 2012).

11. Drawn from personal experience; Robert Muggah, Desmond Molloy, and Maximo Halty, "(Dis)integrating DDR in Sudan and Haiti? Practitioners' Views to Overcoming Integration Inertia," in *Security and Post-Conflict Reconstruction*, ed. Robert Muggah (London: Routledge, 2009); *Final Evaluation of UNIRP* (UNDP, Kathmandu, 2013); and Paul Bonard and Yvan Conoir, *Evaluation of UNDP Reintegration Programmes,* vol. 1 (New York: UNDP, February 2013).

12. *Second-Generation DDR Practices in Peace Operations: A Contribution to the New Horizon Discussion on Challenges and Opportunities for UN Peacekeeping* (New York: UN Department of Peacekeeping Operations, 2010).

13. According to footnote 1 in the Executive Summary of the Report of Security Council Policy Decision 2010/28, November 23, 2010, the DDR Inter-agency Working Group is the vehicle for creating UN coherence.

14. Bonard and Conoir, *Evaluation of UNDP Reintegration Programmes.*

15. The DDR programs reviewed were Burundi, Côte d'Ivoire, DRC, Haiti, Kosovo, Nepal, Somalia, and Sudan.

16. International Labour Organization, *Socio-Economic Reintegration of Ex-Combatants* (Geneva: ILO Programme: Guidelines for Crisis Response and Reconstruction, 2009).

17. Drawn from my discussions with Inter-agency Working Group on DDR representatives from two UN agencies.

18. Guy Lamb, *Assessing the Reintegration of Ex-combatants in the Context of Instability and Informal Economies: The Cases of the Central African Republic, the Democratic Republic of Congo, and South Sudan* (Washington, DC: International Bank for Reconstruction and Development, and World Bank, December 2011), 12.

19. Kilroy, "Disarmament, Demobilisation, and Reintegration."

20. Ibid., citing Eric G. Berman and Melissa T. Labonte, "Sierra Leone," in *Twenty-First-Century Peace Operations*, ed. William J. Durch (Washington, DC: United States Institute of Peace, 2006), who assert that the DDR program in Sierra Leone led to a perceptible reduction in small arms in society.

21. Robert Muggah, "Innovations in DDR Policy and Research: Reflections on the Last Decade" (NUPI Working Paper 774, Norwegian Institute of International Affairs, Oslo, 2010).

22. Ibid.

23. Ibid.

24. Ibid.

25. Nat J. Colletta, Jens Samuelsson Schjörlien, and Hannes Berts, *Interim Stabilisation: Balancing Security and Development in Post-conflict Peacebuilding* (Stockholm: Folke Bernadotte Academy, Ministry of Foreign Affairs, 2008).

26. See Bleie and Shrestha, *DDR in Nepal.*

27. Dean Piedmont, "From War to Peace, from Soldier to Peacebuilder: Interim Stabilisation Measures in Afghanistan and South Sudan," *Journal of Peacebuilding and Development* 7, no. 1 (2012), accessed April 1, 2013, http://dx.doi.org/10.1080 /154231666.3012.719404.

28. Vanessa Prinz, *Group Cohesion in Non-state Armed Groups: Gains and Challenges of Group Reintegration of Former Combatants in Disarmament,*

Demobilization and Reintegration (DDR) Processes (Master's thesis, Hamburg University, July 2012).

29. Elizabeth Molloy, *Gender and the Discourse of DDR: A Post-structural Analysis of the Gendered Discourse of the IDDRS and the Post-conflict Situation* (Master's paper, Education, Gender and International Development, UCL Institute of Education, University College London, 2011).

30. Richard Bowd, *From Combatant to Civilian: The Social Reintegration of Ex-combatants in Rwanda and the Implications for Social Capital and Reconciliation* (PhD dissertation, York, UK: Post-war Reconstruction and Development Unit, University of York, September 2008).

31. Ibid., i.

32. Ibid., 77, drawn from Robert Putnam, *Making Democracy Work: Civic Traditions in Modern Italy* (Princeton, NJ: Princeton University Press, 1993).

33. Ibid., 71, 72, drawn from D. Halpern, *Social Capital* (Cambridge: Polity Press, 2005).

34. Bowd, *From Combatant to Civilian,* 117.

35. The four studies are: Ingvild Magnaes Gjelsvik and Tore Bjørgo, *Ex-pirates in Somalia: Disengagement Processes and Reintegration Programming*; Zuhra Bahman and Stina Torjesen, *Double Disillusionment: Disengaging from the Insurgency in Afghanistan*; Tone Bheie and Ramesh Shrestha, *DDR in Nepal: Stakeholder Politics and the Implications for Reintegration and a Process of Disengagement;* and Tone Bleie, *Post-war Communities in Somalia and Nepal: Gendered Politics of Exclusion and Inclusion*; all (Tromsø, Norway: International Research Group on Reintegration, Centre for Peace Studies, Tromsø University, 2012). All four studies can be downloaded at: https//www.en.uit.no/forskning/forskningsgrupper/medlemmer?p_id=377750.

36. Bleie and Shrestha, *DDR in Nepal.*

37. Zuhra Bahman and Stina Torjesen, *Double Disillusionment.*

38. Ingvild Magnaes Gjelsvik and Tore Bjørgo, *Ex-pirates in Somalia.*

39. Muggah, "Policy Innovations in DDR."

40. Molloy, "The Qualitative Quantitative Dilemma."

41. For "do no harm," see Mary Anderson, *Options for Aid in Conflict: Lessons from Field Experience* (Cambridge, MA: CDA Collaborative, 2000).

42. Eric Y. Shibuya, *Demobilizing Irregular Forces* (Cambridge, UK: Polity Press, 2012).

43. Anders Themnér, "A Leap of Faith: Explaining Ex-combatant Violence" (presentation, International Studies Association Conference, Montreal, March 16–19, 2011).

44. Melanne A. Civic and Michael Miklaucic, eds., *Monopoly of Force: The Nexus of DDR and SSR* (Washington, DC: National Defense University Press, 2011), 265–284.

45. David J. Kilcullen, *Counterinsurgency* (Oxford: Oxford University Press, 2010).

46. Richard Millett, ed., *Demobilization, Disarmament, and Reintegration (DDR): Case Studies of Partial Success and Enduring Dilemmas* (Fort Leavenworth, KS: Combat Studies Institute Press, forthcoming 2017); includes review of DDR by renowned political scientists in nine countries—Haiti, Iraq, Nicaragua, Angola, El Salvador, Bosnia Herzegovina, Liberia, Colombia, and Afghanistan.

9

Crosscutting Issues

Successful DDR should act as a contribution to the delivery of a peace process or to the reduction of armed violence; it should mutually support and affect other practice areas with the same objectives. DDR considerations do not begin with the cessation of violence. Rather, they should be considered by peace mediators during negotiations and be positioned to contribute effectively to the eventual cessation of violence and sustainability of the cease-fire. Justice and transitional justice are two of the most controversial crosscutting issues affecting the postconflict communities' sensibilities, including their perceptions, attitudes, and trust concerning accountability, justice, retribution, reconciliation, and reparations. These issues are the subject of heated debate between the justice/human rights sector and peacebuilders regarding the complementarities, tensions, and relative levels of mutual exclusivity or otherwise between justice and peace. This chapter considers the controversial practice of granting amnesty in the context of DDR—that is, the sacrificing of justice for peace. It includes a review of the controversial amnesty offered to "the boys in the creeks" of the Niger Delta and the innovative partial amnesty being implemented in Colombia.

DDR is a concept under threat. A securitized perspective sees DDR as being synonymous with SSR. This is seen as a function of security and external agency in the "shock and awe" mode and is to be tackled by going in heavy and at scale. Yet such a perspective is missing any commitment to people-centered approaches, which is the overarching agenda of human security. Linked to the threat of oversecuritization is the current tendency to privatize and subcontract the delivery of both in-conflict and postconflict interventions to for-profit-motivated private military and security companies. Is this trend unavoidable, and can the inherent dangers be mitigated?

Within the UN, the response of the Secretariat to resistance by some members of the Security Council and General Assembly to the universal acceptance of the human security agenda and the responsibility to protect

(R2P) concept appears to be carried only in the promotion of a watered-down and less binding version of the human security agenda represented in "The Centrality of Protection in Humanitarian Action" document.[1] Does this response constitute a threat to the overarching human security philosophy that has heretofore driven DDR planning and implementation? Is it a compromise gone too far?

But opportunities for DDR also abound. DDR is often viewed as a Western-oriented concept addressing Western values. Can support for regionally, culturally, and religiously sensitive approaches to DDR, through support for more nationally owned and Islamic-led DDR, eventually contribute to reduction in armed violence in conflict-ridden countries where radical Islam is increasing in dominance, such as in Libya, Syria, Iraq, Mali, the tribal areas of Pakistan, and Afghanistan? What new policy guidance is the UN considering in light of the current focus on the threat posed by violent extremism? Can a heightened sensitivity to local solutions lay the foundations for a next generation of DDR?

Critical Crosscutting Issues Arising in Classic DDR

DDR is not a freestanding practice area being planned and implemented in a bubble. It supports, contributes to, and affects the entire spectrum of critical peacebuilding sectors in bringing about a sustainable cessation of violence and a transition to peace in political and socioeconomic normative environments. Such sectors affected by DDR include the peace negotiations, the implementation of confidence-building and stabilization measures, early recovery, governance, rule of law, security, counterinsurgency, counterterrorism, counter violent extremism, the SSR/DDR nexus, justice and transitional justice, gender perspective and equity, the rights of children, poverty reduction, and knowledge management (together with communications and information technology). The case studies cited so far in this book have addressed, in an incremental way, many of these sectors and their associated concepts. Three sectors that have been inadequately covered so far merit special attention here: DDR during negotiations, amnesty and justice issues, and the essential element of a good communications strategy.

DDR During Peace Mediation

DDR practitioners are summoned to the field as an afterthought in order to deal with the technical aspects of program design and implementation of DDR in a classic environment—that is, postconflict peacebuilding in the context of a comprehensive peace accord ending an intrastate conflict. This occurs usually long after a comprehensive peace agreement has been signed, the prevailing political realities have been established, and even the disarmament has commenced. However, in the absence of DDR expert advice at the precomprehensive peace agreement political mediation, technical aspects of the three processes—the D, D, and R—are often disconnected. It has been assumed that military hands-on technical capacity in security, observation, weapons handling, disposal of ordnance, and logistics support is sufficient to address the immediate needs in the cessation of armed violence. The rationale, which is based in the intense priority to stop the violence, is that the mechanisms to support the reintegration of former combatants can be worked out later. As an example, the UN Assistance Mission in Sierra Leone had been operating for a year and disarmament and demobilization were into the third attempt before a civilian DDR section was established in mid-2001. In the UN Mission in Liberia, the initial attempt at disarmament and demobilization was launched in December 2003, without DDR having been adequately considered during negotiations and without having a DDR expert in the mission.

The application of DDR expertise early in the planning phases for the deployment of a UN mission is now seen as a wise move. In addition to assessing technical requirements, it can also ensure that political aspects and implications of DDR are considered and factored into agreements at the earliest stages of mediation. Due to the context-specific nature, uniqueness, and political complexity associated with each conflict and its immediate aftermath, a customized approach to DDR must be factored into each agreement. Appropriate design and scope, as well as a clear projection of expected outcomes of the program, must be agreed upon. Mediators contributing to peace negotiations must have an integrated understanding of the political and technical implications and must remain discreetly cognizant of the planning considerations for DDR. In general, those considerations should judiciously not be fully shared with the negotiating parties before the time is right. As with amnesties, the provisions of DDR should not be overtly relevant at the early stages of peace negotiations. More relevant security, political, and economic aspects of the end of hostilities should be agreed to first, with the arrangements for DDR following as one of the magnanimous confidence-building measures that contribute to addressing security dilemmas, building trust, and finally sealing the deal.

It is likely that the negotiating parties will have, during the peace process, requested and received nondirective technical advice on DDR, usually by way of international consultants presenting relevant case studies on what has worked elsewhere. They may become acutely aware of examples of practice, the potential shape of institutional structures to support DDR, the implication of cash elements in DDR, how security dilemmas have been addressed, how leaders fared vis-à-vis DDR and amnesties, transitional justice issues, possible reintegration options, and so forth. These issues may be priorities to belligerent group leadership and indeed to the foot soldiers waiting for information, perhaps in difficult circumstances, neither at war nor yet at peace. Yet, mediators must encourage the deferral of DDR matters until close to the final phase of negotiations. The purpose of Kevin Ong's book is to provide peace mediators with the essential information about DDR to allow them to carefully weigh the implications of including the provisions for a DDR process in the final peace agreement, which should assist in ensuring astute judgment in contributing to the political processes and decisions associated with the negotiations.[2] Rarely does the qualified mediator, even one with great political and diplomatic acumen, have a detailed understanding of the implications of the political and technical aspects of DDR. Likewise, an experienced DDR implementer will rarely have the necessary diplomatic acumen and experience to be an effective mediator. They do not need to. An effective compromise during peace negotiations involves the mediation team keeping a DDR expert tucked away on the fringes of the mediation and negotiations to offer discreet technical guidance to the mediation team as required.

Such was the case during peace negotiations brokered by Gabon in the 2007 Global Peace Accord, signed in Libreville, and in the follow-on technical meetings that brought about a temporary cessation of hostilities between belligerents in the Central African Republic.[3] Although the peace eventually fell apart after three years, the associated DDR that resulted from discreet expert input on the fringes of the negotiations made initial rapid progress in developing appropriate and agreed-upon institutional structures, saw beneficiary lists prepared, led to agreed-upon validation processes and eligibility criteria, prepared the program document, and developed a joint operational plan. All of this occurred because of the provisions for DDR that were included in the negotiations. Considering the promising start, the outcomes could have been more successful. However, given the factionalized power maneuvering and the environment of elite rent taking that existed in the failed state of the Central African Republic in 2009, the process failed. Even so, the recommendation here concerning the place of DDR in peace mediation, in light of the evolving theory, is to engage DDR experts early in the mediation process, keeping them as a discreet adviser to the mediators.

Amnesties, Justice, and Transitional Justice Mechanisms

Amnesty. Amnesties have become synonymous with the offer of voluntary DDR programs in postconflict situations or in reducing armed violence by nonstate armed groups in stressed state environments. This is especially so in the context of DDR after a comprehensive peace accord that has resulted in a cessation of violence where there is no clear victor. It is a trade-off of justice over peace that brings the nonstate armed actors (with the victor being, de facto or otherwise, the state) to the negotiation table. It is the "carrot" that sees all or some of the rebel groups, the criminal groups, or the armed dissident groups retain some of their freedom, their civil status, their dignity, and perhaps some of the spoils of war, all in return for participating in the peace process. Thus, they can avoid the "inconvenience" of being held accountable for their actions during the conflict, criminal activity, or dissidence. Amnesties are a mechanism for offering strong negotiating leverage to the legislative authorities; as such, they can bring about an early cessation of violence and encourage political engagement by the nonstate armed groups in the absence of a sense of victor's justice, permitting post-conflict governance to reemerge. Further, an advantage from the state's perspective is that its sins are also overlooked, if not forgiven. Amnesties are mechanisms easily implemented, merely with a declaration and an act of legislation, with huge intrinsic value but little financial cost to the state.

An amnesty, if it is to be used, should be an encouragement to seal the deal that finally ends armed violence; it should not be the reason for ending the violence. The moral arguments associated with the issue of amnesties and the forgoing of justice associated with DDR processes are extraordinarily emotive, complex, and controversial. This is because they demand of the most wronged sector of the community—the victims of the armed activities—to forgo basic justice. The morality of offering amnesty in the context of DDR is not enhanced by the fact that the biggest sacrifice of justice is demanded of the "small" people—the communities, the families of the murdered and disappeared, the amputated, the ethnically cleansed, the kidnapped, raped, and brutalized—while the UN retains the moral high ground for itself and its own sensitivities through the following caveat. Yes, let there be amnesty in the context of a peace process, but the UN will not honor an amnesty that would excuse those "most responsible for war crimes, crimes against human rights or crimes against humanity." Such a clause was the crux for Foday Sankoh of the Revolutionary United Front in Sierra Leone's peace process, who was eventually arrested following an altercation where his bodyguards fired on peaceful protesters, to face transitional justice.[4] It is the foot soldier, the direct perpetrator of the crime, who is resettling back into the community, face to face with the victims, and who is exempted from the administration of justice. Although witnessing the leadership of the crimes face justice may offer some consolation, how difficult is it for victims to observe the actual perpetrators thriving in the very communities that they brutalized, while benefiting from reintegration supports?

Amnesty for the "boys in the creeks."[5] The environment of the Niger Delta of Nigeria is one of historical extreme intertribal violence, including the Biafra War of 1967–1970, and of social injustice. For the past twenty years, the "boys in the creeks"—armed, organized, quasi-political criminal gangs—have been sharing the enormous spoils of *bunkering*, or illegally syphoning off oil from the pipelines of the Niger Delta oil fields. In a conflict-ridden symbiotic relationship, they accommodated not only the Nigerian government's Joint Military Taskforce, which was supposed to end the scourge, but also the notorious elite, government officials, and businesspeople. Nigeria's effort to buy off the "boys in the creek" offers an example of the exclusive use of amnesty in the context of DDR. This amnesty was done in the absence of other effective efforts to address armed violence or extreme social inequity, atrocious environmental conditions, and the related abject poverty of a majority of the delta's forty million people. By 2008, the impact of the organized violence, the theft of the oil, and the kidnapping and intimidation of oil company staff by the gangs, in addition to occasional military atrocities against the civilian population, had brought oil production to 30 percent of capacity. This worried trading partners, particularly the United States, which at the time depended on Nigeria for 18 percent of its oil imports. It also severely threatened Nigeria's foreign reserves.[6]

In 2009, concurrent with robust military attacks on delta gang camps and villages, President Umaru Musa Yar'Adua, cherry-picked from two recommendations of the more than thirty offered by the very credible *Report of the Technical Committee for the Niger Delta*, which had been tasked with finding a solution, and announced a blanket amnesty for those militants who would disarm and enter a DDR process. In a less-than-convincing charade of virtual disarmament, some senior gang leaders and a number of foot soldiers were paraded in front of the media, ostensibly handing in weapons. There are credible claims that the arms displayed to the media were actually supplied by the military and that large sums of money were allegedly paid to senior commanders of the gangs, in addition to other incentives.[7] By September 2010, the government was claiming, to the derision of informed civil society organizations, that 20,000 rebels had been processed through reintegration.[8] Trading partners were temporarily appeased, and prebendalistic cash flows were apparently uninterrupted. However, violence and disruption of oil production rapidly reemerged. Due to the failure to address key elements of the socioeconomic and environmental inequity and lawlessness, increasing tensions related to the spread of Islamic violent extremism from the north, and the reemergence of the unresolved east-west tribal issues of the Biafra War, the powder keg of the Niger Delta, which can spark violent conflict and huge population movements throughout West Africa, remains primed.[9] In this case, in maintaining the status quo for a short period, an amnesty was wasted from the perspective of making a contribution to sustainable peace, though it is evident that its impact on sustaining cash flows to those concerned was as intended.

Nonamnesty in Colombia. For more than fifty years, Colombia has been wracked by armed violence associated with Marxist revolution and organized crime associated primarily with the trafficking of cocaine, of which Colombia produces about 50 percent of global consumption. In the past decade, the state launched four major DDR processes to address the conflict. These efforts up to 2006 included catering for collective demobilization of paramilitary groups, primarily focused on United Self-Defense Forces of Colombia, and offering supports for short-term socioeconomic reinsertion. Since then, the efforts have focused more on offering individuals the opportunity to disassociate from the leftist guerrilla groups (Revolutionary Armed Forces of Colombia and National Liberation Army) and to enter a process of longer-term socioeconomic reintegration. The complexity, uniqueness, and lessons learned in the Colombian DDR processes were reviewed in an earlier chapter; the focus here is on the innovative approach to the concept of amnesty while attempting to retain both a sense of justice and a contribution to the counterinsurgency effort.

Until 2010, President Álvaro Uribe viewed DDR in Colombia as an aspect of a robust counterinsurgency campaign, mixing encouragement to defect with offensive operations. The campaign's chosen "soft" aspect for drawing off members from the guerrilla movement had been to offer incentives and a level of refuge in the state to reticent and more pliable guerrillas who were willing to return to civil society. This tactic was also designed to improve intelligence for targeting incorrigible guerrillas through the interrogation of the deserters. In light of the resources at stake in Colombia's guerrilla activities and considering the confusion of ideological and criminal motivation, the national reach of the guerrilla movements was great, and their response to dissidence brutal. Progress in the peace process has been very slow and costly, exacerbated by intractability and inadequate compromise in negotiations.

The DDR program was somewhat energized in 2006 when responsibility for its management passed to the newly established presidential High Council for Reintegration. From 2011, President Juan Manuel Santos directed that, in addition to military solutions, a more holistic approach to conflict resolution must be strengthened. He saw the need for community security approaches to address bottom-up, community-based contributions and benefits from DDR—that is, a community-centric approach as opposed to a combatant-centric approach.

From the beginning of DDR in Colombia, the implementation of DDR was underscored by a belief on the government side that the guerrillas would eventually be defeated. A full amnesty was not considered appropriate for Colombia's needs. In 2005, a new legal framework—the Justice and Peace Law (Law 975)—was created and promulgated as a mechanism of transitional justice viewed as a "partial amnesty." This act offered to former combatants who would provide "full and frank confessions of the crimes committed and the return of stolen property" the possibility of reduced or commuted jail sentences, along with obligatory community service. This arrangement did not preclude strong-armed military interrogation methods or the allegation of interests-based collusion. There were international doubts about the sincerity of the efforts to find an equitable and just resolution to the conflict in a highly politicized environment, with allegations abounding of criminal collusion in various elements of the processes. However, the DDR community of practice saw the law as a major break with the concept of offering blanket amnesties. Unfortunately, due to a shortage of funds and the legal complexity in implementing it, its impact was limited.[10] This legal framework was strengthened considerably in 2011, however, with the promulgation of the Victim's Law, which offered reparations or the return of land stolen during the conflict.[11]

The legal framework continues to evolve in line with the dynamic environment to better address needs. The current round of negotiations in Havana between the government of Colombia and the Revolutionary Armed Forces of Colombia have resulted in limited agreement, with the target of signing a final comprehensive peace accord by late 2016, which would then be promulgated by national referendum. Four main conflict areas now agreed to are (1) land reform issues that contribute to poverty alleviation in rural areas; (2) political participation once final agreement is reached; (3) elimination of the illegal drugs trade; and (4) the application of transitional justice in offering a limited amnesty for combatants, other than those who have committed the most serious crimes. In the most recent round of negotiations, the Revolutionary Armed Forces of Colombia leadership was not willing to accept reduced sentencing associated with the Colombian non-amnesty arrangement. Despite strong political opposition by those angry at the level of concessions being made to the rebels, the "bullet has been bitten," and government is reconsidering the idea of a broader amnesty as part of the cost of finding a solution to the ongoing conflict. The implementation of the agreed issues and the resolution of those outstanding, including security and DDR issues, are likely to be challenging and arduous.

In August 2016, that accord incorporating elements of the partial amnesty was achieved in Havana. Rebels who admit their role against the people will not be subject to jail time, but to community service and acts of reparation. While both the government and *FARC* claim that this is a win/win result, the opposition are complaining against ratification on the grounds of justice denied.

DDR and mechanisms of transitional justice.[12] Ideally, war crimes and crimes against humanity should be addressed by the state in which they are committed. However, the legislative framework and legal system of a fragile postconflict state are likely to have limited capacity, resources, or political will to address any such crimes that occurred during the war. In such a case, mechanisms of transitional justice, both formal and informal, can provide a way forward to accountability, truth seeking, and, ultimately, reconciliation. The International Criminal Court (ICC), national authorities, and traditional systems often support such mechanisms. In this context, there are considerable potential tensions and complementarities between DDR and transitional justice.[13]

The reduction in the capacity of former belligerents to intimidate society as a result of engagement in DDR can facilitate the implementation of transitional justice mechanisms. However, belligerents may be discouraged from entering DDR if they are concerned that they may be answerable to transitional justice mechanisms, which could delay the cessation of violence. This was the case with Joseph Kony and the Lord's Resistance Army in northern Uganda after his indictment by the ICC in 2005. Timely collaboration between DDR practitioners and ICC prosecutors could offset such outcomes; historically, however, prosecutors have tended not to see things quite this way.

As with Sierra Leone in 2001, aspects of developing a sustainable peace associated with DDR often depend on the ascendancy of a mind-set among the population that it is ready to sacrifice a considerable amount of justice for peace. However, in considering amnesties, the UN draws the line by ensuring that those most responsible for war crimes and crimes against humanity do answer; the ICC can offer an effective mechanism of transitional justice to address such situations. However, DDR implementers are often concerned that the launch of transitional justice mechanisms too early in the DDR process will drive critical leaders underground—this includes those who can deliver their fighters to the program and who are the greatest potential spoilers. This gives rise to tensions between the DDR implementers and the prosecutors in transitional justice and reflects one of the dangers of an uncoordinated, poorly timed launch of transitional justice mechanisms.

Similarly, the ICC prosecutor's office is often frustrated by the reticence of DDR programs, in their serious commitment to confidentiality, to make databases on participants available to any third party, including the Court. Such databases often list details of service, units, locations, armament, and actions in which the participant was engaged, which might contribute to prosecution evidence. Beyond these tensions, complementarities lie largely in the capacity of transitional justice mechanisms to facilitate accountability and reconciliation and to contribute to improved community security as society realizes that the impunity associated with the state of conflict is ended.[14]

Together with the ICC's mechanisms of transitional justice, postconflict countries often consider the mechanism of truth and reconciliation commissions, following the South African model. According to Tim Kelsall, "The unfortunate fact is that it seems that such a mechanism needs the imprimatur of giants such as Nelson Mandela or Bishop Desmond Tutu and a facilitating context before they can be effective. In reality, Truth and Reconciliation Commissions rarely reach the truth."[15] In the case of Sierra Leone, however, it seems that the commission did contribute somewhat to inculcating the concept of reconciliation. The attempt at such a commission in Haiti (1995–1996) was less useful and, eventually, in a cloud of *marronage*, fizzled out without significant publication, following considerable intimidation of some witnesses.

Informal mechanisms of transitional justice—that is, traditional transitional justice mechanisms such as rituals and cultural ceremonies specific to location, community, clan, or tribe—have been used effectively in facilitating an environment for reconciliation in the context of DDR. Such mechanisms include cleansing ceremonies, courts of community elders, and so forth. The most celebrated example of such a community-based transitional justice mechanism used in the context of DDR is probably the grassroots Rwandan Gacaca courts. The government of Paul Kagame developed the Gacaca courts—traditional community courts with local variations in procedure and authority, depending on the region—into a homogenized institutionalized structure of elected members. This move largely dissipated the local legitimacy and community/customary nature by formalizing the practice. Yet, the nationalization and standardization of the traditional practice and the imposition of formal procedures by the Kagame government diminished the effectiveness of this mechanism by distancing it from local ownership, custom, and practice under the control of traditional authority.[16] It is critical to preserve the local ownership of such informal mechanisms of transitional justice to preserve their credibility and local impact in the context of cultural awareness.

A cautionary note to practitioners, however: Emerging anecdotal evidence indicates that in certain cleansing ceremonies associated with the powerful secret community societies of Sierra Leone (the *Poro* and the *Bundu*), reintegrating child soldiers were in fact drowned in water-based cleansing ceremonies and female reintegrating former combatants were subject to female genital mutilation.[17]

Communications Strategies in DDR

Communications must be a fully embedded aspect of any program in a community that is to gain the support of a broad sector of society, in order to gain their positive attitudes, perceptions, and trust. DDR is a practice that occurs in a particularly volatile and sensitive environment. It affects the lives, sensitivities, and sensibilities of entire populations. Communications are a technically complex, professionalized practice area that affects the social response and attitude of stakeholders toward any intervention, especially one with such broad implications as DDR. Yet, communications are consistently the weak link in DDR implementation. Frequently, DDR programs fail to apply the appropriate expertise in planning for, securing, and consistently managing the required resources to implement the appropriate communications strategy that will address the requirements of program stakeholders.

The dissemination of accurate, targeted messages in the management of expectations, perceptions, and attitudes of all sectors of society is a critical aspect contributing to positive outcomes in DDR. Even in a meticulously planned DDR program that has preempted the critical needs and sensitivities of former combatants, program stakeholders are often subject to poor dissemination and misinformation, both malicious and accidental. This creates a negative narrative that undermines the potential of the program to achieve its objectives by deterring support of bilateral actors, donors, government collaborating actors, and parallel programs. Poor communication ultimately undermines the community's perception of the program, destroying the critical asset of public opinion. It further discourages participation by belligerents, which can contribute to volatility in the security environment.

This aspect must be addressed by the development and implementation of an adequately funded, integrated, professionally designed communications strategy. Such a strategy requires input from all relevant stakeholders in DDR, sending agreed messages through appropriate media to targeted audiences to address the specific context of the DDR program. The funding, professional capacities, and energy required to ensure the coherence, efficiency, effectiveness, appropriate integration, and political sensitivity of such a communications strategy are frequently underestimated, leading to further undermining of the DDR program. Underperformance in the area of communications resulting from poor planning, absence of locally informed and conflict-sensitive expertise, and under resourcing is a lesson learned and relearned in the evaluation of multiple DDR programs.[18]

A DDR program's communications strategy must be prioritized in the planning phase, as it is a critical, context-specific element in the management of perceptions and attitudes. The communications strategy requires constant management through dynamic monitoring, evaluation, and adjustment to address the evolving environment and to address specific events. In an era of ubiquitous social media and mobile communications technology, proactive, flexible, rapidly mobilized communications is an essential tool for a DDR program in supporting aspects of program dissemination, in managing targeted information or misinformation, and in rapidly addressing specific events such as security incidents. The development of an effective communications strategy will be broadly consulted; will address the concerns of main stakeholders; will operate through appropriate local media; and will be culturally, religiously, and conflict sensitive. It will ensure that a reputation for broadcasting consistently accurate and timely information will contribute to the program, earning the positive attitudes, perceptions, and trust of stakeholders.

DDR and SSR: Subversion of the Theory

Convergences exist between evolving DDR theory and the doctrine of counterinsurgency.[19] Many of these convergences, if considered and addressed, offer positive potential for both counterinsurgency and DDR. However, the following review focuses on an evolving mind-set within the security sector—particularly, in the United States—that conveniently lumps SSR and DDR together, to be dealt with through an iron fist of mass and agency. Such a mind-set mirrors the current US military-industrial complex polemic highlighting what the conservative side sees as an unwarranted focus on "soft" considerations, such as cultural sensitivities and the time, human resources, and treasure necessary to "win" the people, as advocated in modern counterinsurgency doctrine. Shifting its gaze onto future potential DDR and SSR processes, both of which offer lucrative markets, this mind-set is fusing them together, while ignoring their often independent characters, as well as the principles of the human security approaches to DDR. This for-profit or securitized approach threatens to discredit the practice area and obliterate the overarching imperatives that have guided the evolution of DDR theory to date.

Alison Laporte-Oshiro, writing for United States Institute of Peace (USIP), which is considered a moderate US think tank, and drawing from the findings of a meeting of the USIP Working Group on SSR in September 2011, offered a disturbing insight into the conceptual convergence in the minds of US security professionals toward a hard-line implementation of both SSR and DDR.[20] Such a convergence exposes the preference, even at the level of a moderate organization (assuming that the participants of the meeting can be considered predominantly conservative), of US-security-focused professionals to apply mass, dominance, and agency in its international interventions, including in the DDR sector. The paper's conclusions and recommendations are based on a selective and revisionist spin on recent US experience in SSR and DDR. It implies limited concern for the outcomes of such processes for the host nation, a movement away from a people-centered approach, and an extraordinary sense of agency; it seems to emanate from the perspective of the interests of the post-Afghanistan/Iraq military-industrial services complex.[21] The recommendations by the USIP working group advise that the United States, in a post-Afghanistan period, must prepare to address SSR and DDR scenarios purely in the context of "consolidating legitimate force in the hands of the state" by "going in heavy, tackling DDR and SSR in tandem and consolidating US capacity to implement both tasks in a coordinated, scalable way."[22]

Without specifying the details, the recommendations cite the US experience in Afghanistan, Iraq, Liberia, Haiti, Bosnia, and Kosovo as contributing to these lessons. Certainly there are many lessons to draw from the US engagement in both SSR and DDR processes in these examples. Conceding that the experience is "checkered" is something of an understatement, as most DDR practitioners would contend that the cited engagements were disastrous from a human security perspective. The launch of the Liberian DDR process in 2003 was formally deemed a disaster by UN review.[23] The program, though eventually making a contribution to the stabilization of peace by including huge numbers of beneficiaries, proceeded as a weapons buy-back that grossly overran in budget and time. Likewise, the weapons collected in the US Marine–supported DDR program in Haiti in 1994 are still turning up in gang-related crime in Port au Prince.[24] In Kosovo, the conversion of the criminalized Kosovo Liberation Army into a coherent force has not contributed significantly to improving the quality of democracy or the rule of law in Europe. In Afghanistan, where DDR was implemented under the mandate of the NATO/International Security Assistance Force, elements of the Afghan New Beginning Program could be considered successful if weight of hardware collected were the important factor. But as the disarmament of the selected heavy weapons of the Northern Alliance was underway in Afghanistan in 2004–2005, NATO was busy rearming their favored warlords.[25]

The paper's first lesson citing the necessity for the United States to "go in heavy" ignores the potential for local solutions and denigrates the concept of national ownership.[26] It ignores the fact that US capacity has not delivered positive results in any of the examples cited or even in those not cited, where mass technological superiority and firepower were applied. The rationalization that when you fail with a specific policy, you should keep doing it until you get it right is what Kurt Jacobsen referred to as "repetition compulsion," in referring to the application of firepower and mass in the "shock and awe" policy in Iraq.[27] This "go in heavy" recommendation is coming from the same mind-sets that led to the US defeat in Vietnam and the ambiguity and absence of a long-term vision in both Iraq and Afghanistan.[28] It seems to be directing the United States down the same path of repetition compulsion regarding its future engagements in SSR and DDR, but now it urges the US to do it bigger.

The exhortation that DDR and SSR must be tackled in tandem reinforces the prioritization of an overarching philosophy of the security focus in addressing both processes. DDR is not only a security concept. Although the disarmament and demobilization processes have major security considerations, DDR is primarily a "civilizing" process. It is certainly political, but it is more in the realm of human security. Whereas DDR can be an aspect of SSR, it is not universally addressed in tandem with or dependent on SSR. There are tensions and complementarities between the two, and, where they occur together, each must be designed in cognizance and consideration of the other. They are not interdependent and, though related, should not be intrinsically linked. Although human security outcomes should emanate from successful SSR, it is more about making security forces more effective and context specific or about building the capacity of rule-of-law mechanisms. SSR is a security-driven concept. On the contrary, DDR, as it has evolved, is ultimately a human security–driven concept concerned with putting arms beyond use in the context of developing community security. In such cases, DDR is a parallel process to SSR; it is not convergent. Further, the implementing personalities in both areas are usually from different professional backgrounds—security and humanitarian—and operate with mind-sets that are difficult to reconcile.

Modern approaches to DDR confirm the efficacy of the commitment to bottom-up approaches, to community-based approaches, and to implementing "do no harm" mechanisms in addressing community violence reduction. Although the US Agency for International Development (USAID) can certainly claim significant successes in certain programs that addressed violence reduction through competent implementing partners with a commitment to human security, such approaches are not to the fore in any of the examples cited. Due to severe capacity constraints, USAID and the US State Department, in particular, have been required to subcontract program implementation to a limited number of facilitated-bid, reduced-tendering-process, and rapidly engaged contractors, such as the enormous Chemonics, PAE, or DynCorp International.[29] This commercialization of aid is greatly facilitated by the securitization of humanitarian interventions and is contributing to the subversion of the purpose of peacebuilding and development aid. The Copenhagen School of International Relations sees securitization[30] as a synthesis of constructivist and classical political realism in its approach to international security.[31] It is process orientated—beyond focusing on the material distribution of threat, it considers how the actor can transform certain issues into security matters. It can be used or abused to enable extraordinary means, all in the name of security. Muggah suggested that the practice of DDR is moving beyond the traditional civil-military paradigm, probably reflecting the difficulty of developing the appropriate capacities within the security and development institutions, toward a greater dependence on subcontracting to private security contractors.

From a comparative perspective, the Provincial Reconstruction Team (PRT) experiment in Afghanistan and Iraq demonstrated the organizational and cultural difficulties in an "all of government" (or comprehensive) approach in a civil-military environment. The stuttering attempts to co-opt social science, as with Project Minerva and the Human Terrain System in the US counterinsurgency marriage to the "war on terror," should have proven that civil-military coordination, particularly in the US case, means the dominance of military priorities.[32] This attitude is irreconcilable with either a social scientific approach or the human security motivation of most in the professional social scientific and humanitarian sectors. Taking a step beyond John Nagl's assertion, supported by David Kilcullen, that the US military institution is not a learning organization, we could apply the same idea to the associated support base for the military-industrial services complex.[33] From the cultural- and values-based constraints to the complexity of civil-military cooperation, these recommendations demonstrate that US hawks really haven't "gotten it" yet. Go in heavy, implement in tandem, whole-of-government approach, integrate capacity, US agency and resourcing—essentially this is about a supply-driven approach rather than a demand for results-based interventions or "successful" SSR or DDR.

The UN, in pursuing its efforts to implement the recommendations for civilian capacity development as outlined in the Guéhenno report of 2011, is striving to focus more and operationalize their institutional strengths. Although this effort will certainly necessitate development of an innovative approach to identifying the resources for applying peacebuilding interventions, conceding to a supply-driven approach in a poorly considered way will gradually open the door to less-than-altruistically motivated, private, for-profit contractors. This will soon pose a serious threat to the design, planning, and implementation of both SSR and DDR.

Many private military security companies—mainly US, but also British, South African, Eastern European, and Russian—are facing reduced engagement in Afghanistan, Iraq, and so on. As such, they have expanded their purview and capacities. Some have consolidated cozy relationships with governments and allegedly with senior policymaking UN officers. Many enjoy nebulous accountability, limited legal constraints, and questionable human rights records; are unconstrained by the human security paradigm; and are avaricious.[34] In the US case, some operate lobby groups on Capitol Hill and are not subject to the standards of international law. The infiltration of fundamentally humanitarian program implementation by private military security companies is not an ambiguous threat; it is already happening. Their allocation of formal UN contracts increased by 73 percent from 2009 to 2010.[35] This is happening in an environment of absence of transparency, clear policy, or regulation. The current trend sees the private military security industry also beginning to extend its tentacles beyond defense sector reform related DDR, as in Liberia in 2004–2006, into broader DDR of irregular armed groups. This latter area is seen as a lucrative growth sector, though it is one for which private military security companies are poorly profiled or motivated.[36]

The dangers posed by the use of private military security companies to handle security issues in international interventions are reflected in the debacle of the truncated intervention of US-led private security contractors in Somalia in 2012. (This included interventions led by Erik Prince, former chief executive officer of Blackwater Worldwide, now rebranded as Academi, who is currently CEO of Frontier Services Group, purveyors of "expeditionary logistics.") This intervention saw the creation of the Puntland Maritime Police Force while engaging predominantly South African mercenaries in training. As the funds expired, the teams of Somali military pirate hunters were then abandoned in their camps in the Somali desert. Further, a UN investigative group uncovered a network of collaborating private security companies, led by the secretive Sterling Corporate Services, which has registered offices in Dubai, that colluded to create a "brazen, large-scale and protracted violation" of the arms embargo in Somalia.[37] (Sterling is a reimaging of the notorious mercenary contractor Saracen International.)

The indications are that for-profit-motivated contractors lack commitment, sustainability, human security, or principled consideration—or even basic altruism. They are apparently constrained neither by the parameters of international law nor by international diplomatic protocols. Thus, they are occasionally leaving a bigger problem than they were originally contracted to resolve.[38] In the short term, the threat of a purely security-driven vision and profit motivation, coupled with a proposed sledgehammer power and mass methodology, bodes ill for the prospects of DDR.

Potential Regulation of Private Military Security Company Activities in Conflict or Postconflict Interventions

In 2008, Switzerland and the International Committee of the Red Cross initiated legally nonbinding guidelines to serve as a code of conduct for the activities of private military security companies in armed conflict. The result was the Montreux Document, which was agreed to by seventeen states, including the United States, UK, South Africa, Ukraine, France, and

Germany.[39] This self-regulatory guide, though imposing little compulsion, offers consensus regarding the obligations of states toward international law, international humanitarian law, and human rights law in relation to the activities of private military security companies during armed conflict. The document considers the obligations of contracting states, the states in which private military security companies are operating, and the home states of private military security company actors. However, although it focuses on the responsibilities of states, it does not consider the activities of those private military security companies or rebranded commercial mercenary companies working in postconflict environments or working with the UN.

Ase Gilje Ostensen reviewed how the UN uses private military security companies and recommended a way forward.[40] He noted the increasing prevalence of a broad range of UN family agencies, programs, and funds using such companies and a noted absence of transparency regarding policy or controls in relation to contracting. He specifically mentioned their use in SSR and DDR, apparently conflating the two practice areas just as Laporte-Oshiro's paper does. While suggesting that the UN should be the agency to globally regulate the activities of private military security companies, he felt that it should initially regulate its own practices in contracting private military security companies. In an ideal world, the UN would not be contracting private military security companies; however, in light of capacity constraints, the practice is unlikely to recede in the near future. Thus, Ostensen advised that one way to regulate the practice would be for the UN to endorse the International Code of Conduct for Private Security Service Providers, associated with the aforementioned Montreux Document. The UN would then only contract private military security companies that are signatories to the code. Although this does not address the need for a human security perspective, it would permit the UN to hold private military security companies accountable through contract termination or other sanctions in the event of human rights or international humanitarian law breaches, offering some improved protection to the institution.

The adaption of a code of conduct based on the currently voluntary European Union Strategy for Corporate Responsibility might offer a useful template.[41] Appropriate regulation might be achieved by creating a related code of Corporate Human Security Responsibility to cover the activities of all agencies, funds, programs, and corporate entities working in conflict and postconflict interventions and applying public funds. By making adherence to this code a contractual obligation, the threat of unethical and conflict-insensitive corporate activity that is not people centered can be reduced.

Human Security Agenda and Responsibility to Protect

A critical question currently arises in considering the UN's waning commitment to the human security agenda and to R2P. Human security, having been the humanitarian practitioner's overarching guiding principle since the mid-

1990s, offers something beyond rights-based approaches to human development, as reflected in the achievement of the Millennium Development Goals. However, it is an increasingly disputed concept, particularly so since the post-9/11 refocus on security. Some states are concerned that the implications for these two concepts gaining legally binding status would imply their prioritization over the primacy of state sovereignty. Debate on the concept of human security is also driven by a growing cognizance of the implications of its perceived Western-value relativism on regional cultural and religious sensitivities. Both of the concepts—human security and R2P—are receiving contracting mention in the UN humanitarian action– and protection-focused literature. Despite the General Assembly's commitment in September 2012 to continue to discuss human security, in my discussions with senior UN Secretariat staff in late 2012, I was told that the human security concept is dead. There are suggestions that it was killed by Japanese overpossessiveness and pushiness in promoting the idea in the General Assembly, which undermined the intended more-gradual and nuanced approach favored by Secretariat staff. The difficulty in gaining agreement, either in the General Assembly or the Security Council, to make the concepts legally binding is the implication that the UN could then approve interventions in a state to address issues under either the human security agenda or R2P, without the permission of the relevant state. Thus, both China and Russia, among others, are vehemently opposed to advancing the concepts to a legal status.

The veracity of the claim regarding the demise of the human security concept is somewhat evidenced by publication of two short, related documents—"The Centrality of Protection in Humanitarian Action" and "Rights Up Front: A Plan of Action to Strengthen the UN's Role in Protecting People in Crisis." The two documents were published concurrently in December 2013 by the UN and were endorsed by the Inter-agency Standing Committee principals (the heads of agencies responsible for policy guidance to UN humanitarian activities). The documents served as guidance for UN staff regarding the position of human rights in their work.[42] These guidance documents emphasize the responsibility of states within their own borders and of the UN system to humanity. However, they both pointedly avoid any implication of responsibility of member states to address breaches of international human rights law or humanitarian law in another state.

A cursory review of "The Centrality of Protection..." from the perspective of poststructural analysis (a critical analysis of the language used when "reading between the lines") is telling. The document demonstrates, through a process of linguistic acrobatics, delicate and convoluted dancing around the concepts of human security and R2P, while pointedly ignoring the elephant in the room and retreating from both. It fails to mention the freedoms from fear and want. It fails to espouse the primacy of rights-based approaches to humanitarian interventions in the context of those freedoms. It buries the position of the Universal Declaration on Human Rights in a please-all sea of hypersensitive language in an effort not to discommode those states that are not so committed to the provisions of the UN Charter (that is, the norms of universal values), while still retaining their membership. It omits mention of the word *responsibility,* a notion that might require someone to take action and that might result in someone being held accountable. It returns the institutional position of the UN to the Westphalian notion of the absolute primacy of the state sovereignty over the international responsibility to humanity. The absence of mention of *human security* or *R2P* screams. The Secretary-General's publication of "Rights Up Front" further underlines the failure of R2P to gain traction as a legally binding concept in the General Assembly.[43]

The launch of these two guidance documents is clearly an effort by beleaguered technocrats of the UN Secretariat to pursue an evolutionary path of least resistance by attempting to circumnavigate the intractable constraints thrown up by states' opposition to the language and implications of human security and R2P. However, from the perspective of the DDR field practitioner, they indicate a dilution of the UN's commitment to humanity. They are a further indicator of the loss of strong principled leadership by the UN over the past decade and may well herald the progressive diminution of its relevance to the protection of humanity.

However, the humanitarian commitment to human security and R2P will not go away just because the current leadership of the UN or even the representatives of states find it inconvenient. The concepts have been absorbed and have taken root as the guiding philosophy for humanitarian action by nonstate actors globally. The position, influence, and capacity of the nonstate actors that continue to cherish the concepts of human security and R2P are ascendant. It may be time to reconsider how humanity can be better represented and protected on the global stage.

DDR: The Next Generation

The Arab Spring and Consideration for a Reboot with Islamic-Led DDR

The Arab Spring countries in the Middle East and North Africa saw the uprising of the people against authoritarian regimes that were maintained by the application of the state's security apparatus. From that perspective, changing the system required considerable application of SSR. Such dramatic SSR would need to be closely linked with a supporting DDR process. The nexus is inherent, and in this circumstance, analysts may discuss SSR and DDR as aspects of a joint process, despite reservations regarding the general nexus between the two. Further, whereas much of the Arab Spring's focus was on the secularization of society, much of the post–Arab Spring instability is associated with the tensions between the pro-secularization and pro-Islamist parties. Irrespective of ultimate outcomes, it is likely that eventual solutions will need to be highly culturally and religiously sensitive. Usama Butt approached the SSR/DDR conundrum in the post–Arab Spring countries in this way.[44] His paper is unique in considering this perspective and offers a challenge to the global institutional approach to both SSR and DDR in post–Arab Spring countries; it also flags some critical points suggesting the need for an innovative approach.

In his introduction, he noted a distinct lack of enthusiasm by the international community for SSR in the Middle East and North Africa before the Arab Spring. He asserted that where internationally led SSR and DDR were attempted in the Islamic world, it tended to deteriorate the environment rather than improve it—as in Iraq and Afghanistan. Successful SSR and DDR, however, have tended to be nationally led operations.

The Arab Spring, or Arab Revolution, was not about ousting personalities; it was about "breaking the system" (*isqat al nizam*). Butt says that the security sector is the face of the "system." Put simply, the entire revolution was a "proto-SSR protest" in each respective country. That revolution has since been superseded by a new dynamic and is struggling in most of the countries, including Yemen, Tunisia, Libya, and Egypt. Syria, which had not reached the stage of revolution in mid-2012, is now seeing the civil struggle being overtaken by the threat and transnational ambitions of the Islamic State (IS) in furthering the Caliphate. Butt contended, however, that in 2012, while the Spring was still in the air, SSR and DDR were inseparable from the revolution: "SSR seeks to reform the very system the revolutionaries have fought against. With this cohesion of interest, SSR can become not just any policy but 'revolutionary policy.' . . . Since SSR is a highly political process, . . . it has the potential to become revolutionary politics."[45]

This idea is critical in an environment of poor capacity and with a poor record of implementation of SSR/DDR, along with Western donors' tenuous approach toward SSR since the start of the Arab Spring. If badly implemented, SSR/DDR may undermine the revolution. Although the revolutionary dynamic has changed in the intervening four years, Butt's assertions remain relevant.

Butt suggested that in free and fair elections in Middle Eastern and North African countries, Islamists will come to power.[46] He noted that these Islamists "will be the key actors to implement SSR[/DDR]." Islamists have been the victims of the security system that they will now be required to reform. Because SSR/DDR remains a "Western-driven agenda and practice, . . . the Islamist's relations with the West is a key issue for successful reform." Yet, the security sector remains Islamist-skeptic, which will complicate an SSR process. Civil society itself remains polarized between an Islamic mindset and liberal/secular trends. The potential tensions between civil society and a state with Islamists in power will further complicate the SSR process. In addition, there is the potential that an Islamist victory can ignite a security-sector backlash, as it did in Algeria.

Butt highlighted the fact that the West has tended to misperceive the term *Islamist* as a generic term—a misperception largely stemming from the narrative of George W. Bush's "war on terror." In fact, there exists a spectrum of Islamists, from "modernists, democrats, fundamentalists to Salafist, and militant Jihadists (both national and trans-national)." According to Butt, "the intentions of Islamists are also widely contested." Everything is not about *shariatizing* the state. Butt cited several authors in claiming that "new Islamists" are open to the democratic political process.[47] Butt then undertook a broad literary review in analyzing the complexity of the Islamist relations with the modern nation-state.[48] He summarized:

> Realities may be quite different from the myths. Islamists are not a monolithic entity and predominant Islamists discourse is aware . . . on issues relating to democracy, human rights and pluralism, etc. [They tend to be] more willing to engage with the modern state on a modern footing, however with some clear Islamic reference. However, . . . mostly "regime-security" centric [states are] somewhat "reluctant" to incorporate the Islamists.[49]

This does not preclude the potential for SSR/DDR from an Islamist perspective, whether with international/Western or Islamist government engagement, once the ground rules are clear. Prior to the Arab Spring, "the resurgence of Islamist revival or Islamism" was, in fact, contained by the security sector, often using the most brutal means. However, this situation then gave voice to the Islamists to call for participatory politics and democracy. But regimes and their security sectors tend to harden in reaction. The attacks of 9/11 brought about a less critical form of support, especially from the United States, for this hardening toward securitization; this hardening saw the "foundational tenets of [the] SSR concepts like democratic governance, accountability and transparency being shunted aside in favour of a more militarized form of 'security and development assistance that has often undermined and contradicted principles of democratic governance.'"[50] Butt cited Kenji Isezaki in the context of Afghanistan in saying that this hardening represented a "misjudgement in SSR largely by the US, that causes fundamental damage to stability."

Despite the US drive toward securitization during this post-9/11 period, the European Union in its SSR support tended to retain more focus on controlling migration to the European Union and offering context-specific SSR assistance tailored to the needs particularly of the Maghreb (North African, predominantly Mediterranean) countries. The SSR model being promoted by the West was generally top-down with little input from civil society, specifically the Islamists. Prior to the ignition of the Arab Spring, SSR efforts "were largely symbolic, sporadic, interest-based, securitized and at best, incoherent."

In post–Arab Spring countries, with the exception of Libya, a strong (and contrary) security sector remains intact, which presents a major challenge to any SSR/DDR effort headed by an Islamist-led government. Noting how the West has failed in delivering successful SSR in Islamic countries to date (Iraq, Palestine, Afghanistan), it is wise to consider successful homegrown efforts, such as post-Suharto Indonesia, which had a good start that was retarded by a disproportionately powerful military. The jury is still out on SSR efforts in Turkey, though an "Islamist *lite*" government does seem to be making some headway.

Hamas, with "its ideological roots deeply embedded in the Egyptian Muslim Brotherhood," is a terrorist organization to the United States and the West that has nevertheless gained local legitimacy among its constituency as "a blend of liberation movement and Islamist religious group." According to Butt, Hamas had, to a large degree, performed the SSR job in Gaza, despite the complexity of the conflict relations and overlapping areas of security responsibility with a generally dysfunctional Fatah in the West Bank.[51] Butt assessed in detail the level of the Hamas "success." Using a community-focused security approach, Hamas returned a type of rule of law to Gaza based on Islamic principle and a human security based on Islamic values, and they achieved effective SSR. The key point is that they did this without external assistance.[52] Butt added that SSR efforts have failed in the "corrupt" West Bank, despite Western assistance, which has focused on technical assistance rather than governance and institution building. Butt says that US$450 million has come from the United States and the European Union since 2007.[53]

In relation to SSR/DDR in post–Arab Spring states with Islamist governments, Butt was cautiously optimistic. Despite continuing distrust in these countries, he predicted an improved engagement between the West and Islamists, a move toward realism in addressing polarized civil society, and a more accommodating "new Islamist" perspective leading to levels of "auto-reform." This divergent, changing, and modern form of Islamism offers entry points for Western-supported SSR/DDR, though there are caveats. It must be an Islamic-shared SSR project, and a top-down model must be avoided. One can expect that any Islamic SSR/DDR collaboration with the West will be cautious. SSR/DDR will need a locally driven Islamic-owned approach with less strategic direction than the West has shown heretofore and more political will. A key challenge remains the willingness of the strong security sector to be reformed as it faces the dilemma of seeking both continuing power and a new sense of legitimacy following a revolution that sought to break the system of which they are the face.[54]

In mid-2013, the Muslim Brotherhood was in a delicate environment in Egypt, with President Mohamed Morsi and the Muslim Brotherhood attempting limited top-down SSR to appease the people. We know now that it failed and has been overtaken by a reversion to autocratic military dictatorship. Libya, in chaos, has so far avoided the advances of the United States and the UN in assisting in SSR/DDR and has turned instead to Jordan, Turkey, and Qatar for training. In Tunisia, progress has been relatively smooth, but hostility to the Islamist government is fluctuating. As such, it may eventually be open to Western-supported SSR/DDR. Among Islamists, there is little cohesion and no serious discussion of issues of concern, including the willingness of Islamist governments or those in waiting to undertake SSR/DDR. Butt advised that they need to start talking and that Islamist governments should be undertaking SSR/DDR processes. Such processes would "seek clear reference to Islam or Islamic system of justice (*Adl*) and . . . may remain western-sceptic."[55]

In a discussion on this matter with leading Islamist professor Khurshid Ahmed, secretary-general of the influential Islamic political and social organization, Jama'at Islami, Butt was advised that the Islamist-led SSR ought to conceptualize on three basic principles:

> [The] Islamic concept and practice of Adl (justice) and Ihsan (excellence). Where Adl may stand for deliverance of duty and rights, Ihsan is one step further. It goes beyond deliverance of rights and duties leading to a participatory society. Together an Adl wal Ihsan approach should serve as a fundamental principle for SSR process. He further argued a complete focus on "human security" approaches and the need of securing Islamist governments from the security sector.[56]

Butt concluded that for a successful Islamic-led SSR/DDR experience, Islamists must learn from Western successes and failures, in addition to the limited successes of Hamas and others. He suggested that a "regionally integrated formula, inspired by the principles of Islam and in consultation with western-led SSR donor community may be the right way forward." Within his think tank, the Institute for Islamic Strategic Affairs, this idea is called I-SSR (Islamic world–led security sector reform). He emphasized that the term *Islamic* is a cultural reference rather than a religious one; as such, it encourages Islamic-led formulas and models.

In addressing SSR and DDR processes in the post–Arab Spring countries, the international community—in particular, the Western donors pressing for stabilization and skeptical of the Islamic agenda—must consider a new way to do SSR/DDR that respects the regional culture and aspirations. The embrace of I-DDR (Islamic-led DDR) may offer solutions to complex problems of national and regional security and superpower interests. How divergent cultural approaches to crosscutting issues, such as the gender perspective, are approached and addressed will likely dictate the capacity for intercultural collaboration.

The Department of Peacekeeping Operations and the Next Generation

The UN Department of Peacekeeping Operations (DPKO) has added impetus to its second-generation approach to DDR, going beyond support of the disarmament and demobilization phases of DDR to heightened engagement in the reinsertion phase. The organization insists that the reinsertion phase is associated with demobilization, which was traditionally handled by DPKO and the peacekeeping mission, rather than with reintegration, which would be handled by development actors, such as UNDP. This interpretation of the reinsertion phase takes its disarmament and demobilization programming beyond the time of the departure of former combatants for demobilization centers and into the community where those combatants commence the "civilianization process," along with their engagement of the community. Piedmont suggested that one benefit of the second-generation evolution of DDR is that it works to facilitate enabling conditions by legitimizing the broad interpretation of *reinsertion* in permitting DPKO's encroachment.[57] Further, in orienting itself to address progressive evolution, DPKO is seen to be maneuvering appropriate staff at the headquarters level and developing constructive collaboration throughout the organization, notably with the UN Department of Political Affairs and the World Bank. DPKO is now focusing on the development of a new guiding policy for DDR, referred to as next-generation DDR, to contribute to evolving new contexts of conflict.

In April 2014, in an attempt to preempt the need for a change in direction and the associated policy of this dynamic environment, DPKO called together an eclectic group of experts to a workshop in Oslo to brainstorm the way forward for DDR.[58] This group included DDR practitioners from the UN system and the World Bank, related scholars, lawyers (international and Sharia), military experts, and deradicalization practitioners. Consideration centered on the need to rethink the approach of international organizations to DDR, beyond the contexts covered in the International DDR Standards in addressing emerging global realities. Complex new environments where DDR is being demanded, such as Mali, Libya, Syria, Somalia, and the tribal areas of Pakistan, are arising with increasing frequency. The participants reemphasized the old gems of DDR planning: the importance of good, context-specific analysis; the dangers of the UN and other actors viewing DDR purely as a technical process, rather than as part of a political process; the dangers of failing to define clear objectives, resulting in the whole process being instrumentalized or subverted to address partisan objectives; the need for DDR experts to be engaged in the mediation phase of a peace process; and the vital importance of building trust. Tentative subject areas that will influence the evolution of a new generation of DDR were identified as DDR during conflict—particularly, the counterinsurgency perspective and the question of the effectiveness or otherwise of deradicalization interventions—and DDR in organized crime.

Power relations in evaluation. In reviewing the issue of the scholar/practitioner gap, the negative impact of the power relations between the hirer—usually the headquarters of the implementing agency needing evidence-based research to support their approach—and the scholar, who is contracted to do the research, was discussed. This power relationship can cause the researcher to moderate the critical language to be used in the findings of relevant research to address the perceived sensitivities of the hirer. A new relationship between agency and scholar is needed, one that offers a higher level of independence for researchers, ensuring that their findings are expressed effectively so that their recommendations can be optimized in practice. A closer working relationship between scholar and practitioner in the field is seen as part of the solution to this phenomenon.

Next Generation

Some preliminary conclusions on the realities that affect where next-generation DDR is going expect that it will initially be about managing multiple levels of risk: security, legal, operational, and political. Even as contexts are evolving, the tools and options available to practitioners are not keeping pace. Even though DDR practitioners tend to be problem solvers, the template thinking encouraged by the IDDRS may have retarded the innovative initiative needed by program planners and practitioners to address the dynamic reality of the multiple security dilemmas they face.

The current perceived threat to the West of returning fighters having been indoctrinated and trained with IS has stimulated a high level of research and analysis on policy formulation for DDR to address that threat. Although the military-industrial complex is exerting pressure on the UN to develop policies that address the threat through a securitized approach, many practitioner/scholars advise a more nuanced approach. This approach involves the prevention of the radicalization of susceptible Western youth in the first place or policies advocating innovative practice and cultural sensitivity, which could contribute to a transformation of those radicalized in the areas under the control of violent extremists.

A further influence on the evolution of next-generation DDR is an increasing global concern about the impact on armed violence by transnational and local organized crime, especially among fragile states. Conflict and crime are seen to coexist because "criminal rents generate political power and vice versa."[59] This situation frequently leads to the collusion of political actors with organized crime, including, as in Haiti, the co-option of organized crime in the pursuit of political objectives. The efforts of international agencies to reduce armed violence by dealing with armed criminal gangs through the lens of peacebuilding raises particular conundrums. These conundrums go beyond the obvious legal ones created by the exposure of international actors breaching local criminal law codes by engaging in negotiations with criminal entities. The complexity of the efforts in addressing armed gangs in Haiti (2004–2007) demonstrated the difficulties in identifying the legitimate negotiating partner. First, there is often a multitude of gangs—there were about forty in Haiti. Second, in a criminal gang, the leader is often the biggest killer or the "hardest liner"— the most feared one. Once a leader enters negotiation, he loses aspects of his capacity to control the other members of the gang. A gang leader engaged in negotiations is in a very vulnerable position vis-à-vis his minions and may suddenly lose more than his influence when a more resolute and hard-line subordinate replaces him. Third, if the social benefits are discounted, the proceeds of crime usually outpace what a DDR process can offer as material incentive for participation. Fourth, as with DDR in conflict, the capacity of DDR resources to protect participants who disengage from criminal gangs may be insufficient.

An additional aspect of the conundrum experienced in Haiti in attempting to implement a DDR process during conflict—in this case, criminally motivated armed violence—was associated with the mission's decision to launch robust operations against the gangs in late 2006. The DDR practitioners negotiating discreetly with some of the moderate leaders of the armed gangs, as guided by the human security agenda, were, to some degree, taken unawares and overtaken when the UN force launched large-scale operations into the gang strongholds. This action resulted in DDR teams being caught in live crossfire on at least two occasions, not to mention the destruction of the trust built between DDR negotiators and gang leaders.[60] This event can be attributed to poor communications and high levels of distrust between the DDR Section and the Joint Mission Analysis Cell that was coordinating mission intelligence. This poor communication and distrust were, in part, caused by the DDR team's reticence to share confidential information about their negotiations due to what many of the security-focused mission staff considered misguided thinking—that is, the human security agenda–driven ethics of confidential client relations necessary to build trust within a DDR process.[61]

In a recent report, International Alert considered this nexus of organized crime, armed violence, and fragility and how they might be reduced and transformed through peacebuilding approaches.[62] Noting that there is, as yet, little experience-based evidence to support the theory, the report advises that it will take considerable peer pressure and civic activism to move the necessary political processes to address the issue. International Alert suggested that critical elements of tackling armed violence in the context of organized crime through the process of peacebuilding will include careful conflict analysis for approaches to law enforcement; facilitated dialogue among all actors; innovative and creative approaches to handling predatory power holders; progressive change in addressing crime-incentive structures; and, more controversially, consideration of the need, in this rapidly globalizing world, to actually disrupt globalized market structures.[63]

The leverage that is available to international organizations to successfully deliver DDR in environments of criminal armed violence through "soft" options—that is, socioeconomic enticement beyond the implementation of the rule of law—is limited. Next-generation DDR will have to think outside the box to create innovative, context-specific local solutions to address the multiple security dilemmas that balance credible deterrent with incentive and undermine trust in reducing armed violence.

The questions raised in the Oslo workshop in mid-2014 regarding not only the rapidly growing threat posed by violent extremism as accelerated by the emergence of IS, but also DDR in the context of organized crime, were taken forward by DPKO's collaboration with the UN University in a research project called, "Building New DDR Solutions." Led by James Cockayne and Siobhan O'Neil, the project engaged a team of expert researchers including me.[64] The results of this research were presented at a conference in New York in June 2015, accompanied by the publication of some of the resulting research papers.[65] This research project pulls together a number of think pieces that encourage broad discussion and consultation to contribute to next-generation policy development that will address DDR beyond postconflict environments and, indeed, beyond tested second-generation environments to nonpermissive armed conflict or criminal scenarios, where there is no peace to keep.

In addition to analysis and conclusions, the "think pieces" in the publication consider aspects of DDR in conflict, counterterrorism, counter violent extremism, and other nonpermissive environments. They discussed the relationship between DDR and counter violent extremism in the context of UN peacekeeping operations; the implications of the detention of combatants associated with DDR in the context of UN peacekeeping operations, and the lessons to be learned from a field review of attempts to disengage violent extremists in the unique context of the conflict in Somalia. They also considered the evolving context of violent extremism associated with al Shabaab in Somalia and IS in Syria and Iraq. Specific questions relate to whether DDR can be implemented during offensive operations or during involuntary detention; how regional organizations and private actors can be supported in DDR while maintaining UN principles and human rights standards; and whether DDR methodology can assist UN member states in addressing the rehabilitation of extremists/terrorists in nonconflict contexts, including that of returning foreign fighters.

Five noted scholars, including the editors, contributed think pieces to the research projects. In extracting the primary identified ideas, the editors, in consideration of the complexity of attempting DDR in nonpermissive environments, suggested the necessity to prioritize UN Human Rights Due Diligence Policy as an appropriate starting point.

> [This] constitutes a landmark measure to ensure that the UN lives up to its own normative standards by guaranteeing that its support to security forces and entities around the world is consistent with the organization's purposes and principles in the Charter and its obligations under international law to respect, promote and encourage respect for international Humanitarian, Human Rights and Refugee Law.[66]

The report also considers the need for sustained budgetary support, greater focus on what works in reintegration and reinsertion, the danger of overemphasizing national ownership, and the need for UN member states to champion DDR. In recommending the development of a new conceptual approach for demobilizing and disengaging from violent extremism, it identifies as priorities the creation of (1) "a new practice framework for demobilizing and disengaging combatants and violent extremists, *integrating* both DDR and Counter Violent Extremism"; (2) an appropriate framework for detention and internment associated with demobilization and disengagement from violent extremism; and (3) a "cheap and scalable case management system to track DDR and Counter Violent Extremism participants" to facilitate risk management.

From the perspective of the DDR practitioner, the direction of this study is perplexing. The contributors to this work, which was implemented under the auspices of the UN, are drawn predominantly from the US military-industrial complex, associated think tanks, and security- or justice-focused scholarship. Although all are noted and worthy scholars, none have been DDR scholars or practitioners.

The published result of this research project, *UN DDR in an Era of Violent Extremism,* while probably overstating the level of threat posed by violent extremism as representing an "era" rather than a "context," appears to be directed from a perspective of US security and justice experience.[67] It recommends integrating DDR with counter violent extremism. It convolutes security with human security approaches. It reflects the absence of consideration of the nuanced relationship between DDR theory and practice and of the related overarching position of human security in DDR. There is little tangible DDR practitioner input. The human security perspective for DDR is expunged. The study promotes a rights-based approach rather than a human security–based approach. From my perspective, a rights-based approach limits the parameters of the necessary consideration of decisionmakers and implementing actors and their duty of diligence to the codified lists of legal entitlements and protections of the beneficiary groups and host communities. A rights-based approach can be addressed with a checklist methodology. It represents decisionmaking by exception—that is, if it does not contravene the laws, it can be done.

A human security approach, in contrast, requires broader inclusivity in that every intervention, every decision, every action is considered deeply from the perspective that it is in the interests of the direct beneficiaries (former combatants/gang members) and the host community. This perspective is with respect to their freedom from fear and their freedom from want in the context of the Millennium Development Goals and beyond. The actions must be in the interests of the people. Such an overarching mind-set lays the foundations for a bond of trust between the decisionmakers, the direct beneficiaries, and the host community, which is the ultimate beneficiary group.

In the report, the securitization of DDR in the context of violent extremism and the advice that national ownership should not be overemphasized suggest the appropriateness of foreign agency. Perhaps this is in a context of delivery by a private military security company, or what might be termed as "expeditionary organization" implementing partners. This idea smacks of the recommendations of the USIP Working Group on SSR mentioned earlier in this chapter.[68] Have the foxes already entered the hen house?

Piedmont's work brings a high level of experience and insight in framing the problem and in developing a coherent approach that addresses violent extremism from the perspective of prevention and transformation.[69] As opposed to the Cockayne and O'Neil perspective, Piedmont retained an overarching human security approach. Rather than advocating agency, he agreed that next-generation DDR is an adaptation of the previous generations, while maintaining the basic principles as listed in the IDDRS. However, he warned that the inappropriate implementation of DDR methodologies in the context of evolving conflict dynamics associated with violent extremism—what he terms as "expedient DDR"—in the absence of adequate policy is already exacerbating the conflict in several fields, such as the Sahel and Central African Republic. Similar problems exist in addressing returning fighters where DDR is addressed "through a narrow socioeconomic lens." Concerning political considerations, sound timing is necessary in judging when one can "negotiate, disband or transform non-state armed groups," a skill requiring the assistance of excellent, in-depth conflict analysis. Adequate consideration of the political and socioeconomic push-and-pull factors will be a major variable in contributing to the success or failure of disengagement in the context of DDR.

Piedmont advocated a paradigm shift in addressing a new policy approach to DDR, together with counter violent extremism, along three axes: (1) DDR as a conflict-prevention/radicalization-prevention measure, rather than a postconflict peacebuilding tool; (2) a shift from a focus on socioeconomic reintegration in the case of violent extremism to one of strengthening social cohesion, with an emphasis on community-based reintegration as a precondition to countering violent extremism; and (3) DDR as a transformative medium, recognizing that such social reintegration strengthens "vertical linkages between community and state" and horizontal linkages between individuals and the community and "becomes a vehicle for transformative governance" contributing to national and regional security.

Notes

1. UN, " The Centrality of Protection in Humanitarian Action," December 17, 2013.
2. Kelvin Ong, *Managing Fighting Forces: DDR in Peace Processes* (Peacemaker's Toolkit) (Washington, DC: United States Institute of Peace, February 2012).
3. I was present in Libreville in 2009 as part of a DDR team led by Sophie da Camara of UNDP. I subsequently managed the launch of the DDR process in Central African Republic.
4. Foday Sankoh died in prison in Freetown, Liberia, awaiting the launch of his trial in the Extraordinary Chambers of the Courts of Sierra Leone, associated with the International Criminal Court.
5. Adapted from Desmond Molloy, "DDR in Nigeria and Sri Lanka: Smoke and Mirrors?" *Journal of Conflict Transformation and Security* 1, no. 1 (2011).
6. Ibid.
7. Ibid.

8. Stakeholder Democracy Network in the Niger Delta was one such credible civil society organization that, at the time, expressed its cynicism about these reports.

9. See "Protests in Biafra: Go Your Own Way," *The Economist,* November 28, 2015.

10. Maria Derks, Hans Rouw, and Ivan Briscoe, *A Community Dilemma: DDR and the Changing Face of Violence in Colombia* (The Hague, Netherlands: The Clingendael Institute, Peace Security and Development Network, July 2011), 18.

11. Ibid., 53.

12. Adapted from Desmond Molloy, *The Qualitative Quantitative Dilemma: Analysis of Indicators of Achievement as Used in DDR Programmes* (Tokyo: Tokyo University of Foreign Studies, 2009).

13. Johanna Herman and Chandra Lekha Sriram, "DDR and Transitional Justice" (paper prepared for Tromsø University/NUPI conference on DDR, Tromsø, Norway, August 2008).

14. Ibid.

15. Tim Kelsall, "Truth, Lies, Ritual: Preliminary Reflections on the Truth and Reconciliation Commission in Sierra Leone," *Human Rights Quarterly* 27 (2005), 361–391.

16. Adapted from Herman and Lekha Sriram, "DDR and Transitional Justice."

17. Molloy, *The Qualitative Quantitative Dilemma.*

18. See Desmond Molloy, *An Unlikely Convergence: Evolving DDR Theory and Counterinsurgency Doctrine* (PhD dissertation, Peace and Conflict Studies, Tokyo University of Foreign Studies, 2013); Irma Specht, *Independent Evaluation of the UNIRP* (Kathmandu, Nepal: Transition International, February 2013).

19. Molloy, *An Unlikely Convergence.*

20. Alison Laporte-Oshiro, "From Militant to Policemen: Three Lessons from US Experience with DDR and SSR," *PeaceBrief* 115 (November 17, 2011).

21. See Lou Pingeot, *Dangerous Partnership: Private Military & Security Companies and the UN* (a report, New York: Global Policy Forum and the Rosa Luxemburg Foundation, June 2012).

22. Laporte-Oshiro, "From Militant to Policemen," 1.

23. UN Ad Hoc Interagency Review Team, "UN Interagency Review of the Launch of the DDR Process in Liberia" (New York: DPKO, March 2004).

24. Robert Muggah, *Securing Haiti's Transition: Reviewing Human Insecurity and the Prospects for Disarmament, Demobilization, and Reintegration* (report commissioned by the Firearms and Explosive Control Division, Geneva: Small Arms Survey, May 2005).

25. Kenji Isezaki, *Disarmament: The World Through the Eyes of a Conflict Buster,* published in Japanese by Kodansha Gendhi Shinho (January 2004), translated into English (2011), 122–123.

26. Ibid., 2.

27. Kurt Jacobsen, "Repetition Compulsion: Counterinsurgency Bravado in Iraq and Afghanistan," 179–191, in *Anthropology and Global Counterinsurgency.* eds. John D. Kelly et al. (Chicago: University of Chicago Press, 2010).

28. Larry E. Cable, *Conflict of Myths: The Development of American Counterinsurgency Doctrine and the Vietnam War* (New York: New York University Press, 1986).

29. Ken Dilanian, "US/Afghanistan: Short-Staffed USAID Tries to Keep Pace," *USA Today,* February 1, 2009, accessed September 8, 2012, http://www.corpwatch .org/article.php?id=15288.

30. Ali Diskaya, "Towards a Critical Securitisation Theory: The Copenhagen and Aberystwyth Schools of Security Studies," E-international Relations, accessed November 13, 2015, http://www.e-ir.info/2013/02/02/towards-a-critical-securitisation -theory-the-copenhagen-and-aberystwyth-school-of-security-studies/.

31. J. Samuel Barkin, *Realist Constructivism: Rethinking International Relations Theory* (New York: Cambridge University Press, 2010).

32. Project Minerva was a fund of $50 million launched by US secretary of defense Bob Gates in 2008 to encourage scholarly engagement (particularly social science) to focus on cultural concerns in security-related issues, including the implementation of COIN in Iraq and Afghanistan. From John D. Kelly et al., eds., *Anthropology and Global Counterinsurgency* (Chicago: University of Chicago Press, 2010).

33. John Nagl, *Counterinsurgency Lessons from Malaya and Vietnam: Learning to Eat Soup with a Knife* (Santa Barbara: Praeger Publishers, Santa Barbara, 2002).

34. Global Policy Forum, "PMSCs: Risks and Misconduct," accessed November 26, 2015, http://www.globalforum.org/pmscs.html.

35. Pingeot, *Dangerous Partnership*.

36. The task of SSR-DDR of the Armed Forces of Liberia (AFL) was contracted by the US State Department to the security contractor DynCorp, with the training of the restructured AFL to PAE. From Josef Teboho Ansorge and Nana Akua Antwi-Ansorge, "Monopoly, Legitimacy, Force: DDR-SSR Liberia," in *Monopoly of Force: The Nexus of DDR and SSR*, eds. Melanne Civic and Michael Miklaucic (Washington, DC: National Defense University Press, 2011).

37. Reports of the Panel of Experts and Monitoring Group on Somalia, as well as the Monitoring Group on Somalia and Eritrea, accessed October 5, 2012, http://www.in.org/sc/committees/751/mongroup/shtml.

38. Mark Mazzetti and Eric Schmitt, "Private Army Formed to Fight Somali Pirates Leaves Troubled Legacy," *New York Times*, October 4, 2012.

39. Montreux Document on Pertinent International Legal Obligations and Good Practices for States Related to Operations of Private Military and Security Companies During Armed Conflict, September 17, 2008, accessed November 24, 2012, http://www.icrc/eng/assets/files/other/icrc_002_0996.pdf.

40. Ase Gilje Ostensen, "UN Use of Private and Military Security Companies: Practice and Policies" (SSR Paper 3, Geneva: Geneva Center for the Democratic Control of Armed Forces, 2011).

41. Renewed EU Strategy 2011–2014 for CSR, ISO26000 Guidance Standard on CSR, accessed March 10, 2013, http://www.etuc.org/a/9430.

42. UN, "The Centrality of Protection in Humanitarian Action, Statement by IASC Principals," and "Rights Up Front: A Plan of Action Plan," both released by the UN on December 17, 2013.

43. Kristen Boon, "Assessing the UN's New 'Rights Up Front' Action Plan," *Opinio Juris* (February 27, 2014), accessed November 30, 2014, http://www.opiniojuris.org/2014/02/27/assessing-uns-newrights-up-front-action-plan.http.

44. Usama Butt, "SSR and the Islamists in the Arab-Revolution Countries," *Islamic Institute for Strategic Affairs*, no. 4 (August 20, 2012).

45. Ibid., 4.

46. Ibid., 5.

47. Peter Mandaville, *Global Political Islam* (New York: Routledge, 2007) and Carrie Wickham as cited by Mandaville.

48. Butt, "SSR and the Islamists in the Arab-Revolution Countries," 5–10.

49. Ibid., 10.

50. Ibid., 12, citing Jack Sherman, "The Global War on Terrorism and Its Implications for US SSR Support," in *The Future of SSR Reform*, ed. Mark Sedra (Waterloo, Ontario: The Centre for International Governance Innovation, 2010).

51. Butt, "SSR and the Islamists in the Arab-revolution Countries," 13–14.

52. Ibid., 15.

53. Ibid., 16.

54. Ibid., 18.

55. Ibid., 19.

56. Ibid.

57. Piedmont's comments to an earlier draft, May 2013.

58. DPKO, "Evolving Operational Perspectives on Armed Group Management and Violence Reduction" (Oslo Workshop Report, April 2014). The DDR Section of the Office of Rule of Law and Security Institutions of DPKO at UN Headquarters in New York, together with Norwegian Defense University, organized this meeting of experts. I attended.

59. Ibid., 9.

60. Personal experience, Port au Prince, Haiti, 2006.

61. Ibid.

62. International Alert (IA), *Crime and Conflict: The New Challenges in Peacebuilding* (London: International Alert, 2014).

63. Ibid., Executive Summary.

64. In this project, I was addressing the issue of the potential for the implementation of DDR during war.

65. James Cockayne and Siobhan O'Neil, eds., *UN DDR in an Era of Violent Extremism: Is It Fit for Purpose?* (New York: UN University, June 2015).

66. UN Human Rights Due Diligence Policy, as endorsed by the UN Secretary-General in July 2011, accessed October 3, 2015, http://www.hiiraan.com/news4/2012/nov/26899/human_rights_dilgence_policy_and_the_support_to_security_forces.aspx.

67. Discussions with Professor Tone Bleie of Tromsø University, Centre for Peace Studies, chair of the International Research Group on Reintegration, August 2015.

68. Laporte-Oshiro, "From Militant to Policemen."

69. Dean Piedmont, "The Role of DDR in Countering Violent Extremism," *SSR 2.0 Brief,* Center for Security Governance, no. 3 (June 2015).

10

The Dilemmas of Confronting Risk

This chapter consolidates the cycle of scholarly and practice-based contributions to the evolution of DDR, a human security–based theory, and considers the threats and the opportunities. It advocates the requirement to reboot the theory and practice in order to address a dynamically evolving global environment. It dwells on the predominant practitioner and scholar dilemma of identifying appropriate metrics for evaluation and observes the criticality of using the qualitative metrics of perceptions, attitudes, and trust of the people and stakeholders. It considers twenty security dilemmas inherent in the processes of DDR, identified through tracing the evolution of the theory and practice. The management of these dilemmas will have a decisive impact on those perceptions, attitudes, and trust and ultimately on the outcomes of DDR.

DDR Theory and the Deficit in Practice

From the outset of DDR in the late 1980s in Central America through the post–Cold War reduction in conflict in southern Africa to the present day, DDR theory and practice have evolved dramatically. DDR now reaches beyond a simple confidence-building contribution to a peace process, addressing some short-term security dilemmas, offering political breathing space, and reducing expenditure on security. It is an essential process, approach, vehicle, program or operation offering multiple impacts in contributing to regional and national postconflict recovery; and while DDR can take on any of these characteristics, the configuration depends on the objectives and context. In the complex, dynamic nature of heterogeneous regional and national political, social, and economic contexts, the definitive objectives of specific DDR programs have been difficult to fix or to track; it is difficult to attribute causal effect directly to the DDR program.

Acknowledging that the reintegration aspect of DDR is the most complex of all, much scholarly and practitioner attention has focused on that

191

phase. In developing the theory, the 2006 Integrated DDR Standards (IDDRS) offered a toolbox of lessons learned and best practice to guide the UN approach to DDR program design and implementation. However, the IDDRS process is cumbersome and slow in formulating the required guidance for a dynamically evolving practice area. The institutional will of UN agencies to support the process is strained, and the personal commitment of the founding enthusiasts has likely been exhausted as they progress in their careers. This, together with the dramatic evolution of global and regional conflict and postconflict contexts, means that the continuing relevance of the IDDRS process is in question. Perhaps the most sustainable relevance of the standards is in offering a body of policy guidance that supports the five main principles of the UN approach to DDR: people centered, national ownership, integrated, accountable and transparent, and well planned.

Groups such as the International Research Group on Reintegration at the University of Tromsø in Norway are developing new analytical frameworks for studying the environment for reintegration. This work contributes to planning design, implementation, and evaluation and ultimately will help identify the appropriate metrics, whether qualitative or quantitative. Such indicators of achievement, if they exist in general rather than specific contexts, have not yet been defined to a degree that permits identification of the benefits of the enormous resources being applied to former combatant reintegration in the context of DDR. But at least scholars and practitioners are beginning to consider whether the right questions are being asked.

The changing contexts within the global order are influencing the evolution of multiple conflict issues. There are many potential trouble spots—the impact of the US wind-down in Afghanistan; the prospects for global conflict in the context of the chilly Arab Spring and the emergence of IS in Iraq, Syria, and beyond; nuclear Iran; posturing North Korea; rampant China; and even the specter of a reemerging Cold War. The potential exists for an increasing demand for UN engagement in conflict resolution, including reducing armed violence. There is an arising threat of damaging subversion to DDR theory and practice by diverse global approaches, such as the convergence of security approaches to military interventions to include aspects of DDR implementation and the aspirations of for-profit organizations to impose a very narrow form of DDR/SSR that is devoid of human security motivation. Implementation of DDR programs without due consideration of long-term human security will contribute to future conflict environments. Despite the approaching tsunami of for-profit-motivated implementers in postconflict interventions, the task of altruistic, rights-based, scholarly motivated institutions must be to strive to create an enforceable code of conduct to place DDR where it belongs—being owned by and serving the people of the host nations. It is time to refocus on elements of human security, a currently unfashionable term that has guided the development of many of the better practices of peacebuilding.

A realist constructive approach to DDR is timely. Samuel Barkin defined *realist constructivism* as an approach that balances facing reality head-on and addressing it in a traditional "realist" way with the use of soft "constructivist" approaches to changing (or transforming) the environment to achieve desired outcomes.[1] It is necessary to create the appropriate leverage to clearly demonstrate to political powers, donors, and institutions that the common wisdom that well-implemented DDR is beneficial in the context of human security is based on qualitative or quantitative facts.

The UN Department of Peacekeeping Operations seems confident in its positioning for future engagement in DDR, empowered by the broad acceptance of its second-generation concept. Global circumstances are encouraging the development of a new framework for DDR in addressing evolving contexts. Worryingly, however, DPKO appears to be moving toward securitization rather than human security as it strives to develop appropriate policy for emerging contexts, especially that of violent extremism. Uncorrected, this move will have negative implications for policy development.

UNDP, in line with the current UN institutional consideration of civilian capacities in the organization, is soul searching, while also rapidly distancing itself from DDR per se. Although UNDP may now be beginning to ask the right questions with a view to refining its commitment to the longer-term needs of reintegration and livelihood issues, policy direction may limit its capacity to engage. The organization has already lost most of its experienced, savvy DDR practitioners. It is now in danger of throwing the baby out with the bathwater as it reorients its priorities. The prospects for the UN approach to DDR depend on competent, experienced leadership being placed in key management positions, while maintaining a human security perspective.

Tensions remain within the theory supporting the practice of DDR. Such tensions revolve around the multiple dilemmas and paradoxes that arise in the complexity of dynamic crosscutting security, political, economic, sociocultural, and religious issues that permeate conflict and post-conflict societies. These issues are accentuated by the perception of a clash of civilizations in attempts to apply Western value–laden concepts of DDR in the stabilization of postconflict Arab Spring countries being led by Islamists or associated with the containment of IS.[2] These issues are further complicated by the unpredictability of the most complex of all conundrums—the human condition. Lessons learned from DDR practice are applied more in theory than in practice. The key to gaining positive outcomes in applying the theory of DDR is to address that human condition in order to ensure that locally owned processes address the perceptions, attitudes, and trust of the relevant stakeholders, primarily at a subnational level—that is, the communities. The broad range of security dilemmas often places practitioners in a difficult position with political imperatives and security considerations competing against programmatic factors—time constraints, resources, and professional capacity.

Security Dilemmas: The Decisive Deficit

In this section, "security dilemma" is contextualized beyond the "classic" security dilemma to include those issues that ultimately affect the success of DDR and therefore of human security and security. Security dilemma is a concept relevant to modern international relations that was popularized by John Herz, who described it as "a structural notion in which the self-help attempts of states to look after their security needs tends, regardless of intention, to lead to rising insecurity for others as each interprets its own measures as defensive and measures by others as potentially threatening."[3]

Not exclusive to international relations, such a structural notion as the security dilemma is inherent in the political objectives and design of DDR processes. Dilemmas of various types exist at all stages of planning and implementation and can be collectively construed as security dilemmas. Security dilemma is an aspect of perception; it is an apparently contradictory phenomenon in which decisions implemented to increase security have the opposite effect and, in fact, increase risk. The process of arriving at a decision to implement an activity or procedure while considering the potentially contrary impact is the dilemma. Security dilemmas associated with DDR, beyond security considerations, include issues of morality, culture, ideology, interpretation, and legitimacy. They affect the factors of perception, attitude, and trust of the actors and, if unaddressed, can have a negative impact on the outcomes—and, ultimately, on security outcomes. The contradiction inherent in each security dilemma is a paradox. Awareness of and capacity to address these paradoxes are the keys to success in DDR and represent the primary deficit that has contributed to ambiguity regarding the success of DDR processes to date. The evolving theory specifically identifies a limited number of existing security dilemmas. Table 10.1 draws on experience to expand that list.

1. DDR is a leap of faith; it is a constructivist approach in a realist environment. DDR demands a leap of faith on the part of all stakeholders, including the donors and the international community engaged in funding and delivering DDR. They must believe the following:

- Political will genuinely exists among all stakeholders to deliver DDR.
- The contributions to DDR are not being exploited in a rent-taking opportunity.
- Expectations are neither purposefully nor mistakenly oversold, which would create unrealistic expectations that could subsequently undermine confidence in the process.
- Belligerents are not entangled in a prisoner's dilemma, whether perceived or in fact.
- The promises associated with the DDR process will be delivered.

Table 10.1 Security Dilemmas in DDR

1	DDR is a leap of faith; it is a constructivist approach in a realist environment in gaining the perceptions, attitudes, and trust of the people.
2	DDR cannot lead the political process. It is an element of the political process derived from political agreement.
3	Consistency is king.
4	Local solutions are best.
5	Exclusive use of cash incentives undermines sustainable results and may strengthen the power structures that DDR hopes to dismantle.
6	Placing weapons beyond use is more important than collecting weapons.
7	DDR must prioritize the "carrot" over the "stick."
8	Failure to engage the community in the planning and implementation of reintegration may create social cleavage rather than offer the peace dividend.
9	Building confidence in DDR implies accepting risk.
10	DDR walks a narrow line between security and human security.
11	DDR may be viewed as a foreign and Western colonizing idea.
12	Credible deterrent must be used sparingly and demonstrate proportionality and include soft deterrent.
13	Ex-combatant-centric DDR can lose the community.
14	Peace over justice risks losing the people.
15	Sometimes "doing nothing" in response to threats is best.
16	A host government doing DDR tolerably well trumps the international community doing it excellently.
17	Decentralized DDR facilitates local solutions.
18	Reintegration walks a narrow line between time and resource constraints, management of expectations, and disillusionment of the caseload and the community. The integrated communications strategy is paramount.
19	Bottom-up planning and implementation of DDR facilitates local solutions but risks undermining local government.
20	The people's perception has a predominant impact.

- Belligerents' status as former fighters will be respected in the community.
- The former combatant engaging in DDR will not face retributive justice rather than restorative justice.

DDR is permeated with the expectation of achieving the desired results through the application of soft power, which includes persuasion, harnessing of goodwill, development of win-win scenarios, and facilitating local solutions. Results are derived from the effective application of a "systems thinking approach to conflict transformation" in applying conflict-sensitive analysis.[4] This goes beyond a "do no harm" approach to implementation and can achieve more sustainable socioeconomic and political outcomes in stabilized normative communities. In terms of the overarching philosophy, these ideas fall into the realm of realist constructivism, where traditional political realities (the primacy of the state, sovereignty, hard power, and so on) are tempered by levels of humanitarian idealism strengthened by a sound analysis of causal effect. Barkin saw realist constructivism as combining a political realist approach with social constructivism such that the outcomes predicted by purely realist thinking could be transformed to something of a higher order.[5] Although the realist constructivism concept is much contested, human security often calls for such a cerebral approach to mobilize the more qualitative elements of human nature and morality in achieving results. DDR is prone to taking that leap of faith in accepting and expecting trust.

2. *DDR cannot lead the political process; it is an element of the political process derived from political agreement.* The uninitiated frequently perceive DDR as a quick fix used to stabilize a postconflict environment in the absence of broad political agreement addressing the source of conflict. This was the case in Nigeria, with President Yar'Adua's offer of amnesty and incentives to the "boys in the creeks," the oil "bunkerers," and guerrilla groups in the Niger Delta in 2009. This amnesty constituted a buy-off that consolidated the status quo and permitted elite and military beneficiaries—and, indeed, the "boys in the creeks"—to continue criminal activity, while offering the impression of taking action.[6] This mistake is currently coming back to haunt the Nigerian government.

Classic DDR is implemented as an aspect of political agreement. The evolution of the theory and practice into second-generation DDR has seen a shift toward attempting elements of DDR in unconventional environments—for example, DDR in counterinsurgency, in conflict, and in radicalized environments of violent extremism. Although DDR requires trust building and the transformation of a conflict environment, it cannot create the environment for political solutions. This idea is counterintuitive; removing arms from the environment does not open doors for politics. However, attempting to rebalance the armed environment prior to political agreement may also court disaster. One or both sides, experiencing prisoner's dilemma, may be discreetly preparing for war. Whether it is a perception or reality, this may destroy the confidence-building aspects of DDR. Thus, DDR must follow the political solutions, often as an agreed-upon aspect of a comprehensive peace accord.

In Haiti in 2005, as chief of the Integrated DDR Section of the UN Stabilization Mission, I came under great pressure to get early results in a totally miscued DDR effort. Mission leadership had initially misidentified the main threat to the reemerging state as the posturing of a now aging group of previously demobilized members of the former army of Haiti. In reality, the reactivation and mobilization of this group was initiated as a façade through the manipulation of certain notorious members of the Haitian elite and their agents. These were the same ones who had toppled Aristide in pursuing their personal interests, both political and economic.

Mission leadership believed that disarming and demobilizing this perceived threat would constitute early political success and would contribute to confidence in the stabilization effort. But the real threat was subsequently identified as the activities of the multitude of diversely motivated urban criminal gangs, mainly associated with narco-trafficking, which were controlling and abusing the cities and communities. It took a costly false start to realize that DDR would not solve the issue of armed violence in Haiti in the absence of integrated political solutions that would offer socioeconomic and political inclusion, poverty reduction, rule of law, and economic stimulation.

3. Consistency is king. Flexible management in the context of mainstreamed dynamic monitoring and evaluation of DDR is vital. Concurrently, clear consistency in the delivery of benefits across the program avoids misunderstanding between beneficiaries and program implementers. Such consistency reduces the risk of former combatants threatening power games to leverage benefits. In an environment of social communications capacity, local solutions that contradict program policy can be exploited by very savvy, organized caseloads. In offering local solutions to specific contextual difficulties that address local problems, implementers may undermine program policy and cause a snowball effect of undeliverable demands among the broader caseload.

Appropriately shaping and then addressing the expectations of all actors through consistent application of policy is vital. Inconsistency leading to misunderstandings during the disarmament and demobilization phases can be explosive. Elements demanding consistency include entry criteria, weapons criteria, identification procedures, timing, entry benefits, transportation support, and transitional security allowances.

Dogged consistency must also be ensured in the early stages of the reinsertion and reintegration phases. This includes adherence to policy and timing in the delivery of benefits, levels of consultation, health and psychosocial support, gender perspective, standards of training, entrepreneurial or agricultural support, mentoring, and so on. A well-planned and well-executed integrated communications strategy must effectively manage those issues to avoid unrealistic expectations or willful misrepresentation of the program. The underestimation of the required planning, resourcing, and effort to develop and implement an effective communications strategy is a frequent failing in the implementation of DDR. Once policy is disseminated, the program must be implemented with strict adherence, ensuring consistency, even at the expense of losing short-term local advantages.

Early in the UN Interagency Rehabilitation Programme in Nepal (2010–2013), Maoist former combatants occasionally besieged local UN offices and threatened staff, insisting on increased benefits. Any level of concession in addressing what might be considered a special case in a local context was rapidly communicated via mobile phone to the caseload nationwide, resulting, within hours, in widespread demands for similar concessions. Over time, however, once program participants realized that policy regarding benefits was being implemented consistently across the country, such incidents abated. When the program staff judged claims for increased benefits or additional supports to participants or their immediate dependents to be legitimate for addressing specific rehabilitation needs, program policy was adjusted centrally through a dynamic management process, and the changes were applied nationwide.

4. *Local solutions are best.* Local solutions to difficulties in DDR that do not undermine program policy can often address problems and improve goodwill. Whereas classic DDR processes were designed with a top-down impetus, second-generation DDR, in its many context-specific permutations, promotes the virtues of bottom-up participation in planning, designing, and implementing DDR at a local level. This approach is vital in gaining the perceptions, attitudes, and trust of the people. The dilemma associated with such an approach is related to the time, expertise, and resources required to develop local solutions through a broadly participative process. Operationalizing local solutions may also activate the security dilemma associated with consistency of policy and implementation. However, the overarching wisdom of prioritizing the development of local solutions to aspects of design and implementation, while carefully avoiding inconsistency, is clear. This danger is addressed by applying a systems approach that facilitates local solutions while also ensuring a process of ascending consultation through the local and national actors that will influence the eventual political outcomes.

Success here tends to have a snowball effect in demonstrating to adjacent communities that the program is a listening and conflict-sensitive entity. This can help dispel fears in the community that a foreign or external solution is being imposed on them. The community-based disarmament program implemented in Sierra Leone after the implementation of the combatant-focused DDR process focused on surplus small arms retained in the community. The Chiefdom Arms for Development program achieved a positive reputation and was welcomed by adjacent chiefdoms.

5. *Cash incentives must be considered with caution.* The use of cash incentives in DDR is an attractive option for implementers in many circumstances. It can simplify management and administrative procedures and reduce support costs. Cash is a basic subsistence requirement of former combatants and their dependents after demobilization. It may also be a vital component of a reintegration option, such as entrepreneurial support, where microfinance is needed for a start-up. The provision of cash support can contribute to beneficiary empowerment and offer greater choices to former combatants regarding their reintegration trajectory, thus showing respect for their dignity. However, the exclusive provision of cash incentives to former combatants poses risks.

Consideration of the pros and cons of cash incentives is an old chestnut for DDR. Cash is often an easy option in buying off immediate short-term acquiescence. The dangers include creating the impression of cash for arms and inflating the market for weapons, which could undermine the value of the other benefits offered by the DDR program. Further, when cash is offered in lieu of personal socioeconomic capacity building, such as education, skills training, or entrepreneurial support, there exists the danger of the inflationary impact on local markets where the former combatant is spending, along with the related danger of recidivism once the cash is spent. Where cash incentives have been prevalent, rent taking and exploitation have also been high. Cash incentives offered against very low-level entry criteria in the Liberia DDR process were a notorious mistake in the annals of DDR and are well documented as "how not to do DDR."

Cash can also create negative perceptions in the community, with the perpetrators of the conflict being seen to benefit disproportionately from their violence, while the community members—the victims of the violence—continue to struggle, seeing relatively little of the peace dividend. Returning former combatants may also be in a position to exert excessive leverage as a result of their new resources and may upset the community's traditional or natural social structures. Former combatants may be inexperienced in financial management and may quickly spend their nest egg irresponsibly, becoming destitute without having invested in sustainable livelihoods. The security dilemma arises in weighing the attractiveness of cash benefits, both in easing implementation and in their acceptability to the beneficiaries, against the inherent risks that their introduction can undermine the DDR process.

Certain levels of cash incentive to former combatants are necessary as an initial enticement into the program and to address subsistence needs for them and their dependents, especially during demobilization and the transition period before they are established into the reintegration phase. There is indeed a case for cash incentive, but it must be managed judicially, sparingly, and clearly to address needs.

6. *Placing weapons beyond use is more important than collecting weapons.* Although collecting weapons does not offer sustainability in reducing armed violence, it does offer a metric that is popular with donors and lead nations in funding and encouraging DDR. Yet, even a successful DDR process is likely to collect fewer than 25 percent of the illicit arms in the theater.[7] Collected weapons can easily be replaced. Further, belligerents will often cache spare weapons, maybe their best weapons, in the bush, pending confirmation of their perception of DDR. If the perception is that those weapons are no longer necessary, then they will likely remain in the bush beyond use and will pose little threat to the DDR process or the peace process. This represents disarmament of the mind in placing weapons beyond use.

The primary objective of DDR is to place weapons beyond use by peaceful means. This implies the creation of a normative environment in which people can live with levels of predictability and the evolution of arms-free mind-sets among former belligerents and their communities. Forgoing the impact of the metric of the number of weapons collected requires bringing about a culture change among the primary actors in

DDR—in particular, donors, bilateral lead countries, and host governments. It requires fostering the realist constructivist approach in considering the broader, longer-term causal effects through a qualitative approach to DDR.

7. DDR must prioritize the "carrot" over the "stick." DDR is a voluntary process that former combatants enter into with free will, perhaps under the direction of former commanders, to participate in a process that is based on goodwill. Excessive use of force, as in President René Préval's 2006 public threat to criminal gangs in Port au Prince to "join the DDR or we will kill you," likely contributes to setting up DDR efforts to fail. A "stick" that is applied in DDR must include soft pressure in addition to credible deterrent. The "carrot," in addition to the benefits of the program, must include peer and community acceptance in an environment of community security. Second-generation DDR, in working in unconventional contexts, requires high levels of confidence building to achieve workable levels of acquiescence.

On entering a DDR program, former combatants or gang members are expected to fully cooperate with the DDR implementation. The best results will be achieved when encouragement to participate is beyond the threat associated with remaining outside the program—that is, the carrot is preferred over the stick. The advantages to be gained from participation must be well articulated, disseminated, and accepted. The threat—the capacity to deter spoilers—must be held in reserve. How much stick, how visible it is, and how proactively and timely this deterrent can be deployed must be considered when trying to maintain a passive attitude within the community; the required reserve of force must be considered in relation to perceived threat by spoilers. Disproportional use of force will alienate the communities and undermine the legitimacy of the DDR processes.

In Haiti in late 2006, the UN force used robust military action against armed criminal gangs in an attempt to wrestle control of Port au Prince from the gangs. Many in the community and resident international NGOs perceived the level of kinetics as disproportional,[8] despite the fact that the UN force commander emotionally reported that his troops had an estimated 30,000 rounds of ammunition fired at them during its first day of operation.[9] The broadly held perception that the action had been disproportional severely undermined the UN mission's relationship with the communities and generated something of a "metropolitan effect" among donors in the coming years.[10]

8. Failure to engage the community can create social cleavage. A community that is fully engaged in a reintegration process and that does not consider the return of former combatants as a threatening imposition is likely to support, or at least not oppose, its implementation. Second-generation approaches to DDR focus on operationalizing local ownership that is likely to deliver sustainable results. DDR must be seen to bring elements of the peace dividend directly to the community. Otherwise, the resettlement of former combatants into the community may contribute to social cleavage. A conflict-sensitive approach working closely with the community will contribute more to connectors than to dividers.

9. Building confidence implies accepting risk. DDR, in the context of its leap of faith, implies accepting risk. This risk must be informed and carefully managed. Mechanisms for managing risk involve formal and informal communications and information gathering through the development of relationships of mutual respect. That respect must initially be demonstrated by the program through humility, patience, consistency, and professionalism. Despite threats and aggressive behavior, a light-foot security presence may be necessary to avoid undermining relationships. Failure to maintain these relationships can see apparent minor incidents or delays in service delivery escalate rapidly into serious security threats.

Accepting levels of risk is inherent in a DDR process. Risk is inevitable when undertaking a program that is offering a way out to former armed elements. DDR means different things to each actor. In a conventional postconflict environment, it may offer to the victor (or host) government the opportunity for the cessation of violence, while a credible armed opposition remains intact. It may facilitate the reassertion of the monopoly in the use of force, the rule of law, and legitimacy. For the defeated or postconflict nongovernment side, it offers an avoidance of total destruction; victors' justice in consideration of crimes committed during the violence; the opportunity to offload, reasonably cheaply, a surplus mass of former combatants; and the potential to retain some of the spoils of war and perhaps some levels of prestige and authority.

Although comprehensive peace accords may outline the main policies of DDR processes, the devil is in the detail to be thrashed out through negotiations after the signing. Maneuvering and power plays can continue even after the comprehensive peace accord is signed, and violence could reemerge. This is a highly volatile environment. For DDR to progress under such conditions, all actors must assume adequate levels of goodwill. This requires risk taking to nurture that goodwill and strengthen trust among actors. In either classic or second-generation DDR, without goodwill among stakeholders, bottom-up impetus will not contribute, and local solutions will not emerge. Goodwill is nurtured by stakeholders taking mutually reinforcing calculated risks.

10. DDR walks a narrow line between security and human security. Significant political pressure generally supporting security approaches often comes from the dominant components of a UN mission—senior management, force, and police. If sustainable DDR results are to be achieved, DDR must retain levels of mutual trust between leaders of armed factions or gangs and the program in the context of human security. Tensions and complementarities associated with decisions on the application of overarching human security or security approaches in DDR may lead to the conundrum that encapsulates most of the related security dilemmas. These tensions between approaches exist in DDR in the context of a peacekeeping operation, especially where a Chapter VII approach has been mandated.[11] The use of UN force in implementing robust operations against recalcitrant armed militants can contrast with the DDR team's approach of wooing those recalcitrant elements into the DDR process, often through discreet negotiations. When the robust operations are concurrent with DDR negotiations, the tensions are accentuated.

In Haiti in late 2006, with encouragement from the government of President Préval, the UN force lost patience with the audacious criminal activities of the gangs in Port au Prince and launched attacks on their strongholds. Concurrently, the DDR team was engaged in negotiations with those same gangs in the strongholds. On two occasions, in the absence of adequate communications, DDR staff were caught in the crossfire of those attacks and beat a hasty retreat, luckily without casualties. Tensions arose at the Joint Mission Analysis Cell where military and police analysts were processing information and intelligence in support of those operations. Trust between the DDR team and the Joint Mission Analysis Cell was lost. The DDR team was kept in the dark about these operations, despite having embedded military liaison officers. This failure in communication was largely due to the DDR team's human security approach and its mutual reluctance to share information regarding the movements and locations of the gang leaders with which it was negotiating. This raised suspicion, particularly by the former US military head of the Joint Military Analysis Centre, of an apparent policy of noncooperation.

Complementarities do exist in how the credible deterrent facilitates the DDR process by both discouraging spoilers and increasing the relative benefit to former combatants of participating in the DDR process. In Sierra Leone in 2000, the robust actions of British Special Air Service troops against the notorious armed gang, West Side Boys, in Operation Barras brought the Revolutionary United Front to heel and opened the doors to the third and successful phase of DDR.

Both human security and security constitute more than cold concepts. They also reflect the mind-sets that direct how the practice is approached. Opposing mind-sets are difficult to reconcile in the context of predominant doctrines. The decisive factor is in how this dilemma is managed, knowing that the appropriate balancing of human security over security in DDR will have a critical impact on outcomes.

11. DDR may be viewed as a foreign and Western colonizing idea. DDR, especially in African postconflict environments, has been viewed as a specifically Western concept that is imposed upon a vanquished insurgency to support the resurgence of a devastated state. Initially, classic DDR was driven by pressure of the Bretton Woods institutions on bankrupt postconflict countries to address their fiscal stress through mechanisms of structural adjustment and conversion of security-focused expenditures to social issues. The practice and theory of DDR evolved, largely through the study of World Bank– and UN-driven DDR processes primarily in Africa and South and Central America. The process is perceived to be inculcated by Western values and cultural phenomena. Further, nonstate actors, who are frequently the vanquished in the conflict, often perceive the term *DDR* derogatorily, seeing it as surrender rather than as a negotiated postconflict win-win solution allowing them to retain their dignity in avoiding an ignominious zero-sum finale. It may also be perceived as a cookie-cutter approach to dealing with surplus arms and combatants that is rarely adapted to local realities. Currently, DDR, or at least the term *DDR,* is frequently rejected as a solution contributing to a comprehensive peace accord. However, when it is adapted locally and presented as a nationally owned and community-focused concept—for example, as "rehabilitation" in Nepal (2010–2013) and "normalization" in the Philippines (2014)—it can become acceptable. This success can be coupled with well-informed conflict sensitivity and light or invisible foreign footprint support in implementation.

Usama Butt highlighted the difficulty in harnessing the expertise and experience of Western institutions—namely, the UN and World Bank—in implementing DDR/SSR in Islamic countries, particularly in conflicted post–Arab Spring countries. His implication is that while needing the donor support, Islamic-led countries will tend to reject Western value and moral systems, which could lead to the danger of rejecting a wealth of technical experience. He advised that all relevant institutions, including the emerging Islamic states, must start thinking of the priorities of Islamic-led DDR/SSR and find the required accommodation with the supporting global institutions that have the funds and the necessary technical expertise. The security dilemma arises in finding the common ground that the human security approach is compatible with or adaptable to a local value-driven system. DDR must contribute to the establishment of normative systems through respect for local values. Dealing with such a complex dilemma offers an extraordinary challenge.

12. Credible deterrent must be used sparingly and demonstrate proportionality. High-profile deterrents will indicate an absence of trust. Strengthening trust implies the acceptance of elements of risk. A high visibility of force or police and apparent high levels of enforcement, rather than tangible enhanced security, may damage public perception that the DDR process is based on agreement or that it is a voluntary process. This dilemma offers particular difficulties in implementing DDR, a peacebuilding activity, in ongoing conflict—as in Afghanistan, where there is not yet peace to build.

Beyond considering soft over hard approaches, credible deterrent has proven to be an essential reserve capacity in the delivery of DDR programs. However, it is one that projects trade-offs and opportunity costs both in the context of winning the people—their perceptions, attitudes, and trust—and in garnering their contribution to the sustainability of the reintegration of former combatants. Movement toward bottom-up implementation of second-generation DDR reduces the necessity for the use of blunt force as a credible deterrent, which should be a last resort. It advocates the strengthening of community-based deterrent, including peer pressure, community acceptance, and advice and guidance from respected elders in the community, family, or religious leaders. The Community Violence Reduction program in Haiti in mid-2005 facilitated the development of Community Violence Reduction Committees. However, continuing recalcitrance by urban gangs necessitated the application of robust military force (the "stick") in late 2006.

The main trade-off regarding deterrent in DDR is that if participants enter the program motivated by fear, rather than voluntarily motivated by a commitment to alternate livelihoods and reintegration into the community, the chances of their reintegration being sustainable are greatly reduced. Further, deterrent in DDR must be subtler than simply applying force, as a perception of disproportional use may lose community support.

Peacekeeping operations committing extraordinary resources to address concurrent priorities of the UN Security Council are severely time bound. Three or four years are usually the optimistically projected period to achieve the desired outcomes. In practice, most peacekeeping operations require much longer than that. As time goes by and new global threats arise, the interest and commitment of the Security Council diminishes. Criminal gang members, radical extremist groups, or insurgents—particularly those with a cause—may have time to waste while international attention focuses on their turf. They can go to ground and wait to reemerge once the dust of international attention has settled. Credible deterrent must come from indigenous sources, preferably from within the community, and must be sustainable. A dilemma exists in the effort required to empower this local credible deterrent and harmonize it with the various elements of deterrent supporting the DDR process.

13. Ex-combatant-centric DDR can lose the community. Community-based approaches to the reintegration of former combatants that share the peace dividend with the broader community offer better chances of success. In practice, however, DDR tends to focus resources on the former combatant caseload, with the broader community receiving spin-off as an afterthought. Community-based approaches contribute to the establishment of normative systems through conflict-sensitive considerations. Bottom-up participation in the crucial planning stages contributes to more sustainable results in DDR and the reemergence of normative environments by focusing attention on the context-specific conflict issues in the community. This, in turn, contributes to positive community perceptions, attitudes, and trust toward DDR. Community security approaches, including second-generation approaches such as community violence reduction, require a commitment in resources, including time, money, and human capacity, to facilitate community capacity and activities. The dilemma is in weighing broader perception and more sustainable long-term reintegration against the achievement of short-term quantitative metrics, often to satisfy political interests.

The emergence of new and complex conflict and postconflict environments, such as addressing urban gang violence, has given rise to the evolution of a second-generation theory that has reemphasized and elevated the importance of bottom-up approaches that include the broader community.

Now, with broader scholarly interest in the evolution of DDR theory and practice, a transformative theory of change is recommended that implements a systems approach to conflict sensitivity that goes beyond Mary Anderson's "do no harm" theory.[12] This new theory aims for broader positive socioeconomic and political outcomes by harmonizing bottom-up engagement with a top-down effort.

Second-generation DDR is striving to apply the evolving theory in practice in appropriate environments with better results and is better managing the security dilemma. The next generation of DDR must reconsider the approach in light of the increasing complexity of post–Arab Spring confusion and of radicalized and criminalized conflicts to address violent extremism.

14. Peace over justice risks losing the people. An amnesty as an aspect of a comprehensive peace accord is often instrumental in bringing rebels to the peace table and is often a prerequisite to rebels agreeing to enter a DDR process. Many senior actors in civil war may have engaged in serious crimes, including war crimes and crimes against humanity. The UN draws the line at condoning general amnesties by requiring that "those most responsible for war crimes or crimes against humanity" cannot be granted amnesty. However, the majority of foot soldiers do escape formal justice for their part in such crimes. Despite the welcome end of hostilities, this sends a mixed message to people who have been the victims of war. Their frustration can increase as the environment moves away from the initial cessation of violence. Those who perpetrated such crimes are now not only exempt from retribution for those crimes within the rule of law but are also benefiting from supports rehabilitating them back into society. The frustration generated can undermine the DDR process by turning popular perception against it.

However, Kenji Isezaki contended that such amnesty does not consist of sacrificing justice; rather, it represents a "temporal void of justice that is necessary for peace, [a void that we] solemnly and silently conceive strategies to remedy."[13] The issue has been mitigated in some cases by requiring those accused of crimes to undergo local forms of community justice, including traditional justice mechanisms such as the Gacaca system in Rwanda or traditional cleansing ceremonies such as in Sierra Leone. However it might be addressed, sacrificing justice for peace at any level poses a security dilemma and can undermine the achievements of acceptable outcomes.

In readjusting concerns regarding this void of justice and in discouraging crimes against humanity and war crimes, transitional justice mechanisms may be applied. These mechanisms are often in the context of the provisions of the International Criminal Court, where the fragile postconflict justice system of the state has limited capacity. On the one hand, from the DDR perspective, the timing of the indictment of leaders of belligerent forces is critical, as leaders concerned about prosecution are slow to lead their forces into the DDR process. On the other hand, the perception of a just peace will increase the stability of the peacebuilding environment and will broaden the support for the DDR processes, including the reintegration of former combatants into the community. Managing these tensions and complementarities creates a serious dilemma for DDR. This dilemma lies in the answer to the question, Is peace worth the sacrifice of justice? Balancing the pay-off with the cost as regards perceived justice is the conundrum.

15. Sometimes "doing nothing" in response to threats is best. Former combatant caseloads are a volatile group of people with which to work. Cease-fires can be broken. If dissatisfied with the DDR process, former combatants can revert to form by offering threats or violence toward those implementing the process. Prescriptive security reaction is rarely constructive. Occasionally, no immediate security reaction is wise, while a process of mediation and political action is smarter.

Former combatants are easily tempted to use muscle over brainpower when expectations are not met or in their attempts to extract improved benefits. This often occurs early in the program before a sound, trusting relationship has been built with DDR program actors, staff, and implementing partners. Careful threat analysis and local consultation must inform any level of reaction to such occurrences. Local staff and partners must be protected. However, in most DDR environments into which former combatants have entered voluntarily, after the combatants recognize it as the best option open to them, they will quickly realize the negative consequences of executing threats against DDR actors. In strengthening human relations, doing nothing, or at least considered nonreaction, might be the right action. Employing the reserve deterrent, UN force, or local rule-of-law forces may contribute to a deterioration in human relations and to an escalation of action, both locally and farther afield. Experience suggests that application of local peer pressure, counseling, improved information, and consistency of program policy, together with a demonstration of respect for the former combatants' predicament, can defuse a tense situation.

This does not constitute "doing nothing"; rather, it shows the intelligent and well-considered application of calculated nonreactive action. This action goes beyond the concept of proportionality, or reaction scaled to neutralize a particular threat, and falls into a category in which the very threat is transformed into a confidence- and relationship-building opportunity. The dilemma arises in knowing when this nonreactive action is the wise course. It involves strong vertical and horizontal trust and confidence among the DDR team, good local knowledge, and community engagement. Successfully applied, such nonreactive action can have a huge impact on respect and confidence building among the DDR team, the participants in the DDR program, and the broader community.

16. A host government doing DDR tolerably well trumps the international community doing it excellently. In an immediate postconflict environment, DDR processes are vital for contributing to the reestablishment of the host government's legitimacy. Often the capacity of that postconflict government, or indeed a government during conflict, to implement DDR efficiently, effectively, or with any level of accountability and transparency is limited. International facilitators often have a tendency to take a position of agency in delivering the process. While this can contribute to effective delivery of the process, it may not enhance the host government's legitimacy in the perception of its people. Thus, it will undermine the sustainability of outcomes, particularly once the international partner is no longer present. Being prepared to accept less-than-perfect delivery of DDR in projecting the host government as the prime implementer and to accept the associated fall-off in quality of delivery is a significant security dilemma. However, the investment in building government capacity and legitimacy can far outweigh the risks in terms of sustainability of DDR outcomes and stability of governments.

The temptation in DDR, in the context of a peacekeeping operation or an internationally supported counterinsurgency campaign, is to directly apply the international resources—human, logistical, and technological—in order to achieve rapid results that will deliver quantitative indicators of achievement to demonstrate "early wins." Although such an approach may deliver the required short-term outputs, it is unlikely to contribute to desirable outcomes. International actors applying exceptional resources to address the processes of DDR will not contribute to local capacity to address the needs using local resources, nor will they prepare local actors—the government and community—to sustain the effort after the international actors depart. Implementation by the relevant national actors, even if the quality of the program delivered is inferior from an international perspective, has multiple benefits that contribute to positive outcomes. Such outcomes include strengthening government and local capacity; reestablishing or strengthening the legitimacy of government or local leaders; ensuring that the local cultural, religious, and social sensitivities receive due attention during implementation; and contributing to the sustainability of results. This tactic assists in building confidence and in bolstering issues of perception, attitudes, and trust within the national and local population.

The trade-off of facilitating the local capacity rather than applying international know-how and resources is a slower and less-efficient or less-effective implementation, at a time when some early political gains are critical. This implies an increased exposure to risk for the DDR program. Consideration and careful analysis of this dilemma is crucial in making the right decisions regarding the wisdom of facilitating national or local implementation of DDR.

The DDR process in Sierra Leone (1999–2004), despite the presence of a large peacekeeping operation, was seen as a national process being implemented by national institutions. As such, it gained legitimacy and, eventually, for the most part, succeeded in delivering acceptable outcomes. On the contrary, the series of DDR programs implemented in Afghanistan since 2004 was heavily supported by the resources of the international counterinsurgency campaign. The outcomes there have generally been poor; with the progressive NATO withdrawal since 2015, it can be expected that there will be limited national capacity to develop an effective approach to DDR in what will likely be a deteriorating security environment.

17. Decentralized DDR facilitates local solutions. DDR must demonstrate trust in regional and local managers, those who understand the local context and are ready to work with the local community in addressing local concerns, while also maintaining consistent program policy. The risk in offering subordinate authority for decisionmaking in a decentralized manner is that local managers are often exposed to local security, political, and social pressures.

DDR tends to be planned in a top-down process, which gives rise, as the planning moves toward implementation, to a centralized command, control, and decisionmaking environment. Regional, provincial, or district offices are established to spread the implementation capacity and create a functional structure that appears to be decentralized. Conflict and immediate-postconflict environments often reflect a fragmentation of society and community structures and widely varying local conditions that require locality-sensitive approaches to DDR. Local understanding of conditions and sensitivities must be reinforced and reflected through local interpretation in the application of policy. However, frequently, the decisionmaking processes remain centralized at a headquarters level, even when rapid, conflict-sensitive response is essential.

DDR occurs in a dynamic environment where local events can quickly affect the strategic situation. This is especially true in this era of immediate communications that includes mobile phones and social media. Heads of decentralized offices must be fully competent with the DDR program's strategic intentions and empowered to make rapid decisions to address current local developments in a dynamic environment in an effective, conflict-sensitive way. Such decisions must not undermine the program by invoking the negative impact of other dilemmas, such as the need to implement policy consistently and the wisdom of nonreactive action. All of this requires excellent briefing and training, effective real-time communications, and high levels of trust and confidence between headquarters and the heads of decentralized offices. It is about the existence of healthy relationships within organizations.

The dilemma arises as a conundrum in considering the potential operational cost of forgoing the opportunity for headquarters to shape local conditions in events needing immediate responses, albeit through the application of levels of micromanagement that may reflect unhealthy working relationships. Such micromanagement, though occasionally necessary when local security is compromised or capacity to act effectively is lost, can be a destructive phenomenon that undermines subordinate confidence and severely impairs the quality of response when there is no choice but for local immediate, unconsulted action.

18. Reintegration walks a narrow line between time and resource constraint and disillusionment. Management of stakeholder expectations in all aspects of DDR is heavy in time and resources. Failure to apply the necessary time and resources risks stakeholder disillusionment. Such management implies the implementation of strong, integrated communications strategies, the absence of which has been the crux of many DDR processes. In the delivery of DDR, major constraints are inevitable due to budgetary and operational limitations. Cash flows can be delayed. Staff can be overwhelmed in addressing a surge of participant needs. Capacity can be stretched beyond the limit by the demands of community facilitation. Time and resources to devote to the appropriate planning of integrated approaches, including the communications strategy for managing expectations, can be lacking. The communications strategy is probably the most frequently neglected element in a DDR program. This undermines the program's capacity to shape the environment to ensure effective management of any possible frustration and disillusionment in both the former combatant caseload and participating communities that can result from delivery not meeting expectations, misinformation, or perceptions of inadequate consultation.

19. Bottom-up planning and implementation facilitates local solutions. Top-down efforts at reintegration tend to prioritize security objectives and are focused on former combatants. A bottom-up approach with broad community engagement is necessary to ensure that the population's human security needs are considered. If the DDR effort is to derive sustainable socioeconomic and political outcomes, this bottom-up approach must meet and synergize with the top-down effort in a systems approach to conflict sensitivity This is recognized within the evolution of DDR theory in second-generation approaches, community security, and community violence reduction. Despite this recognition, the dilemma remains due to the additional resources, time, expertise, and sensitivities required to facilitate or mobilize that bottom-up effort. Further, empowering the local civil capacity for violence reduction, even as local government is under-resourced or has limited presence or capacity to strengthen its legitimacy, can create insurmountable official resistance to the program. This was the case during the launch of the Community Violence Reduction Program in Haiti.

In considering delivery of a systems approach to conflict sensitivity that offers results beyond doing no harm, the bottom-up approach to DDR implementation must meet and synergize with top-down efforts from the outset of the planning process. Noting that communities may be fragmented in the immediate postconflict environment, commitment is required to develop the local capacity and to mobilize the required human capital to ensure a community-based approach. This implies that the community has participated at an early stage in planning the DDR program to ensure that dividers have been addressed and connectors accentuated. This, in turn, should lead to the consideration of local sensitivity in the program design, addressing local contextual conditions with local solutions.

The time and resources required to develop effective bottom-up approaches in an effective, conflict-sensitive way are considerable and fraught with potential pitfalls, including the identification of appropriate local opinion leaders; inclusion of all relevant parties; the use of locally acceptable methodologies, such as participative rural analysis; cultural and religious sensitivity; sensitivity to traditional and local elites and authorities; local government buy-in to community-based approaches; and so on. Stakeholders, especially those at the top (national actors, mission leadership, and lead countries), must exercise patience and flexibility while the foundations for a functional and effective systems-based, bottom-up approach are established with the facilitation of the DDR team.

20. *The people's perception has a predominant impact: "The mother of security dilemmas."* Scholars such as Robert Muggah frequently lament the failure of DDR practitioners to find the appropriate metrics to indicate the real achievement of a DDR process. Popular quantitative metrics include the number of former combatants entering the process, the number of guns and amount of ammunition collected, the number of former combatants completing the reintegration process, the percentage of graduates of reintegration with sustainable livelihoods, and so forth. However, the level of relativity of these metrics to stabilization of the peace process has been difficult to fix. Further, the direct relationship between participation in a DDR process and sustainable livelihoods, as opposed to the impact of the general "peace dividend" and improving socioeconomic environment, is difficult to attribute. Richard Millett, Eric Shibuya, and I have independently suggested that the wrong questions have been asked. The most critical indicator of achievement in DDR is a qualitative one; it is the perception of the people, as reflected in their attitudes and levels of trust, that DDR contributes to sustainable peace in their community, or at least to an environment of survivable predictability—that is, a normative system. This security dilemma echoes the difficulties that arise between the security approach and the human security approach in DDR. The political search for quick fixes prefers concrete quantitative metrics to demonstrate progress, as opposed to the nebulous quality of perception.

Gaining the perceptions, attitudes, and trust of the host people is a critical objective of DDR. In practice, the effort to "win the people" gives rise to significant costs in terms of political will, planning, resources, time, and increased exposure to security risks, thus converging the potential impact of all the security dilemmas. It requires the pursuit of qualitative, intangible indicators over the popular quantitative ones. The quantitative approach focuses on indicators of achievement that are specific, measurable, achievable, relevant, and time bound (SMART), whereas the desired qualitative approach will prioritize indicators of achievement that are subjective; participative; interpreted; communicable, cross-checked, and compared; empowering; and diverse and disaggregated (SPICED).[14] This dilemma—the cost and effort required to gain the attitudes, perceptions, and trust of the people—is the "mother of all dilemmas" in DDR, the management of which will have a decisive impact on outcomes.

Unexpected Findings

I set out to trace the evolution of the practice of DDR and its related body of theory. This did not intend to test a scholarly hypothesis. However, in incrementally piecing together the jigsaw, a consistent reality has emerged. The findings indicate that in attempting to apply the evolving theory of DDR, security dilemmas associated with addressing the perceptions, attitudes, and trust of the people, predominantly in subnational communities, consistently arise. The failure to address these dilemmas appropriately and thereby neglecting the perceptions, attitudes, and trust of the stakeholders—primarily, the "receiving" communities, the local populations—is the decisive deficit element in most observed practices of DDR. This failure in practice is contrary to the guidance of the evolving theory. These findings point to the urgent necessity to reconsider the application of the theory of DDR to overcome the impact of this decisive deficiency. The failure has been in marshaling the political will and the considerable resources necessary to apply the theory. It therefore follows that management of the security dilemmas in practice within the context of the evolving guiding policy will converge to affect perceptions, attitudes, and trust and therefore outcomes. Thus, through management of the security dilemmas, negative outcomes will be avoided.

The theory of DDR has gradually evolved. It started from the studies and evaluations of the early practitioner/scholars, who were mainly working for the World Bank or Bonn International Center for Conversion, in post–Cold War security considerations in South and Central America and southern Africa. At that time, the need for people-centric implementation was emphasized. However, it was only in the search for appropriate metrics in judging the impact of DDR early in the new millennium, often where analysis of the quantitative metrics defied the common wisdom that DDR is effective, that the appropriateness of those metrics came under scrutiny. An emerging school of DDR scholars has asserted that the most critical metrics are qualitative and point especially to the requirement for a sustained focus on addressing and evaluating the elements of the perceptions, attitudes, and trust of the people at a local, subnational level.

It is time to refocus on applying the guidance of the theory to recommit to winning the people in practice areas, including their perceptions, attitudes, and trust. Such a refocus requires an improved capacity to appropriately weight prioritization in the application of political imprimatur and resources as opposed to seeking quick wins, quick fixes, and early political progress. Approaching the security dilemmas from the perspective of risk management and with a prioritization on gaining the positive perceptions, attitudes, and trust of the people will contribute to improved outcomes. It will contribute to lives saved and to the establishment of appropriate normative systems for people in the stabilizing postconflict environments. Delivering second-generation and next-generation DDR as an aspect of peacebuilding will result in the enhancement of both human security and security.

Notes

1. J. Samuel Barkin, *Realist Constructivism: Rethinking International Relations Theory* (New York: Cambridge University Press, 2010).

2. Samuel P. Huntington, "The Clash of Civilizations," *Foreign Affairs* (Summer 1993), accessed April 16, 2013, http://edvardas.home.mruni.eu/wp-content/uploads/2008/10/huntington.pdf.

3. John Herz, *Political Realism and Political Idealism* (Oxford: Cambridge University Press, 1951), 7.

4. "Systems thinking approach to conflict transformation" is drawn from Peter Woodrow and Dian Chigas, "Connecting the Dots: Evaluating Whether and How Programmes Address Conflict Systems," in *The Non-linearity of Peace Processes: Theory and Practice of Systemic Conflict Transformation*, eds. Daniela Körppen, Norbert Ropers, and Hans J. Giessmann (Leverkusen, Germany: Barbara Budrich, 2011), accessed May 15, 2014, http://www.cdacollaboratice.org/publications/reflections-on-peace-practice/rpp-articles%.

5. Barkin, "Realist Constructivism."

6. Desmond Molloy, "DDR in Nigeria and Sri Lanka: Smoke and Mirrors?" *Journal of Conflict Transformation and Security* 1, no. 1 (2011).

7. Desmond Molloy, *The Qualitative Quantitative Dilemma: Analysis of Indicators of Achievement as Used in DDR Programmes* (Tokyo: Tokyo University of Foreign Studies, 2009).

8. Médicins Sans Frontières, which managed a hospital in Cité Soleil, was particularly strident in its criticism of the robust force operations of the UN Stabilization Mission in Haiti.

9. I was present to hear the force commander, Brigadier General Carlos dos Santos Cruz of Brazil, brief the mission's senior management.

10. James Cockayne, "The Futility of Force? Strategic Lessons for Dealing with Unconventional Armed Groups from the UN's War on Haiti's Gangs," *Journal of Strategic Studies* 37, no. 5 (June 2014).

11. Chapter VII of the UN Charter details the UN Security Council's powers to maintain peace and to take military and nonmilitary action to "restore international peace and security." Basically the UN can authorize the use of military force in implementing peacekeeping mandates.

12. Woodrow and Chigas, "Connecting the Dots."

13. My discussions with Kenji Isezaki, May 2013.

14. Chris Roche, *Impact Assessment for Development Agencies: Learning to Value Change* (Oxford, UK: Oxfam Publishing, 1999).

11

The Next Generation

The nature of violence in the future will dictate how DDR, as one aspect of a multidimensional approach, must adapt to contribute to the reduction of armed violence. Consider how global violence is evolving. Is the world becoming a more violent place? Pope Francis, in light of the incidence of crime, massacres, destruction, and fear, warned that "a piecemeal World War III" may already be upon us.[1] While concurring that the world of 2014 was a "messy place," Stephen Pinker, the controversial cognitive scientist and author, insisted, in line with the thrust of his 2011 book, *The Better Angels of Our Nature*,[2] that despite Ukraine, Syria, Iraq, Gaza, and so on, the current trend continues to be that the world is becoming less violent. During World War II, he explained, the death rate was 300 per 100,000 per year. In 2014, even having crept up a little during the past twelve months, it was slightly more than one per 100,000 per year.[3] But the body count, albeit a handy metric, has never been very useful for measuring reality. Further, Pinker's assertion does not seem to be reflected in the broadly held despondent perception, in line with Pope Francis's view, that levels of violence in the world are currently out of control. Since 9/11, the sense of threat generated by an evolving network of international terrorism mobilized by nonstate actors—in particular, Islamic fundamentalist terrorism—has reached its tentacles into the entire world. The post–Arab Spring chill in multiple Middle Eastern and North African states has dispelled much optimism regarding the potential for reducing levels of violence and threat in what could have been a gradually democratizing world.

The very brief close-to-unipolar era after the collapse of the Soviet Union, which falsely heralded, from the Western perspective, a utopian Pax Americana, has indeed ended. China is rising, and the hopes in the West of a Xi Jinping–led détente regarding East or West hegemonic influence are evaporating as he assumes a robust stance in international relations and the projection of Chinese influence. Russia, in what could be mistaken for a spate of Putin-led populist thuggish megalomania, is belligerently striving to regain some of the influence of the Soviet Union days. In November 2015, Putin bombed anti–Islamic State

(IS) and anti-regime rebel forces and cheekily probed Turkish airspace, while offering close support to Bashar al-Assad's offensive operations in Syria. Putin's stated objective was to prevent the total implosion of Syria as a sovereign state, as happened in Libya and Yemen. An enhanced Russian submarine fleet and increased patrolling in the North Atlantic drew NATO focus and fueled an increase military spending. Competition for influence and resources is driving the reemergence of a recalibrated multipolar global environment led by China, the United States, and Russia. Europe, an element of US polarity, is resecuritizing in the context of Russia's strategic maneuvering in Ukraine and its expanding influence and operations in Syria, not to mention in response to the increasing threat of violent extremism.

The current dynamic of increasing competition and the associated security dilemma is spawning the specter of a new arms race, potential massive espionage intrigue, and multiple proxy intra- and perhaps even interstate conflicts. All of this will see interests-based engagement in the development of compliant regional security-complex partners and the associated interests-based peacebuilding. The tensions evolving among the main protagonists are likely to be maintained as a cool, if not totally cold, war. Mutually assured destruction has not gone away; it is just out of sight.

Disputing this analysis of the possible return to geopolitics with a rising multipolar hegemonic influence, Amitav Acharya, in an article focusing on the future of the East Asian regional economic cooperation block (the Association of Southeast Asian Nations), claimed that the emerging order is "multiplex" rather than multipolar. This idea reflects a growing interdependence marked by "complex global and regional linkage."[4] Multiplexity reflects that interdependence in the context of "trade, finance and transnational production networks" interacting through the agency of "not just great powers and nation states but also by international institutions, NGOs, multinational corporations and [other] transnational networks."[5] The potential impact of the Chinese-led Asian Infrastructure Investment Bank, the US-led Trans-Pacific Partnership, the discreet renegotiation of the Trans-Atlantic Free Trade Agreement, and a broader Transatlantic Trade and Investment Partnership between the United States and the European Union can be considered topical primary examples in this context. Acharya claimed that an old-style hegemonic order, even in the context of multipolarity, could never reemerge.

Evolving separately and apparently independently from this traditional style of international relations is the rising global importance and impact of the Islamic violent extremism perpetrated by a network of nonstate actors mobilized by information technology. This evolution appears not to be influenced by the global order that emerged among nation-states, which was to a large degree associated with the demise of the bipolar hegemonic order. Islamic fundamentalism has seen al-Qaeda and its affiliates moving throughout the Middle East and North Africa, in addition to threatening the Western world; that fundamentalism is now turning in on itself in a regionwide Sunni-Shiite confrontation. In Afghanistan, failure by the West and the Karzai regime to create sufficient governance capacity may see a rapid reversion to a large degree of control by the Taliban, including those combatants reemerging from the tribal areas of Pakistan. This is despite a much-publicized recent Pakistani army offensive in the tribal areas. If this occurs, it will offer an even broader spawning ground for Islamic fundamentalism and will contribute to the further internationalization of Islamic violent extremism.

The new caliphate emerging in Iraq and Syria was, to some degree, facilitated by the George W. Bush (Dick Cheney and Donald Rumsfeld) regime's decision to assign proconsulship to Paul Bremer in Iraq. Bremer's mandate was to summarily demobilize the Ba'athist Army and Ba'athist state institutions, colloquially termed as "Decision #2," leaving masses of disgruntled military experts with their weapons to find their own solutions. Condemned to the shadows, they have brought much of their military fighting skill and organizational capacity to IS.[6] With compassionless atrocity and the obliteration of historical evidence of earlier civilizations, IS is brandishing its sharpened saber at the world and sowing panic, while brutalizing those unfortunate enough to fall within its influence.[7] Masses of refugees are being driven west toward Europe.

In 2015, with their operations in Iraq and Syria under constant bombardment by Western and Russian air forces and with access to their youthful recruits from the West tightening, IS demonstrated its capacity to encroach into unstable Islamist environments, such as in Nigeria, Libya, and Mali.[8] Further, it hit soft targets outside of its heartland, including in the centers of Western society. In June 2015, an attack on a Tunisian beach resort killed thirty-eight tourists; in October, in Turkey, an attack on a pro-Kurdish peace rally killed 102 people; again in October, a Russian airliner was brought down in Sinai, killing 224 people; on November 12, the Hezbollah stronghold in Beirut was hit, with forty-four killed; the attack on Paris on November 13 killed 129 people. These attacks continue to this day, ever more audacious and atrocious, reaching deeper into Western society. Most of these attacks were proudly claimed by IS. The threat is not directed exclusively toward the West; rather, it is globally directed. Islamic violent extremism offers a haven to marginalized minorities and individuals and to religious fundamentalists concerned with secular encroachment—in China's far-western Xinjiang Province,[9] throughout South and East Asia, the Middle East, Africa, the Caucasus, and even within the Islamic communities of European cities.

Pinker would have us believe that much of this sense of threat is media driven and that violence is, in fact, reducing. The immediacy and starkness of the IS decapitation video clips and social media witnessing of unfolding atrocities bring the horror of violence not just to the security analysts but directly into each sitting room. Images demonstrating the free and expanding range of Boko Haram in northern Nigeria, marauding militias in Libya, the advances of IS in Iraq and Syria, the atrocities in our own cities, naval and aerial cold confrontation in the South China Sea, massacres in Mexico, the opaque war in Ukraine, a confusion of both US and Russian engagement in Syria, the reversion to civil war in South Sudan, the unpredictability of North Korea—all of this and more crowds the media.

The images overshadow the progress being made around the world in protracted peace processes. Nepal found a sort of accommodation with its Maoists, perhaps a buy-off, that eventually led to the delivery of a new federal constitution—though it is one that has not pleased its influential neighbor, India. Colombian peace talks in Havana are progressing. Significant political accommodation with the biggest and most intractable rebel group, the Revolutionary Armed Forces of Colombia, will perhaps draw the curtain on most of that conflict. In the Philippines, in 2014, the Moro Islamic Liberation Front signed a peace accord with the government that was expected to end decades of strife, though this agreement is currently in limbo pending the resolution of outstanding matters of trust. Myanmar suffered sixty years of military dictatorship and struggle by a myriad of armed groups representing different ethnic minorities in the frontier hills; it is now crawling laboriously toward a preliminary national cease-fire agreement. Indeed, after the electoral landslide victory of Aung San Suu Kyi's National League for Democracy party over the reclothed military party in November 2015, it is moving toward a more democratic government. After a process of intensive political dialogue and mutual accommodation, Myanmar may move on to a comprehensive peace accord that should offer broader democracy and reconciliation of the ethnic groups in the context of agreed-upon federal solutions. Although painfully slow and multifaceted, a great deal of potentially progressive peacebuilding is happening.

Beyond 2016

The United States, while struggling with its internal politics, will continue to lead the Western world and those aligned in offering a foil to Chinese and Russian influence. This does not mark a return to the geopolitics of the old-fashioned hegemonic order; as Acharya suggests, even allowing for superpower economic dominance, the nations are operating in a flatter, more broadly influenced multiplex order.[10]

The likely path of violence into the next decade may well be predominantly structural rather than kinetic—the continued suppression of dissidence in China, Russia, and elsewhere; the reemergence of despotic autocracies; the reemergence of more oppressive regimes in Egypt, Thailand, Malaysia, Turkey and Brunei, among others; the retrograde lurch to the right and the rise of neo-fascism in EU countries in response to economic austerity and the perceived threat of massive immigration from the Middle East and Africa. Indeed, threats include the heightened possibility of the breakup of the EU itself, as foreshadowed by "Brexit." This signals the reemergence of a more assertive approach to a globalized take on a Westphalian style of national sovereignty that shuns the imposition of foreign or inconvenient values. The word is out that there is no penalty for driving reversals in humanitarian law, human rights, or civil liberties.

The assault on perceptions will continue through the expansion of network-mobilized Islamic violent extremism and high-profile acts of terrorism by

Islamic nonstate actors throughout the world. This trend is fueled by increasing numbers of radicalized, disgruntled Islamic youth from all countries. As they meet increasing difficulties in reaching territories claimed by the caliphate, they are organizing and committing atrocities within their own or neighboring countries.

An integrated, multidimensional, and globally cooperative approach is needed to address this threat. The application of a systems approach to conflict sensitivity and violence prevention should involve security and intelligence assets; rule-of-law capacity; social capital development; social, political, and economic inclusion; and education. This approach will need multidirectional horizontal and vertical considerations among local communities, the state, and the international community. It will also require the demonstration of a single-mindedness that the UN has as yet failed to garner.

. . . And DDR?

It is not clear at this stage what options might be available to violence reduction interventions such as DDR in dealing with network-mobilized Islamic violent extremism. Claims of successful deradicalization of Islamic fundamentalists over the past decade, including in Pakistan, Yemen, Saudi Arabia, and Singapore, which have mixed vocational training with counseling "designed to challenge the 'single narrative' of Islamic extremism," seem exaggerated and have little supporting evidence.[11] In addition, despite their popularity with policymakers in that the claims offer an opportunity to appear to be doing something, some of these efforts have been derided as scams. Even some of the well-publicized Saudi deradicalization camps for al-Qaeda members are reputedly now providing leaders to IS.[12]

The threat is not confined to the geographical area of intense operations in Syria and Iraq—"the geographical caliphate"—or to those areas from which IS is projecting its ever-increasing atrocities to the world. Those drawn to IS include youth of all social classes with broad levels of stake in Western society, as well as men and women who feel alienated and marginalized, who see themselves as outsiders in a less-than-pluralist Western environment, where they view their religious practice as oppressed or their fervor threatened by the secularization of Islamic society. Mobilized through the calling of fundamental imams in their local mosques or by the network mobilization of the highly professional IS communications machine, coupled with a higher calling to devote their lives to God in martyrdom, large numbers have been finding their way to the battlegrounds.[13] Many left Europe for Syria to fight against President Assad's forces and have since been absorbed into the Islamic State.[14] Others are attracted to IS by the heady vision of a utopian fundamental Islamic caliphate spreading across the world—"the global caliphate," which offers them a place of their own. While hardly beyond the threat posed by climate change, the United States and Europe are awakening to the realization that a long-term, insidious threat to their respective national security will include the activities of radicalized youth at home. Whether as radicalized sleepers—"ticking time bombs" in their communities[15]—or ostensibly disillusioned and exhausted former combatants seeking disengagement, their exposure to IS means that they pose a latent threat of terrorism into the future.[16]

The United States, Great Britain, France, Canada, and Norway, in particular, are scaling up their assessment of the threat created by the potential return of radicalized youth to the West and have been arresting those individuals upon arrival.[17] Greater difficulty exists concerning those radicalized in situ. Belgium, in addition to arresting returnees, has been pursuing those who may have encouraged the departure. Netherlands has barred some jihadists from returning at all or has imposed electronic tracking devices on those who do. Denmark has been piloting an enlightened approach in supporting the rehabilitation of returning jihadists and those susceptible to recruitment.[18] Based on mechanisms tested and applied in the reorientation of far-right hooligans associated with the Aarhus football club, this policy offers a secure refuge to those who are vulnerable and seeking disengagement. It offers, in an integrated systems approach, reorientation counseling, family outreach, and livelihood/vocational training or education, combined with an overarching rule-of-law encouragement. These efforts are coupled with engagement and negotiation with the institutions to which the original radicalization may be attributed, such as a particular mosque or imam. In addition to discouraging engagement, the process centers on decriminalizing the returning jihadist, neutralizing radicalization influences, and permitting gradual reabsorption into society.[19] While initial results indicate that this is working, it will take decades to confirm its impact in that jihadi returnees who undertake the processes do not subsequently attack their communities. In the meantime, the underlying risk persists.

In terms of prevention of recruitment, efforts must focus on the development of counternarratives to the heady "positive, empowering, personalized and intimate" attraction to Muslim youth of the caliphate.[20] Solutions will address the effects of marginalization, providing a sense of belonging, self-worth, and relevance.

How does one address a theologically motivated, network-mobilized movement of zealots driven to a higher calling—the creation of the global caliphate and martyrdom—who are led by their perception of the word of God? Rational theory does not function here. Dean Piedmont's advice is for a movement to prevention and transformation directed toward returning foreign fighters or those radicalized without ever traveling—the global caliphate. In addressing the geographical caliphate, however, there seems to be little option but to fight and destroy this force, which seems immune to compromise and determined to destroy all that is not with it. This indicates limited scope for the application of DDR within the conflict zone under present circumstances and the necessity to focus prevention and transformation efforts on the countries of origin.

Can the emerging competing multipolar world, or even a multiplex world, address the rising panic among its citizens and offer an effective and integrated response to what might be seen as a threat against all order—that is, the Islamic State? How the United States and Russia can cut a deal to create some level of symbiosis in addressing IS in Syria might well shape the model for an integrated approach to network-mobilized terrorism and violent extremism into the future.

In considering how the emerging global order must respond, it is becoming clear that the evolving threat of violent extremism is globalized and must be addressed with a coherent, coordinated globalized and multidimensional strategy. It seems that the spawning grounds of the caliphate in Syria and Iraq and their strong points in the unstable countries of encroachment, such as Libya, Nigeria, Egypt, and Mali, must be attacked and destroyed with sound intelligence-based targeting. This cannot be achieved by airpower alone but may ultimately need a massive number of "boots on the ground," either from internal resources or through an expeditionary force. But this is only one dimension of the solution. The threat of radicalized youth entering the caliphate from outside and then returning or being radicalized in their home countries to wreak havoc must be stemmed. An effective multidimensional strategy that addresses the homegrown aspect of this threat will draw from many areas, including effective counterinsurgency methodology. Even as the fight is taken to the caliphate, innovative methods must shape the environment at home.

1. The caliphate's network-mobilized expansion must be addressed through advanced information technology–applied intelligence to address its communications, radicalization, and recruitment capacity.

2. Sound intelligence-based knowledge of the human terrain must be developed. The vulnerable communities of recruitment must be well understood and addressed through human intelligence and rule-of-law mechanisms that offer early warning and that point to an effective response to recruitment and radicalization. This response will include appropriate psychosocial and social strategies. All sectors of society must give pragmatic consideration to how such strategies—especially intelligence driven and psychosocial strategies—will affect issues of civil liberties.

3. DDR methodologies can be adapted and applied to the various national psychosocial and socioeconomic support strategies to help address issues of education; social, economic, and political inclusion; and the enhancement of social capital to stem destructive marginalization, exclusion, and exposure to recruitment to violent extremism.

Such a coordinated globalized strategy will require strong global diplomacy to develop broad political will among the leaders of the global order.

The conundrum of how best to address this phenomenon is as yet unanswered. Whether the process is to prevent radicalization in the first place or accept returning jihadists or those radicalized locally and establish the potential for their reintegration into Western society, it will involve complex matters of trust. A recent UN study advocated the securitization of the threat posed by increasing Islamic violent extremism using a rights-based approach;[21] Piedmont, however, suggested that a human security approach targeting the prevention of engagement and the application of conflict transformation mechanisms through effective governance is appropriate. Addressing this conundrum will pose a major challenge for next-generation DDR.[22] Counter violent extremism, if it is to contribute to a more peaceful world, will need to be much more subtle than it has been.

The UN and Violent Extremism

Where the capacity for such a global strategy lies is as yet unclear. Can the broken institutions of an ailing UN system, including a moribund and anachronistically structured Security Council, be made fit for this purpose? Can the UN retain relevance, legitimacy, and credibility in addressing the imperative of its foundation "to reaffirm faith in fundamental human rights and in the dignity and worth of the human person"?[23] The HIPPO Report of 2015 warned that "the changes in conflict are outpacing the capacity of the UN to respond," particularly in the case of addressing violent extremism and in implementing peace operations where there is no peace to keep. In this dynamic environment, the strain on the UN is enormous. Future peace operations must engage more in politics than in military action. The UN must be capable of applying a full spectrum of interventions in an appropriately sequenced and prioritized way. Broader partnerships in peace and security that offer shared responsibility and mutual respect must be operationalized.

Future peace operations will focus on prevention and mediation, drawing on the knowledge of civil society. While protection of civilians must remain a priority, the limits of UN capacity must be recognized. Perhaps alluding to the debate and difficulties experienced in the employment of the Force Intervention Brigade in Democratic Republic of Congo, the HIPPO Report calls for clarity regarding the use of force. The UN is not suited for war, and UN troops are not counterterrorists. The report advises that the recommended re-profiling of the UN mind-set in mobilizing global partnerships will be better prepared to address the dynamic changes in the nature of violence into the future.

Richard Atwood of the International Crisis Group doubts that in attempting to operationalize these HIPPO recommendations to prevent violent extremism, the UN Secretary-General has appropriately framed the problem.[24] First, while attributing the accelerated mobilization of violent extremism to "short-sighted policies, failed leadership, heavy-handed approaches, a single-minded focus on security measures and utter disregard for human rights," the Secretary-General has not adequately defined *violent extremism* in legal terms. This failure can contribute to skewed international policy and malevolent manipulation by states.

In considering a second "misframing," Atwood says that the catalyst for this escalation in violent extremism is clearly "the Middle East's convulsions"— Iraq, Syria, Sunni suffering, Yemen, Palestine, sectarian Saudi/Iranian rivalry, etc. Ban Ki-moon has rightly called for efforts to end these conflicts, but he confused the "underlying causes of those wars with the dynamics that enable extremists to gain force within them." This envisages a problem that may be too broad to address.

Third, the UN Secretary-General presents a long list of seventy necessary actions for addressing violent extremism, including youth employment, gender equality, education, support for marginalized communities, human rights, inclusion, and reform. This list reflects many of the Sustainable Development Goals. Atwood believes that such expansiveness muddies the waters, while suggesting that the Secretary-General's greatest fault is in buying into the concept of framing the conflict as being between governments and violent extremists. In warning against such an idea, Atwood avers that Ban Ki-moon's statement "divorces policy from politics" and implies the justification of hard security measures by states. This could end up creating opportunities for states to abuse the terms in waging war against their own citizens, as has happened in Syria.

Atwood suggests that the UN would have been better off identifying the root causes of violent extremism and articulating why it is a new phenomenon. By not doing so, the UN is painting itself into a corner. Unable to address violent extremism through diplomacy or with "blue helmets" and by suggesting goals that are unachievable in the short to medium term, it leaves open only the option of effective military force to destroy violent extremists.[25] If this is really the only option, the UN, debatably as the only reasonably credible representative of humanity, needs to prepare a coherent global strategy to address the aftermath. It should also keep in mind that the environment that has facilitated the creation of IS is largely the result of poorly planned short-term massive expeditionary military interventions.

Ban Ki-moon has been loath to define the nature of violent extremism, much less to focus on the major threat of Islamic violent extremism. This resistance may reflect the politically correct passivity of the UN Secretariat in dancing around linguistic issues to avoid raising the wrath of irascible states, including those who will purposefully misconstrue broad terms and apply them to addressing their narrow political interests. Yet, an official definition of violent extremism is necessary—and soon. The definition will need to emphasize, in particular, the threat of Islamic violent extremism.

Despite Atwood's reservations, Ban Ki-moon is not wrong. In laying the foundations for addressing the global threat of the spread of Islamic violent extremism and in containing the problem, the "stick" is unavoidable. Ban Ki-moon admits that we need to hit the main spawning ground of Islamic violent extremism hard. Only a kinetic security approach, a robust hard line, can curtail the expansion of the geographic caliphate and reduce its network capacity to recruit susceptible members. Better global agreement and coordination regarding the objectives can narrow the scope and term of such destructive force. Between the West and Russia, a resolution to the confusion of objectives in Syria—the destruction of IS or the preservation of the Assad regime—will permit concentration on the target. Turkey must also be persuaded to contribute to joint objectives, rather than using the conflict as a cover to pursue narrow internal political objectives. Accommodation between Saudi- and Iranian-driven sectarianism, including in Yemen, must take the steam out of the Middle East's bubbling cauldron. Although Israel under Benjamin Netanyahu cannot be persuaded much, progress in the solutions previously agreed to regarding the Palestinian issue—that is, a two-state solution based on 1967 boundaries—will offer respite to this thorny catalyst and create the scope to redress gross injustice on both sides.

There is no quick fix for addressing Islamic violent extremism. As in the past, the "stick" can change the environment but not always for the better. The new environment, which may perhaps be a temporary vacuum, must be filled by a long-term strategy toward normalization using a full-spectrum approach. This is an adaptation and expansion of the maximalist approach. The evolved methodologies of second-generation DDR must rise to address the next generation. Noting the inherent incompatibility, the security approach (war) must be followed by a human security approach in an appropriately sequenced way, on a scale never seen before—the Aarhus approach adapted and applied a million times over. It will need innovative creativity in finding a million local solutions for local elements of marginalization, of political, social, and economic exclusion. As Ban Ki-moon expressed, it is going to take global coordination, unprecedented political will, broadened partnerships, and the achievement of many of the Sustainable Development Goals. It is going to take generations to apply next-generation DDR to deliver the results of Piedmont's prevention and transformation of violent extremism, not just to the West but globally.

Drawing from the evolution of DDR through its second generation, and considering the growing commitment to bottom-up facilitation and empowerment, it is possible to envisage how these methodologies will be applied to addressing Islamic violent extremism on a global scale. It will need a focus on multiple intersecting communities, soft options driven by the needs and direction of civil society, all coordinated and supported by top-down imprimatur from states and regional bodies in a broad international systems approach. I am not offering a blueprint or a road map on how to address global Islamic violent extremism; that is for others to do. If the leadership to take up the challenge can be found, they will do well to consider how evolved DDR methodologies can be adapted and applied in contributing to a global long-term strategy for transforming and preventing Islamic violent extremism.

Conclusions

The Status of the Evolution

Second-generation DDR looks at the means of addressing violence reduction in nonpermissive environments other than classic postconflict DDR. Such environments include interventions during conflict or situations that call for a systems approach to grassroots participation in addressing conflict-sensitive community security. New levels of conflict complexity, associated with armed violence, network-mobilized violence, violent extremism, organized crime, and disengagement during ongoing conflict, offer new strategic challenges. These situations require broader integrated, collaborative strategic approaches, combined with improved and innovative local approaches, to find solutions.

Already, DDR no longer refers to a set of processes involving only disarmament, demobilization, and reintegration of armed groups to reduce conflict and contribute to peacebuilding. The range of subsidiary activities and crosscutting issues has expanded along with the complexity of contexts being addressed. From the perspective of the planner and practitioner, the second-generation approach has broadened into a genre of practice rather than a range of activities. It includes greater emphasis on a wide spectrum of multidimensional approaches to support violence reduction associated with armed groups and the stabilization of peacebuilding environments—the maximalist approach. The existence of irregular armed groups, surplus combatants, or radicalized youth and the desire to transform their social capital through soft means for a positive contribution to the community remain the common denominator for the term *DDR*. Although DDR continues to include a set of interrelated processes, it also encapsulates a mind-set that integrates global efforts at addressing these strategic challenges, while also searching for context-specific, innovative approaches that will support local solutions to armed violence. It incorporates security considerations with an overarching sensitivity to the human security agenda.

Within the UN system, the shift from classic DDR to the second-generation approach to armed violence reduction was not so much a gradual evolution as a panic-stricken leap to repair the results of poor conflict analysis and rushed deployment and to address the reality of nontraditional environments, initially in Haiti. Classic DDR falls into the parameters outlined within the Integrated DDR Standards, which still cites postconflict preconditions and suggests some aspect of template approaches. However, the needs eventually identified in Haiti could not be shoehorned into such approaches; as such, beleaguered program planners, filling whiteboards in team discussion groups, brainstormed a more effective approach tailored to the Haitian reality. Lessons learned in attempting DDR in Afghanistan and Somalia contribute to the impetus for further rethinking and evolving the approach. Consideration is moving toward addressing conflict sensitivities with the inclusion of bottom-up inputs to develop and implement a systems approach to local solutions to armed violence and to address environments where the classic conditions do not exist.

The repetition compulsion in achieving failure when applying mass and technology to subdue armed threat has not contributed to creating normative systems for host communities in the short term. This securitized approach has been about addressing external interests and stoking the industry. Securitization of DDR practice by the application of military "expertise" or encroachment by the inappropriately motivated private military security sector threaten to undermine a heretofore human security–motivated practice. There is little evidence of implementation of DDR by for-profit-motivated organizations yielding positive outcomes.

Complex and intractable violence caused by Islamic radicalization, hydra-headed leadership, transglobal network mobilization, and the confusion of ideological motivation with organized criminal interests limits the potential for the design of local political and security solutions. Geopolitical considerations are now complicated by current dynamic realignment of the global order—by the post–Arab Spring (the great investigative political author Robert Fisk would prefer it be called the Arab Awakening), flux and instability in the Middle East and North Africa, the impact of broadening radical Islam, intra-Islamic sectarianism, and the sense of threat created by the massive movement of refugees resulting from this instability. Evolving global conditions of conflict are moving beyond national borders to network-initiated violent extremism. In these new contexts, the DDR interventions being demanded in select cases, driven by the diverse interests of the UN Security Council, go beyond the parameters of the Integrated DDR Standards. In view of the changing, apparently diminishing, capacities of the UN and other international organizations that are being asked to address complex new environments, an innovative pragmatism is required that will open the possibility for a coordinated globalized strategic response. This is driving a new phase of brainstorming within those leaders of the emerging global order and those international organizations, moving toward next-generation DDR.

. . . And Where Is It Going?

Despite a current increase in the amount of rigorous scholarly research into the theory of DDR in identifying the multiplicity of variables affecting its success, it is difficult to predict how the tracing of past trends in a rapidly evolving dynamic environment will affect the practice. According to Robert Muggah, "DDR is growing up, [but for it] to be fully mature . . . greater investment and attention to measuring outcomes is warranted."[26] The availability of an enormous new database from the World Bank's Great Lakes Region Multi-country Demobilization and Reintegration Program may keep scholars busy for decades analyzing these variables and identifying new ones in exclusive case-specific contexts.[27] This may raise relevant concepts that are unlikely to be ready for operationalization by program planners and practitioners in the short term. Planning for next-generation DDR is taking an integrated approach. Focusing on quantitative indicators of achievement alone will not offer the answers to improving outcomes.

A recognition of the convergence in the theories of DDR and the doctrine of counterinsurgency identifies that the mutual necessity of "winning the people"—their trust and positive perceptions—will influence next-generation DDR.[28] This common deficit revolves around the concept of losing the people, their perceptions, attitudes, and trust, by failing to address a broad range of security dilemmas that undermine their perceptions. Similar security dilemmas occur in the practice of counterinsurgency, and how they are addressed there has a similar decisive impact on outcomes. This deficit has been neglected in practice in both DDR and counterinsurgency. Recognition of the decisive impact on outcomes of this deficit will motivate the reorientation of resources and efforts in planning and implementing DDR to address the security dilemmas and to "win the people," contributing to both strategic and local solutions in achieving sustainable results.[29]

Is DDR implemented in the context of the human security agenda at all compatible with the perpetration of war, counterinsurgency, or counter violent extremism that are implemented in the security agenda context? Does potential for inclusion in the "comprehensive" approach, as attempted in Afghanistan, actually exist? There is little evidence to support the concept of achieving successful outcomes by integrating DDR into an ongoing conflict in a security-driven environment. Issues of the voluntary nature of DDR in conflict and of the capacity of fighting forces to support psychosocial, socioeconomic, or political reintegration in a conflict environment—or, indeed, to protect participants in DDR from the retribution of their former insurgent comrades—are unresolved. It can be expected that this dilemma will be greatly accentuated in the context of the practice of counter violent extremism in addressing not only the emergence of IS but also the return of foreign jihadists to their home countries and the disengagement of indigenous radicalized youth. It is early days, and the jury remains out.

In facing reality, next-generation DDR theory will be forced to admit to the incompatibility of applying a human security approach in the context of ongoing war. As Ban Ki-moon said, the war on violent extremism must be addressed with a full-spectrum approach, mobilizing broad partnership and drawing in the collaboration of civil society through a process of global coordination and political will. It must see the security approach of applying force followed rapidly by a globalized process of human security interventions—soft approaches applying context-specific local solutions to local problems. This integrated approach will necessitate a long-term strategy of addressing the marginalized at the level of the community to prevent radicalization and to transform conflict, structural or otherwise, through the delivery of the Sustainable Development Goals.

The Aarhus model of prevention and transformation of radicalization may provide an adaptable and replicable model for an integrated approach that combines intelligence-based rule of law with soft strategies in an accepting pluralist environment. This will include support for psychosocial, socioeconomic, and political reintegration, together with peer community pressure, all within the communities at risk. It is a new generation of DDR.

Next-Generation DDR: A Matter of Trust

In the geographic caliphate, a normative and permissive environment under the control of the state must be regained. The focus of attention must then be on the global caliphate, or those areas susceptible to reestablishment of the caliphate or youth radicalization. The current evolution of second-generation DDR, which involves community security and community violence reduction, does offer a possible solution to stabilizing normative environments in areas susceptible to violent extremism. There is a way forward, if there is the leadership to coordinate it on a global level. Trust between the state, civil society, and the youth must be fostered in marginalized areas that are at risk of radicalization. The focus must be on gaining positive perceptions. Integrated systems approaches must address horizontal and vertical concerns and must emphasize prevention of engagement and conflict transformational aspects of program delivery that focus on developing social capital, or "disarming the mind." This implies a reemphasis on the human security agenda–driven approach. It must be more about winning the trust of stakeholders, with the Sustainable Development Goals being the stake. States and civil society must partner with communities to facilitate either local solutions, in order to prevent engagement in conflict, or disengagement, by addressing the full spectrum of local dividers and connectors. Appropriate qualitative indicators of achievement that will be devised in each specific case to measure the impact of these soft benefits will focus on perception, attitudes, and levels of trust.

For two decades, scholars and practitioners have been pursuing the achievement of quantitative indicators in striving for "successful" DDR. The coherent thread in this book, however, has been that the critical independent variable in achieving successful DDR is the qualitative aspects of the environment—that is, the perceptions, attitudes, and elements of trust of the stakeholders. Yet, these qualitative elements, which have an overwhelming impact on outcomes, have been neglected. The wrong questions have been asked. Now, as we move forward into next-generation DDR, it is time to refocus. DDR is, after all, a matter of trust.

Notes

1. BBC News online, Europe, September 13, 2014. Also, in response to the escalation of audacious and atrocious attacks in Europe claimed by IS, Pope Francis reiterates that the "world is at war; [. . . a conflict over] interests, money, resources." BBC News online, Europe, July 27, 2016.

2. Stephen Pinker, *The Better Angels of Our Nature: The Decline of Violence in History and Its Causes* (London: Penguin, 2011).

3. Stephen Pinker, interviewed by Arun Rath, NPR, 2014. Drawn from a posting on Stephen Pinker's official Facebook site, accessed September 17, 2014.

4. Amitav Acharya, "ASEAN Can Survive Great-Power Rivalry in Asia," *East Asia Forum* online, October 4, 2015.

5. Ibid.

6. Liz Sly, "The Hidden Hand Behind the Islamic State Militants? Saddam Hussein's," *Washington Post,* April 4, 2015.

7. Paul Krugman, "Fearing Fear Itself," *New York Times,* November 17, 2015.

8. David D. Kirkpatrick, Ben Hubbard, and Eric Schmit, "ISIS' Grip on Libyan City Gives It a Fallback Option," *New York Times,* November 28, 2015.

9. Although China claims the existence of this threat, there is little tangible evidence. Chris Buckley, "China Responds to Paris Attacks Through a Domestic Lens," Sinosphere, *New York Times,* November 17, 2015.

10. Acharya, "ASEAN Can Survive Great-Power Rivalry in Asia."

11. Jason Burke, "Fighting Terrorism: Do 'Deradicalisation' Camps Really Work?" *The Guardian,* June 9, 2013, accessed September 29, 2014, https://www.theguardian.com/world/2013/jun/09/terrorism-do-deradicalisation-camps-work.

12. Discussion with Jonathan Gornall, on Middle East matters, September 29, 2014.

13. Dominic Casciani, "How Serious Is the IS Threat to the UK?" *BBC World News*, November 18, 2014.

14. About 3,000 Europeans are believed to have made their way to Syria to fight Assad. Melissa Eddy, "Nations Ponder How to Handle European Fighters Returning from Jihad," *New York Times*, November 23, 2014.

15. Johanna Mikl-Leitner, Austria's interior minister, quoted in Eddy, "Nations Ponder How to Handle European Fighters."

16. Casciani, "How Serious Is the IS Threat to the UK?"

17. In France, according to the interior minister, 138 French veterans of the Syrian conflict have been arrested on return to France, ninety have been charged, and sixty-eight jailed. *Washington Post*, November 24, 2014.

18. Andrew Higgins, "For Jihadists, Denmark Tries Rehabilitation," *New York Times,* December 13, 2014.

19. Ibid.

20. Drawn from Scott Atran, "Islamic State Has a Plan and That Plan Is Working," *Irish Times,* November 17, 2015.

21. James Cockayne and Siobhan O'Neil, eds., *UN DDR in an Era of Violent Extremism: Is It Fit for Purpose?* (New York: United Nations University, June 2015).

22. Dean Piedmont, "The Role of DDR in Countering Violent Extremism," *SSR 2.0 Brief,* Center for Security Governance, no. 3 (June 2015).

23. Cited from the preamble of the UN Charter as in the HIPPO Report 2015.

24. Richard Atwood, "The Dangers Lurking in the UN's New Plan to Prevent Violent Extremism," *The Great Debate* (Reuters), February 8, 2016.

25. Ibid.

26. Robert Muggah, "Next Generation DDR," *World Politics Journal* (June 17, 2014).

27. Randolph Wallace Rhea, *Ex-combatant Reintegration in the Great Lakes Region: Processes & Mechanisms, Trajectories & Paradoxes* (PhD dissertation, Center for Peace Studies, Tromsø University, Norway, January 2016).

28. Desmond Molloy, *An Unlikely Convergence.* (PhD dissertation, Peace and Conflict Studies, Tokyo University of Foreign Studies, Tokyo, July 2013).

29. Ibid.

Acronyms

ANBP	Afghan's New Beginning Program
APRP	Afghanistan Peace and Reintegration Program
BICC	Bonn International Center for Conversion
DAC	Development Assistance Committee
DDR	disarmament, demobilization, and reintegration
DfID	Department for International Development
DIAG	Disbandment of Illegal Armed Groups
DPKO	Department of Peacekeeping Operations
DRC	Democratic Republic of Congo
DSRSG	deputy special representative of the UN Secretary-General
ECOWAS	Economic Community of West African States
FARC	Revolutionary Armed Forces of Colombia
FMLN	Frente Farabundo Marti para la Liberation Nationale
GTZ	German Technical Cooperation Agency
HIPPO	High-Level Independent Panel on Peace Operations
ICC	International Criminal Court
IDDRS	Integrated DDR Standards
ILO	International Labour Organization
IS	Islamic State
M-19	19th of April Movement
M23	Mouvement du 23-Mars
MDG	Millennium Development Goals
MDRP	Multi-country Demobilization and Reintegration Program
MILF	Moro Islamic Liberation Front

MINUSTAH	UN Stabilization Mission in Haiti
MONUSCO	UN Organization Stabilization Mission in the Democratic Republic of Congo
NGO	nongovernmental organization
OECD	Organisation for Economic Co-operation and Development
ONUCA	UN Observer Group in Central America
PRT	Provincial Reconstruction Team
R2P	Responsibility to Protect
SDGs	Sustainable Development Goals
SNG	specific-needs group
SPLA	Sudan People's Liberation Army
SSR	security sector reform
SWOT	strengths, weaknesses, opportunities, and threats
TCC	troop-contributing country
TDRP	Transitional Disarmament and Reintegration Program
TPO	Transcultural Psychosocial Organization
UN	United Nations
UNAMA	UN Assistance Mission in Afghanistan
UNAMSIL	UN Assistance Mission in Sierra Leone
UNDP	UN Development Programme
UNFPA	UN Population Fund
UNICEF	UN Children's Emergency Fund
UNIRP	UN Interagency Rehabilitation Programme
UNMIL	UN Mission in Liberia
UNMIN	UN Mission in Nepal
USAID	US Agency for International Development
WFP	World Food Programme

Bibliography

Abinales, Patricio. "Missing the Peace in Muslim Mindanao." *East Asia Forum* (May 6, 2015). http://eastasiaforum.org/2015/05/06/missing-the-peace-in -muslim-mindanao.

Acharya, Amitav. "ASEAN Can Survive Great-Power Rivalry in Asia." *East Asia Forum* 7, no. 3 (July–September 2015).

Adams, Natasha T. "Policy Options for State Building in Afghanistan: The Role of NATO PRTs in Development in Afghanistan," Johns Hopkins School of Advanced International Studies (SAIS), Washington, DC, 2009.

Anderson, Mary B. *Do No Harm: How Aid Can Support Peace—or War.* Boulder, CO: Lynne Rienner Publishers, 1999.

———. *Options for Aid in Conflict: Lessons from Field Experience.* Cambridge, MA: Collaborative for Development Action, 2000.

Ansorge, Josef Teboho and Nana Akua Antwi-Ansorge, "Monopoly, Legitimacy, Force: DDR-SSR Liberia." In *Monopoly of Force: The Nexus of DDR and SSR,* edited by Melanne Civic and Michael Miklaucic, 265–284. Washington, DC: National Defense University Press, 2011.

Atran, Scott. "Islamic State Has a Plan and That Plan Is Working." *Irish Times* (November 17, 2015).

Atwood, Richard. "The Dangers Lurking in the UN's New Plan to Prevent Violent Extremism." Reuters (February 18, 2016).

Bacon, Paul, and Christopher Hobson, eds. *Human Security and Japan's Triple Disaster: Responding to the 2011 Earthquake, Tsunami, and Fukushima Nuclear Crisis.* London: Routledge, 2014.

Bahman, Zuhra, and Stina Torjesen. *Double Disillusionment: Disengaging from the Insurgency in Afghanistan.* Tromsø, Norway: International Research Group on Reintegration, 2012.

Barkin, J. Samuel. *Realist Constructivism: Rethinking International Relations Theory.* New York: Cambridge University Press, 2010.

Bebber, Robert J. "The Role of Provincial Reconstruction Teams (PRTs) in Counterinsurgency Operations: Khost Province, Afghanistan." *Small Wars Journal.* Accessed April 1, 2012. http://www.smallwarsjournal.com/blogs /journal/docs-temp/131-bebber.pdf.

Bell, Edward, and Charlotte Watson. *DDR: Supporting Security and Development— The EU's Added Value.* London: International Alert, 2006.

Benner, Thorsten, Stephan Mergenthaler, and Philipp Rotmann. *The New World of UN Peace Operations: Learning to Build Peace?* Oxford: Oxford University Press, 2011.

Berdal, Mats. "Disarmament and Demobilisation After Civil Wars." Adelphi Paper 36, Oxford University Press, 1996.

Berman Eric G., and Melissa T. Labonte. "Sierra Leone," in *Twenty-First-Century Peace Operations*, edited by William J. Durch. (Washinton, DC: United States Institute of Peace, 2006).

Bhatia, Michael Vinay, and Robert Muggah. "The Politics of Demobilization in Afghanistan," in *Security and Post-conflict Reconstruction: Dealing with Fighters in the Aftermath of War*, ed. Robert Muggah (Oxon, UK: Routledge, 2009), 126–164.

Bigdon, Christine, and Benedikt Korf. *The Role of Development Aid in Conflict Transformation: Facilitating Empowerment Processes and Community Building.* Berlin Berghof Research Center for Constructive Conflict Management, 2004.

Blanfield, Jessie. *Crime and Conflict: The New Challenges in Peacebuilding.* London: International Alert, 2014.

Bleie, Tone. *Post-war Communities in Somalia and Nepal: Gendered Politics of Exclusion and Inclusion.* Tromsø, Norway: International Research Group on Reintegration, Centre for Peace Studies, Tromsø University, 2012.

Bleie, Tone, and Ramesh Shrestha. *DDR in Nepal: Stakeholder Politics and the Implications for Reintegration as a Process of Disengagement.* Tromsø, Norway: International Research Group on Reintegration, Centre for Peace Studies, 2012.

Bonard, Paul, and Yvan Conoir. *Evaluation of UNDP Reintegration Programmes,* vol. 1. New York: UN Development Programme, February 2013.

Boon, Kristen. "Assessing the UN's New 'Rights Up Front' Action Plan." *Opinio Juris* (February 27, 2014). http://www.opiniojuris.org/2014/02/27/assessing-uns-newrights-up-front-action-plan.http.

The Border Consortium. *Protection and Security Concerns in Southeast Burma/Myanmar.* Bangkok, Thailand: The Border Consortium, November 2014.

Bowd, Richard. *From Combatant to Civilian: The Social Reintegration of Ex-combatants in Rwanda and the Implications for Social Capital and Reconciliation.* PhD dissertation, University of York, 2008.

Bryan, Ian. "Sovereignty and the Foreign Fighter Problem." *Orbis Journal* 54, no. 1 (2009): 115–129.

Buckley, Chris. "China Responds to Paris Attacks Through a Domestic Lens." *New York Times* (November 17, 2015).

Burke, Jason. "Fighting Terrorism: Do 'Deradicalisation' Camps Really Work?" *The Guardian* (June 9, 2013).

Butt, Usama. "SSR and the Islamists in the Arab Revolution Countries." *Islamic Institute for Stategic Affaris,* no. 4 (2012).

Cable, Larry E. *Conflict of Myths: The Development of American Counterinsurgency Doctrine and the Vietnam War* (New York: New York University Press, 1986).

Canadian Army, Land Force. *B-GL-323-004/FP-003 Counter Insurgency Operations.* Chief of Staff, Canadian Forces Headquarters, Ottawa, Canada (December 13, 2008).

Caramés, Albert, Vicenç Fisas, and Daniel Luz. *Analysis of Disarmament, Demobilisation, and Reintegration (DDR) Programmes Existing in the World During 2005.* Barcelona: Escola de Cultura de Pau, 2006.

Carter, Jimmy. "A Five-Nation Plan to End the Syrian Crisis." *New York Times* (October 23, 2015).

Casciani, Dominic. "How Serious Is the IS Threat to the UK?" *BBC World News* (November 18, 2014).

Cepeda, Fernando. *Democracia y Desarrollo en America Latina.* (Buenos Aires: GEL, 1985).

Chambers, Robert. "The Origins and Practice of Rural Participatory Appraisal." *World Development* 22, no. 7 (1994): 953–969.

Chief of Staff, Canadian Army, Land Force. *B-GL-323-004/FP-003 Counter Insurgency Operations (English)*. Canadian Army, Ottawa, December 13, 2008.

Child, Jack. "Confidence-Building Measures and Their Application in Latin America." In *Confidence-Building Measures in Latin America: Central America and the Southern Cone* (Report No. 16), edited by Augusto Varas, James A. Schear, and Lisa Owens. Washington, DC: The Henry L. Stimson Center, February 1995.

Child Protection Unit, UN Assistance Mission of Sierra Leone. *Lessons Learned and Best Practice on DDR Children with Fighting Forces and on Negotiating the End of Recruitment/Release of Child Soldiers*. UN Assistance Mission of Sierra Leone (June 2003).

Chomsky, Noam. "Humanitarian Imperialism: The New Doctrine of Imperial Right." *Monthly Review* 60, no. 4 (September 2008).

Civic, Melanne A., and Michael Miklaucic, eds. *Monopoly of Force: The Nexus of DDR and SSR*. Washington, DC: National Defense University Press, 2011.

Cockayne, James. "The Futility of Force? Strategic Lessons for Dealing with Unconventional Armed Groups from the UN's War on Haiti's Gangs." *Journal of Strategic Studies* 37, no. 5 (June 2014).

Cockayne, James, and Siobhan O'Neil, eds. *UN DDR in an Era of Violent Extremism: Is It Fit for Purpose?* New York: United Nations University, June 2015.

Colletta, Nat J., Markus Kostner, and Ingo Wiederhofer. *The Transition from War to Peace in Sub-Saharan Africa*. Washington, DC: World Bank, 1996.

Colletta, Nat J., and Robert Muggah. "Rethinking Post-war Security Promotion." *Journal of Security Sector Management* 7, no. 1 (2009): 1–25.

Colletta, Nat J., Jens Samuelsson Schjörlien, and Hannes Berts. *Interim Stabilisation: Balancing Security and Development in Post-conflict Peacebuilding*. Stockholm: Folke Bernadotte Academy, Ministry of Foreign Affairs, 2008.

Confederation Syndicat European Trade Union. "Renewed EU Strategy 2011–2014 for Corporate Social Responsibility (CSR)." http://www.etuc.org/a/9430.

Dalrymple, Sarah. *Common Ground: Gendered Assessment of the Needs and Concerns of Maoist Army Combatants for Rehabilitation and Integration* (Kathmandu, Nepal: Saferworld, November 2010).

DDR 2009, Analysis of World's DDR Programs in 2009. Barcelona: Escola de Cultura de Pau, July 2009.

DDR Coordination Section. *DDR in Sierra Leone* (presentation to UNAMSIL staff). UN Assistance Mission in Sierra Leone (June 2003).

———. *Evaluation of Human Security Fund Program*. UN Assistance Mission in Sierra Leone (August 2003).

———. *Preliminary Report of the Disarmament and Demobilisation in Sierra Leone*. UN Assistance Mission in Sierra Leone (April 6, 2002).

———. *The Stopgap Program Evaluation Report*. UN Assistance Mission in Sierra Leone (August 2003).

DDR Coordination Section and UN Volunteer Programme. *Reintegration and Transition to Peace Building* (collaborative program document). UN Assistance Mission in Sierra Leone (December 2002).

Dembinski, Matthias, and Theresa Reinold. *The Culture of Regional Security: EU and AU Approaches to Responsibility to Protect (R2P)*. Accessed June 27, 2012. http://www.scribd.com/doc/54737305/AU-and-R2P.

Dennys, Christian. "For Stabilization." *International Journal of Security and Development* 2, no. 1 (2013). Accessed July 27, 2016. http://doi.org/10.5334/sta.an.

Derks, Maria, Hans Rouw, and Ivan Briscoe. *A Community Dilemma: DDR and the*

Changing Face of Violence in Colombia. Peace Security and Development Network, (Clinendael and IKV Pax Christi) Netherlands, July 18, 2011.

Derksen Deedee. "Reintegrating Armed Groups in Afghanistan: Lessons from the Past," USIP Peace Brief, March 7, 2014. Accessed August 19, 2014. http://www.usip.org/publications/reintegrating-armed-groups-in-afghanistan.

Dilanian, Ken. "US/Afghanistan: Short-Staffed USAID Tries to Keep Pace," *USA Today,* February 1, 2009, accessed September 8, 2012, http://www.corpwatch .org/article.php?id=15288.

Diskaya, Ali. "Towards a Critical Securitisation Theory: The Copenhagen and Aberystwyth Schools of Security Studies." Accessed November 13, 2015. http://www.e-ir.info/2013/02/02/towards-a-critical-securitisation-theory-the -copenhagen-and-aberystwyth-school-of-security-studies/.

Douglas, Ian, Colin Gleichmann, Michael Odenwald, Kees Steenken, and Adrian Wilkinson. *Disarmament, Demobilization, and Reintegration: A Practical Field and Classroom Guide* (Frankfurt: German Technical Cooperation Agency, Norwegian Defence International Centre, Pearson Peacekeeping Center, and Swedish National Defence College, 2004).

Dower, John W. *Embracing Defeat: Japan in the Wake of World War II.* London: Allen Lane, 1999.

Eddy, Melissa. "Nations Ponder How to Handle European Fighters Returning from Jihad." *New York Times* (November 23, 2014).

Edwards, Lucy Morgan. *The Afghan Solution: The Inside Story of Abdul Haq, the CIA, and How Western Hubris Lost Afghanistan,* chapter 17, "Return to Kandahar," (London: Bactria Press, 2011).

Encyclopedia Britannica Mobile. "The Hague Conventions." Accessed June 27, 2012. m.eb.com/topic/251644.

———. "Open Door Policy." Accessed June 27, 2012. m.eb.com/topic/429642.

European Community and the Government of Sierra Leone. *Country Strategy Paper and National Indicative Program for the Period 2003–2007.* Freetown: European Community Cooperation Office, 2003.

Farmer, Paul. *The Uses of Haiti.* Monroe, ME: Common Courage Press, [1994] 2005.

Fatton, Robert. *Haiti's Predatory Republic: The Unending Transition to Democracy* (Boulder, CO: Lynne Rienner, 2002).

Felbab-Brown, Venda. "DDR, a Bridge Not Too Far: A Field Report from Somalia." *UN DDR in an Era of Violent Extremism* (New York: United Nations University–Centre for Policy Research, June 2015).

Ferks, George, Geert Gompelman, and Stefan van Laar, with Bart Klem. *The Struggle After Combat: The Role of NGOs in DDR Processes.* Afghanistan Case Study (The Hague, Netherlands: Cordaid, 2008).

Freire, Paulo. *Pedagogy of the Oppressed.* London: Herder and Herder, 1972.

Galtung, Johan. *Conflict Transformation by Peaceful Means (The Transcend Method): Participants' and Trainers' Manual.* Geneva: United Nations Disaster Management Training Programme, 2000.

Galula, David. *Counterinsurgency Warfare: Theory and Practice.* Westport, CT: Praeger Security International, 1964.

Gjelsvik, Ingvild Magnaes, and Tore Bjørgo. *Ex-pirates in Somalia: Disengagement Processes and Reintegration Programming.* Tromsø, Norway: University of Tromsø, Centre for Peace Studies, 2011.

Global Policy Forum. "PMSCs: Risks and Misconduct." Accessed November 26, 2015. http://www.globalforum.org/pmscs.html.

Government of Sierra Leone. *Minutes of Sierra Leone Tripartite Group Meetings on DDR* May 2001–March 2002. Unpublished, Government of Sierra Leone.

Guéhenno, Jean-Marie. *The Report on Civilian Capacity in the Aftermath of Conflict* ("The Guéhenno Report"). New York: United Nations, March 2011.

Hammes, T. X. "Attempting Disarmament Without Peace," in *Disarmament, Demobilization and Reintegration (DDR): Case Studies of Partial Success and Enduring Dilemmas,* ed. Richard Millet (Fort Leavenworth, KS: Combat Studies Institute Press, forthcoming 2017).

Herman, Johanna, and Chandra Lekha Sriram. "DDR and Transitional Justice: Bridging the Divide?" *Conflict, Security, and Development* 9, no. 4 (2009).

Herz, John. *Political Realism and Political Idealism.* Oxford: Cambridge University Press, 1951.

Higgins, Andrew. "For Jihadists, Denmark Tries Rehabilitation." *New York Times* (December 13, 2014).

Humphreys, Macartan, and Jeremy M. Weinstein. "What the Fighters Say: A Survey of Ex-combatants in Sierra Leone, June–August 2003." CGSD Working Paper 20, Columbia University, Center on Globalization and Sustainable Development, New York, 2004.

Huntington, Samuel P. "The Clash of Civilizations." *Foreign Affairs* (Summer 1993). http://edvardas.home.mruni.eu/wp-content/uploads/2008/10/huntington.pdf.

Ibish, Hussein. "Putin's Partition Plan for Syria." *New York Times* (October 19, 2015).

International Alert (IA). *Crime and Conflict: The New Challenges in Peacebuilding.* (London: 2014).

International Committee of the Red Cross. "Geneva Conventions and Commentaries." Accessed June 25, 2012. http://www.icrc.org/eng/war-and-law/treaties-customary-law/geneva-conventions.

International Committee of the Red Cross and Swiss Government. *Montreux Document on Pertinent International Legal Obligations and Good Practices for States Related to Operations of Private Military and Security Companies During Armed Conflict.* Geneva: ICRC, September 17, 2008.

International Labour Organization. *Socio-Economic Reintegration of Ex-combatants: Guidelines.* Geneva: ILO Program for Crisis Response and Reconstruction (ILO/CRISIS), 2009.

Ireland, Department of Foreign Affairs and Trade. "Good Friday Agreement." Accessed July 6, 2012. http://www.dfa.ie/home/index/asdex?id=335.

Isezaki, Kenji. *Disarmament: The World Through the Eyes of a Conflict Buster.* Published in Japanese by Kodansha Gendhi Shinho, Tokyo, January 2004, translated into English by Shinho, Tokyo, 2011.

Jacobsen, Kurt. "Repetition Compulsion: Counterinsurgency Bravado in Iraq and Afghanistan." In *Anthropology and Global Counterinsurgency*, edited by John D. Kelly, Beatrice Jauregui, Sean T. Mitchell, and Jeremy Walton. Chicago: University of Chicago Press, 2010.

James, Paul. "Human Security as a Military Security Leftover, or as Part of the Human Condition?" In *Human Security and Japan's Triple Disaster,* edited by Paul Bacon and Christopher Hobson. London: Routledge, 2014.

Kelly, John D., Beatrice Jauregui, Sean T. Mitchell, Jeremy Walton, eds. *Anthropology and Global Counterinsurgency.* Chicago: University of Chicago Press, 2010.

Kelsall, Tim. "Truth, Lies, Ritual: Preliminary Reflections on the Truth and Reconciliation Commission in Sierra Leone." *Human Rights Quarterly* 27, 2005.

Kendall, Bridget. "Syria Conflict: John Kerry Seeks End to Civil War 'Hell,'" *BBC World News* (October 29, 2015).

Kilcullen, David J. *Counterinsurgency.* New York: Oxford University Press, 2010.

Kilroy, Walt. "DDR: The Co-evolution of Concepts, Practices and Understanding." Program on States and Security, Ralph Bunche Institute for International Studies, The Graduate Center, City University of New York, February 2009.

Kingma, Kees, and Vanessa Sayers. "Demobilisation on the Horn of Africa." Proceedings of the International Resource Group on Disarmament and Security in the Horn of Africa, Workshop Brief No. 4, Addis Ababa, Ethiopia, December 4–7, 1994 (published June 1995).

Kirkpatrick, David D., Ben Hubbard, and Eric Schmit. "ISIS' Grip on Libyan City Gives It a Fallback Option." *New York Times* (November 28, 2015).

Kiszely, John. "Counterinsurgency in the 21st Century: Creating a Comprehensive Approach—A British View." Paper presented at the US Government Counterinsurgency Conference, Washington, DC, September 2006. Accessed February 1, 2013. http://www.au.af.mil/au/awc/awcgate/uscoin/kiszely _sept2006.pdf.

Klem, Bart, and Pyt Douma, with Georg Frerks, Geert Gompelman, and Stefan van Laar. *The Struggle After Combat: The Role of NGOs in DDR Processes (Case Studies and Synthesis Study).* The Hague: Cordaid, 2008.

Krugman, Paul. "Fearing Fear Itself." *New York Times* (November 17, 2015).

Kurtz, Gerrit, and Philipp Rotmann. "The Evolution of Norms of Protection: Major Powers Debate the Responsibility to Protect." *Global Public Policy Institute E-Newsletter* (November 24, 2015).

Lamb, Guy. *Assessing the Reintegration of Ex-combatants in the Context of Instability and Informal Economies: The Cases of the Central African Republic, the Democratic Republic of Congo, and South Sudan.* Washington, DC: International Bank for Reconstruction and Development and World Bank, December 2011.

———. "Demilitarisation and Peacebuilding in Southern Africa: A Survey of Literature." CCR Staff Papers, Center for Conflict Resolution, University of Cape Town, South Africa, 1997.

Laporte-Oshiro, Alison. "From Militant to Policemen: Three Lessons from US Experience with DDR and SSR." *PeaceBrief* 115 (November 17, 2011).

Leao, Isabela. *Swimming Against the Stream: DDR in Sierra Leone.* PhD dissertation, State University of Milan, Italy, January 2011.

Loutis, Wiza. *Evaluation de la situation des femmes dans le cadre de la violence armée en Haïti,* trans. Natalie Mann (Port au Prince: MINUSTAH, 2006).

Mao Tse-tung on Yu Chi Chan *(Guerrilla Warfare),* 1936. Translated by Samuel B. Griffith, 1940. Quantico, VA: US Marine Corps, 1961.

Martin, Mike. *An Intimate War: An Oral History of the Helmand Conflict, 1978–2012.* London: Hurst, 2014.

Mazzetti, Mark, and Eric Schmitt. "Private Army Formed to Fight Somali Pirates Leaves Troubled Legacy." *New York Times* (October 4, 2012).

McChrystal, Stanley. *Commander's Assessment: International Security Assistance Force Commander Recommendations for Achieving Victory in Afghanistan.* Geneva: International Security Assistance Force, August 2009.

Meek, Sarah. "Confidence-Building Measures as Tools for Disarmament and Development." *African Security Review* 14, no. 1 (2005).

Millett, Richard, ed. *Demobilization, Disarmament, and Reintegration (DDR): Case Studies of Partial Success and Enduring Dilemmas.* Fort Leavenworth, KS: Combat Studies Institute Press, forthcoming.

Mitonga, Zongwe. *DD Program in Sierra Leone, Executive Assessment and Lessons Learned for Workshop in Paris.* Washington, DC: World Bank and National Committee for DDR, July 2002.

Molloy Desmond. "DDR: A Shifting Paradigm and the Scholar/Practitioner Gap." Occasional Paper 1, Pearson Peacekeeping Centre, Ontario, Canada, 2008.

———. "DDR in Nigeria and Sri Lanka: Smoke and Mirrors?" *Journal of Conflict Transformation and Security* 1, no. 1 (2011).

———. "DDR in Sierra Leone 2001–2005 and the Pitfalls of DDR in Liberia 2003–2009," unpublished. Tokyo University of Foreign Studies, 2009.

———. *The DDR Process in Sierra Leone: An Interim Report: Lessons Learned.* DDR Section, UNAMSIL, Freetown, August 28, 2003.

———. "The Evolving Nature of Integrated DDR." *Hiroshima Review of Peacebuilding Studies,* Hiroshima Institute of Peace Science (April 2010).

———. "The Gender Perspective in DDR: Lessons from Sierra Leone." *Conflict Trends 2004/2,* Accord, Mt. Edgecombe, March 31, 2004.

———. *The Qualitative Quantitative Dilemma: Analysis of Indicators of Achievement as Used in DDR Programmes.* Master's thesis, Tokyo: Tokyo University of Foreign Studies, 2009.

———. *Sierra Leone and Discovering DDR: Conflict Resolution and Peace Building in Africa: Lessons Learned,* translated by Yujiro Tokumitsu. Kyoto: Ryukyu University Kyoto, March 2011.

———. *An Unlikely Convergence: Evolving DDR Theory and Counterinsurgency Doctrine.* PhD dissertation, Peace and Conflict Studies, Tokyo University of Foreign Studies, Tokyo, July 2013.

———. *Update on DDR Process, Central African Republic: 29 Apr 2009.* New York: UN Development Programme and UN Peacebuilding Commission.

Molloy, Elizabeth. *Gender and the Discourse of DDR: A Post-structural Analysis of the Gendered Discourse of the IDDRS and the Post-conflict Situation.* Master's thesis, Education, Gender and International Development, UCL Institute of Education, University College London, 2011.

Morgan Edwards, Lucy. *The Afghan Solution: The Inside Story of Abdul Haq, the CIA and How Western Hubris Lost Afghanistan.* London: Bactria Press, 2011.

Morier, Florian. *Reduction de la Violence Communautaire Dans L'Ouest De La Cote d'Ivoire.* Abidjan: International Organisation for Migration, 2013.

Morse, Ted. *Lessons Learned from Sierra Leone DD of Combatants.* DfID UK, Freetown, April 2002.

Muggah, Robert. "Innovations in DDR Policy and Research: Reflections on the Last Decade." NUPI Working Paper 774, Norwegian Institute of International Affairs, Oslo, 2010.

———. "Next Generation DDR." *World Politics Journal* (June 17, 2014).

———. *Securing Haiti's Transition: Reviewing Human Insecurity and the Prospects for Disarmament, Demobilization, and Reintegration* (a report commissioned by the Firearms and Explosive Control Division). Geneva: Small Arms Survey, May 2005.

———, ed. *Security and Post-Conflict Reconstruction: Dealing with Fighters in the Aftermath of War.* London: Routledge, 2009.

Muggah, Robert, Desmond Molloy, and Maximo Halty. "(Dis)integrating DDR in Sudan and Haiti? Practitioners' Views to Overcoming Integration Inertia." In *Security and Post-Conflict Reconstruction: Dealing with Fighters in the Aftermath of War,* edited by Robert Muggah. London: Routledge, 2009.

Muggah, Robert, and Albert Souza Mulli. "Rio Tries Counterinsurgency." *Current History* (February 2012).

Munive, Jairo. "DDR in South Sudan: Feasible Under Current Conditions?" African Arguments, Royal African Society, February 6, 2013. Accessed March 18, 2013. http://www.africanarguments.org/2013/02/06/disarmament-demobilisation-and-reintegration-in-south-sudan-feasible-under-current-conditions.

Nagl, John. *Counterinsurgency Lessons from Malaya and Vietnam: Learning to Eat Soup with a Knife.* (Santa Barbara: Praeger Publishers, Santa Barbara, 2002).

Nilsson, Manuela. "Conflict, Peace, and DDR in Angola." In *Demobilization, Disarmament, and Reintegration (DDR): Case Studies of Partial Success and*

Enduring Dilemmas, edited by Richard Millett. Fort Leavenworth, KS: Combat Studies Institute Press, forthcoming.

Nye, Joseph S., Jr. "Think Again: Soft Power." *Foreign Policy* (March 1, 2006). Accessed June 28, 2012. http://www.yaleglobal.yale.edu/content/think-again -soft-power.

The Office of the President of Sierra Leone, and partners (including UN, WB, DfID). *National Recovery Strategy for Sierra Leone.* Freetown: Government of Sierra Leone, December 2001.

Olyemu, Adeniji. *End of Mission Report.* UNAMSIL internal document, August 2003.

Ong, Kelvin. *Managing Fighting Forces: DDR in Peace Processes.* Washington, DC: United States Institute of Peace, 2012.

Opération des Nations Unies en Cote d'Ivoire. *Projets Réinsertion communautaire: PRC de l'ONUCI, Bilan del' exercise 2013–2014.* Abidjan: ONUCI, 2013.

Organisation for Economic Co-operation and Development, Development Assistance Committee. *Handbook on Security System Reform: Supporting Security and Justice.* Paris: Organisation for Economic Co-operation and Development, 2008.

Ostensen, Ase Gilje. "UN Use of Private and Military Security Companies: Practice and Policies." SSR Paper 3, Geneva Centre for the Democratic Control of Armed Forces, 2011.

Oswald, Bruce (Ossie). "The UN Security Council and the Force Intervention Brigade: Some Legal Issues." In *Strengthening the Rule of Law Through the UN Security Council,* edited by Jeremy Farrall and Hilary Charlesworth, Chap. 17, Challenges to Globalization Series. New York: Routledge, 2016.

Paes, Wolf-Christian. "Eyewitness: The Challenges of DDR in Liberia." *International Peacekeeping* 12, no. 2 (Summer 2005).

Pastreich, Emanuel. "Interview with Francis Fukuyama on 'The Rise, East Asia Tensions, and the Role of the US.'" *The Diplomat* (October 15, 2015).

Petraeus, David H., and James A. Amos. *FM3-24 MCWP 3-33.3 COIN: Manual of Offensive, Defensive and Stability Operations.* Washington, DC: Headquarters, Department of the Army, December 2006.

Piedmont, Dean. "From War to Peace, from Soldier to Peacebuilder: Interim Stabilisation Measures in Afghanistan and South Sudan." *Journal of Peacebuilding and Development* 7, no. 1 (2012). Accessed April 1, 2013. http://dx.doi.org/10.1080/154231666.3012.719404.

———. "The Role of DDR in Countering Violent Extremism." *SSR 2.0 Brief,* Center for Security Governance, no. 3, June 2015.

Pinker, Stephen. *The Better Angels of Our Nature: The Decline of Violence in History and Its Causes* (London: Penguin, 2011).

Pingeot, Lou. *Dangerous Partnership: Private Military & Security Companies and the UN.* New York: Global Policy Forum and the Rosa Luxemburg Foundation, June 2012.

Post-conflict Reintegration for Development and Empowerment (PRIDE). *Ex-combatant Views of the Truth and Reconciliation Commission and Special Court in Sierra Leone.* Freetown: PRIDE, September 12, 2002.

Prinz, Vanessa. *Group Cohesion in Non-state Armed Groups: Gains and Challenges of Group Reintegration of Former Combatants in Disarmament, Demobilization and Reintegration (DDR) Processes.* Master's thesis, Hamburg University, July 2012.

"Protests in Biafra: Go Your Own Way." *The Economist* (November 2015).

Pugel, James. *What the Fighters Say: A Survey of Ex-combatants in Liberia, February–March 2006.* New York: UN Development Programme and African Network for the Prevention and Protection Against Child Abuse and Neglect, April 2007.

"Re: Foreign Fighters Returning from Syria." *Washington Post* (November 17, 2014).

Rehn, Elisabeth, and Ellen Johnson Sirleaf. *Women, War, Peace: The Independent Experts' Assessment of the Impact of Armed Conflict on Women and Women's Role in Peacebuilding.* New York: UNIFEM, 2002.

"Reintegration of Armed Groups Eludes Most Policy Fixes." *Oxford Analytica* (September 28, 2012).

Rhea, Randolph Wallace. *Ex-combatant Reintegration in the Great Lakes Region: Processes & Mechanisms, Trajectories & Paradoxes.* PhD dissertation, Center for Peace Studies, Tromsø University, Norway, January 2016.

Roberts, James, and Andrew Markley. "CRS: New EU Strategy Threatens US and European Companies." The Heritage Foundation. http://www.heritage.org /research/reports/2011/11crs-new-eu-strategythreatens-us-and-european -companies.

Roche, Chris. *Impact Assessment for Development Agencies: Learning to Value Change.* Oxford, UK: Oxfam Publishing, 1999.

Rosenberg, Matthew, and Michael D. Shear. "In Reversal, Obama Says US Soldiers Will Stay in Afghanistan to 2017." *New York Times* (October 15, 2015).

Rotmann, Philipp. "Built on Shaky Ground: The Comprehensive Approach in Practice." NATO Defense College Research Paper 63, NATO Defense College, Rome, December 2010.

Rubin, Alissa J. "Karzai Bets on Vilifying US to Shed His Image as a Lackey." *New York Times* (March 13, 2013).

Ruiz, Moses T. *Sharpening the Spear—United States Provincial Reconstruction Teams in Afghanistan.* PhD dissertation, Texas State University, Department of Political Science, Public Administration Program. Accessed April 4, 2012. https://digital.library.txstate.edu/handle/10877/3586.

Ryan, Simon and Owen Greene. "Disarmament, Demobilization, and Reintegration in Nepal: A Mini-study." Saferworld and Centre for International Co-operation and Security, University of Bradford, UK, July 2008.

Saferworld. *Community Security Handbook.* London: Saferworld, 2014.

Scanteam. *Final Report on the Multi-country Demobilization and Reintegration Program: End of Program Evaluation* (an independent evaluation). Oslo: Scanteam, June 2010.

Schmitt, Carl. *The* Nomos *of the Earth in the International Law of* Jus Publicum Europaeum. Candor, NY: Telos Press, 2006.

Secretary-General's Senior Advisory Group, *Report on Civilian Capacity in the Aftermath of Conflict Within the UN System (The Guéhenno Report).* New York: UN Headquarters, March 4, 2011.

Sedra, Mark. "Afghanistan and the DDR-SSR Nexus." In *The Monopoly of Force: The Nexus Between DDR and SSR,* edited by Melanne Civic and Michael Miklaucic. Washington, DC: National Defense University, 2011.

Sepp, Kalev I. "From 'Shock and Awe' to 'Hearts and Minds': The Fall and Rise of US Counterinsurgency Capability in Iraq." *Third World Quarterly* 28, no. 2 (2007).

"Sharif Condemns US Drone Strike." *BBC News* (June 1, 2013).

Sheeran, Scott, and Stephanie Case. *The Intervention Brigade: Legal Issues for the UN in the Democratic Republic of the Congo.* New York: International Peace Institute, November 2014.

Sherestha, Subina. "The Disillusioned Soldier." *Witness Report,* Al Jazeera, December 31, 2012. http://www.aljazeera.com/programmes/witness/2011/11 /2011112813233689170.html.

Sherman, Jack. "The Global War on Terrorism and Its Implications for US SSR

Support," in *The Future of SSR Reform*, ed. Mark Sedra (Waterloo, Ontario: The Centre for International Governance Innovation, 2010).

Shibuya, Eric Y. *Demobilizing Irregular Forces*. Cambridge, UK: Polity Press, 2012.

Sierra Leone, Ministry of Youth and Sport. *National Youth Policy for Sierra Leone*. Freetown: Ministry of Youth and Sport, June 2003.

Simon, Arthy. *Ex-combatant Reintegration: Key Issues for Policy Makers and Practitioners, Based on Lessons Learned from Sierra Leone*. London: Department for International Development, 2003.

Sitaraman, Ganesh. "Counterinsurgency, the War on Terror, and the Laws of War." *Virginia Law Review* 95 (2009): 1746–1747.

Sly, Liz. "The Hidden Hand Behind the Islamic State Militants? Saddam Hussein's." *Washington Post* (April 4, 2015).

Specht, Irma. *Independent Evaluation of the UNIRP*. Kathmandu, Nepal: Transition International, February 2013.

Stapleton, Barbara. "A Means to What End? Why PRTs Are Peripheral to Bigger Political Challenges in Afghanistan." *Journal of Military and Strategic Studies* 10, no. 1 (2007).

Stelios, Comninos, Aki Stavrou, and Brian Stewart. *Assessment of the Reintegration Programmes of the NCDDR*. Washington, DC: World Bank, October 25, 2002.

Stiles, Thomas Shannon. "DDR in El Salvador." In *Demobilization, Disarmament, and Reintegration (DDR): Case Studies of Partial Success and Enduring Dilemmas*, edited by Richard Millett. Fort Leavenworth, KS: Combat Studies Institute Press, forthcoming.

Subedi, D. B. "War to Peace Transition in Nepal: Success and Challenges Ahead." *Small Wars Journal*, November 9, 2013.

Themnér, Anders. "A Leap of Faith: Explaining Ex-combatant Violence." Paper presented at ISA Conference, Montreal, Canada, March 16–19, 2011.

Transcultural Psychosocial Organization (TPO). *A Longitudinal Psychosocial Assessment Among VLMRs During Reintegration*. Kathmandu: TPO, 2012.

Transitional Disarmament and Reintegration Program. *Overview*. Washington, DC: World Bank, November 2011.

———. *Quarterly Report, October–December 2011*. Washington, DC: World Bank, 2012.

———. *Quarterly Report, July–September 2012*. Washington, DC: World Bank, 2012.

Trinquier, Roger. *Peacekeeping in Sierra Leone: UNAMSIL Hits the Home Straight*. Training for Peace in Southern Africa Project (a study sponsored by government of Norway), November 18, 2001.

UK Department for International Development, West and North Africa Department. "Comments on Ted Morse's Lessons Learned Report," August 2, 2002.

UN Ad Hoc Interagency Review Team. "UN Interagency Review of the Launch of the DDR Process in Liberia." New York: DPKO, March 2004.

UN Assistance Mission in Sierra Leone and Economic Community of West African States Monitoring Group. *DDR Information Sheet*. Freetown: UNAMSIL, 2000.

UN Department of Peacekeeping Operations (DPKO). *DDR in a Peacekeeping Environment: Principles and Guidelines for the Collection and Destruction of Ammunition* (draft). New York: DPKO, August 28, 2002.

———. *Guidelines for DDR Process*. New York: DPKO, 2000.

———. *Second-Generation DDR Practices in Peace Operations: A Contribution to the New Horizon Discussion on Challenges and Opportunities for UN Peacekeeping*. New York: DPKO, 2010.

UN Department of Peacekeeping Operations, Best Practices Unit. *Lessons Learned from UN: Peacekeeping Experience in Sierra Leone Draft Report.* New York: DPKO, June 2003.

UN Development Programme. *Destroying Illicit Small Arms* (press kit). New York: UNDP, 2001.

———. *Development Held Hostage: Assessing the Effects of Small Arms on Human Development.* New York: UNDP, April 2002.

———. *Final Evaluation of UNIRP.* Kathmandu: UNDP, 2013.

———. *Final Report of the Community Arms for Development Program Pilot Phase.* New York: UNDP, July 2003.

———. *A Handbook on Reintegration.* New York: UNDP, 2000.

———. *Mano River Union Arms for Development Program.* New York: UNDP, June 2003.

———. *Post-Rehabilitation Participant Satisfaction Report.* Kathmandu, Nepal: UN Interagency Rehabilitation Programme, September 2013.

———. *Practice Note on DDR of Ex-combatants.* New York: UNDP, 2005.

———. *Report on the Reintegration of Demobilised Soldiers in Mozambique, 1992–1996.* New York: UNDP, 1999.

UN Development Programme, Bureau for Crisis Prevention and Recovery. *Terms of Reference for DDR Multi-programme Evaluation.* New York: UNDP, September 2012.

UN Development Programme, Asian Development Bank, and World Bank, Afghanistan. *Demobilisation: Toward a Programme for Reintegration of Ex-combatants* (draft sector report). Kabul: UNDP, December 2001.

UN Executive Committee on Humanitarian Affairs. *Harnessing Institutional Capacities in Support of the DDR of Former Combatants* (final report of the DDR Working Group). New York, 2000.

UN General Assembly. "World Summit Outcome Document 2005," UN A/60/L.1, 60th Session. Accessed July 27, 2012. http://www.who.int/hiv/universalaccess2010 /worldsummit.pdf.

UN High Commissioner for Human Rights. "The International Bill of Human Rights." Accessed June 27, 2012. http://www.unhchr.org/documents/publications /factsheet2rev.1en.pdf.

UN Office of Internal Oversight Services. *Review of the Role of UNAMSIL in the Implementation of GoSL's DDR Program.* New York: United Nations, June 16, 2003.

UN Research Institute for Social Development. *The Social Impact of Light Weapons Availability and Proliferation.* Geneva: UNRISD, March 1995.

UN Secretary-General. "Agenda for Peace: Preventive Diplomacy, Peacemaking and Peacekeeping," by Boutros Boutros-Ghali, 17 June 1992.

———. *Implementation of the Recommendations of the Special Committee on Peacekeeping Operations.* New York: United Nations, January 16, 2003.

———. *Secretary-Generals Quarterly Reports on Sierra Leone to the Security Council, 2002 to 2003.* New York: United Nations, 2003.

UN Security Council. Resolution 1325. "Women, Peace and Security." October 2000.

———. Resolution 1366. "Promoting a Greater Perspective of Gender Issues in Peacekeeping / Peace Building Mandates." August 2001.

van Burgen, Peter. "We Meant Well: How I Helped to Lose the Battle for Iraq Hearts and Minds." Accessed July 7, 2012. http://www.wemeantwell.com.

Varas, Augusto, James A. Schear, and Lisa Owens, eds. *Confidence-Building Measures in Latin America and the Southern Cone.* Report No. 16, Henry L. Stimson Center/FLACSO-Chile. Washington, DC: The Henry L. Stimson Center, February 1995.

Verhoeven, Harry, Ricardo Soares de Oliveira, and Madhan Mohan Jaganathan. "To Intervene in Darfur, or Not: Re-examining the R2P Debate and Its Impact." *Global Public Policy Institute E-Newsletter* (November 24, 2015).

Villanueva, Ceasar, George Aguilar, and Niall O'Brien Center, *The Reintegration of the Moro National Liberation Front in Mindanao.* Bradford, UK: Centre for International Security, University of Bradford, July 2008.

Villarino, Eliza. "House Proposal: Bigger Private Sector Voice in USAID." August 3, 2012. Accessed September 14, 2012. http://www.devex.com/en/news/blogs /house-proposal-bigger-private-sector-voice-in-us-aid-programs.

Williams, Rens, Willemijn Verkoren, Maria Derks, Jasper Kleingeld, Georg Frerks, and Hans Rouw. *Security Promotion in Fragile States: Can Local Meet National? Exploring the Connections Between Community Security and Disarmament, Demobilisation and Reintegration (DDR).* Working Group on Community Security and Community-Based DDR in Fragile States, Netherlands, August 2009.

Willibald, Sigrid. "Does Money Work? Cash Transfers to Ex-combatants in DDR Processes." *Disasters* 30, no. 3 (2006).

Wolf, Charles. *Insurgencies and Counterinsurgencies: New Myths and Old Realities.* New York: RAND, 1965.

Woodrow, Peter, and Dian Chigas. "Connecting the Dots: Evaluating Whether and How Programmes Address Conflict Systems." In *The Non-linearity of Peace Processes: Theory and Practice of Systemic Conflict Transformation*, edited by Daniela Körppen, Norbert Ropers, and Hans J. Giessmann. Leverkusen, Germany: Barbara Budrich, 2011. http://www.cdacollaboratice.org/publications/reflections-on-peace -practice/rpp-articles%.

World Bank, "Demobilization and Reintegration of Military Personnel in Africa: The Evidence from Seven Country Case Studies" (discussion paper, Africa Regional Series No. IDP-130, October 1993).

————. *Quarterly Reports on DDR Process in Sierra Leone, 2001–2004.* Washington, DC: World Bank, various years.

Index

About the Book

Disarmament, demobilization, and reintegration, or DDR, has been widely advocated for decades as an essential component of postconflict peacebuilding. But DDR in practice has generated more questions than answers. Does the approach work, contributing to postconflict stabilization and the reintegration of former combatants? Can it work better? What constitutes success? What accounts for failures? Do the potential risks outweigh the potential benefits?

Drawing on his extensive experience in the field, Desmond Molloy considers these questions and more as he traces the evolution of DDR theory and practice from the mid-1980s to the present and projects its potential direction in contributing to addressing violent extremism.

Desmond Molloy is program director in the Myanmar Liaison Office of the Nippon Foundation, where he focuses on the design and management of integrated peacebuilding programs.